The Color of Gender

The Color of Gender

Reimaging Democracy

Zillah R. Eisenstein

UNIVERSITY OF CALIFORNIA PRESS
Berkeley · Los Angeles · London

University of California Press
Berkeley and Los Angeles, California

University of California Press, Ltd.
London, England

© 1994 by
The Regents of the University of California

Library of Congress Cataloging-in-Publication Data

Eisenstein, Zillah R.
   The color of gender : reimaging democracy / Zillah R. Eisenstein.
      p.   cm.
   Includes bibliographical references and index.
   ISBN 0-520-08338-5 (alk. paper). — ISBN 0-520-08422-5 (pbk. :
alk. paper)
   1. Sexism.   2. Racism.   3. Patriarchy.   4. Democracy.
5. Feminism.   I. Title.
HQ1237.E58   1994
305.3—dc20   93-23836
                                                             CIP

Printed in the United States of America
9 8 7 6 5 4 3 2 1

For my daughter Sarah

Contents

Acknowledgments

As always, I have incurred many debts while researching and writing this book. Thanks to Nina Martin, a Dana Student Fellow at Ithaca College, for assisting me in my initial researching of AIDS. Thanks to Cornell law students Amy Weissman, Patricia Barasch, and Ann Saponara for locating Supreme Court decisions and updating legal footnotes; Ann also provided me with exceptional assistance in the final stages of copyediting. Thanks to Jim Meyers for his speedy book ordering, and to John Henderson, librarian at Ithaca College, for his gracious reference assistance.

I thank Hilda Scott for her complete generosity in sharing her Eastern European feminist network with me. Thanks also to Florence Howe of the Feminist Press, Marian Chamberlain of the National Council for Research on Women, Debbie Rogow of the International Women's Health Coalition, and Elizabeth Gardiner, all of whom helped me collect information on Eastern European women, and to Ann Snitow, who provided information on the Network of East-West Women. Alena Heitlinger and Slavenka Drakulic were most helpful in sending me their unpublished papers. I could not have completed my final chapter without the assistance and enthusiasm of Luz Alvarez Martinez of the National Latina Health Organization.

Several people provided me with helpful criticism on specific chapters of the book. Special thanks to Barbara Smith, Asma Barlas, Tom Shevory, and Patricia Zimmerman.

Rosalind Pollack Petchesky, Miriam Brody, and Mary Katzenstein read the entire manuscript, sometimes several times over. My debt to each of them is enormous, in terms of both friendship and scholarship. Ros Petchesky critiqued the discussion of privacy and improved it. It is not so easy to say where her thoughts end and mine begin. Miriam Brody used her keen eye to spot points that required further explanation, but also let me know when it was time to move on. Mary Katzenstein loyally insisted that I not narrow my audience unnecessarily.

Many people enriched our family and domestic life, enabling me to write. Thanks to Diane Tripodi, Marj Babcock, and Marsha Lucas for tending to the needs of our daughter Sarah between 3:00 and 5:00. Teachers Pat Holmes (kindergarten) and Laurie Rubin (first grade) allowed Sarah to love school and to love writing so that she encouraged me to do my own. Thanks to Tony House for her attention to the home front.

I would not have had the peace of mind necessary to write without Richard or Ellen or my mother, Fannie Eisenstein.

In the age of computers, I always seem to need help. Jonathan Plotkin figured out my outdated software for me when no one else could. Donna Freedline always volunteered her secretarial and administrative skills before I even asked. Sarah Dean provided much-needed assistance. Dorothy Owens once again edited and processed the final copy. My editor at the University of California Press, Naomi Schneider, was key in bringing this book to fruition. My copy editor, Liz Gold, forced me to rethink my choice of words and often created clarity when I was unable to do so. Tony Hicks oversaw the last stages of book production.

I also wish to acknowledge the support of several faculty research and summer grants and the reassigned time program at Ithaca College, which allowed me to write this book. I want to thank my colleagues in the Politics Department, as well as my students at Ithaca College, for providing such a rich and supportive atmosphere in which to do this writing.

Finally, I wish to thank the Hunter College Women's Studies Program (1989), the organizers of the Women and AIDS Conference (Boston, 1991), and the Third Women's Policy Research Conference (Washington, 1992) for allowing me to present and discuss many of the arguments found here.

Some of the initial ideas, now much revised, were first published in

"Specifying U.S. Feminism in the Nineties: The Problem of Naming," *Socialist Review* 20, no. 2 (April–June 1990): 45–56; "Privatizing the State: Reproductive Rights, Affirmative Action, and the Problem of Democracy," *Frontiers, A Journal of Women's Studies* 12, no. 1 (1991): 98–125; and "Fetal Position," *Nation* 249, no. 17 (20 Nov. 1989), 12–13.

Introduction

Ideas begin in personal experiences and circumstances and then move outward. When we write theory, we need to start from the self, move in and through it, and then go beyond this narrow starting place of simple identity.

I grew up in the 1950s, one of four daughters of parents who had been members of the Communist Party. My childhood was defined by the civil rights movement. My earliest political memory is of my sister Sarah and me carrying picket signs outside of Woolworth's. I graduated from high school in 1964, and I came to adulthood active in the women's movement of the 1970s. The 1980s felt politically dismal and very different from the preceding decade, as the gains toward racial and sexual equality were systematically attacked. With the election of Clinton, the 1990s look more hopeful: for the first time in over a decade, it is not a foregone conclusion what politics will look like. One is allowed to hope that the "new" Democrats will retrieve democracy from its rightward drift.

My imagining of democracy begins here, between the legacy of the Reagan-Bush decade and the possibility of change. It responds to a politics heavily racialized and encoded through the gender imagery of black women, a politics also defined by the internationalization of the United States economy, which excuses less equality in the name of greater competitiveness.

Over the past decade in the United States, there has been an unnoticed revolution of a sort. It culminated in the spring of 1989 with a series of Supreme Court decisions which have all but destroyed civil rights and abortion law. Even as the Bush administration embraced the revolutions of 1989 in Eastern Europe as a victory for "democracy," it continued to oversee the demise of democracy at home.

The Gulf War was supposedly an attempt to protect democracy in the Middle East. But how can one term Kuwait or Saudi Arabia democratic, even in a narrow sense? Better than 90 percent of the population of both countries is not allowed to vote. Few observers made much of the issue that U.S. military women were risking their lives for countries where women could not even drive, let alone vote.

My discussion also takes us to Eastern Europe and to the revolutionary struggles of 1989. Eastern Europe popularized the idea of democracy anew. Totalitarian statism was rejected, and the discourse of liberal democratic rights was adopted. Yet even within this discourse, women's rights have not been viewed as essential to the construction of democracy. Unfortunately, since 1989, ethnic warfare has all but stalled any reenvisioning of democracy. In Eastern Europe, the imaginings remain patriarchal and ethnocentric. These limitations in democratic vision reflect and reverberate back on neoconservative assaults against racial and sexual equality within the United States.

I write this book as a white woman of the middle class (hazy concept as that is) in a society where whiteness (a much less hazy concept) is privileged through a racialized system of difference threaded through economic class and gender privilege. In such a society, difference reflects power and structures of oppression more than the richness of diversity. I take this problem of racialized patriarchy and push it to reinvent the way we think about democracy. This is a book about democratic theory which does *not* discuss the literature of white men on democracy. There are many books already written of this sort.[1] I instead take the language of universal democratic rights and demand that they be reconceptualized to include women of color.

RACIALIZED PATRIARCHY

Patriarchy differentiates women from men while privileging men. Racism simultaneously differentiates people of color from whites and privileges whiteness. These processes are distinct but intertwined. Like any structuring of power, the racializing of gender is a process that always needs to be renegotiated. I use the term "racialized patriarchy" to bring attention to the continual interplay of race and gender in the structure of power.

Language is already racialized and engendered (i.e., coded with gender) at the start. Toni Morison argues that language is so threaded in and through racial imagery that we can subvert ourselves without knowing it.[2] Evelyn Brooks Higginbotham believes that gender has always had a racial meaning, that it is constructed in and through racialized contexts, and that gender is both constructed and fragmented by race.[3] Donna Haraway says that feminists must recognize that there is a race/gender system both similar to and different from the sex/gender system.[4]

Economic class is completely embedded in the way race and gender play themselves out. When we speak of "racism and sexism and economic class," it sounds like the systems are more separate than they are. (The same is true of phrases like "women and blacks.") I hope to show how a racialized and sexualized gender system is differentiated by economic class to create complicated processes that often stand in for each other, as in the racial coding of family issues or the gender coding of race in much abortion rhetoric. As we shall see, one only needs to reflect on the Anita Hill/Clarence Thomas hearings to recognize the complex relations of racialized gender privilege.

NEOCONSERVATISM AND THE MYTH OF UNIVERSAL RIGHTS

My rethinking of democracy requires the deconstruction of universalism. The doctrine of universal rights must be reinvented through a recognition of individual needs. I want to work from this position of specificity to radicalize liberal rights discourse.

The neoconservative attack on affirmative action and abortion rights has operated in exactly the opposite direction, embracing universal rights while silently privileging the white male. Although neoconservatives claim to be defending the rights of the individual—meaning, presumably, *all* individuals—in fact the individual they have in mind is always a white male. From this point of view, affirmative action programs are allegedly unfair because they privilege "difference" of gender and/or race. They represent "special" interests rather than "universal" (i.e., white male) ones. Abortion rights are suspect as well, because the "universal" rights guaranteed by the "founding fathers" were in fact based on a man's body, which cannot be pregnant. Any reproductive rights for women are inherently different from the traditionally recognized rights guaranteed to men.

In most theory, the universal and the abstract are preferred for their supposed neutrality and objectivity. They are also assumed to be more democratic, encompassing everybody in their nonspecificity. But nonspecificity is really quite specific when it is revealed to mean "white male." Instead of speaking of individuals but really meaning white men, I will speak of women of color. By stipulating both "women" and "of color," I move toward a more inclusive meaning of "individual," one that includes previously invisible categories of gender and race. Thus, to become more specific, in this case, is actually to encompass more of humanity. Universal categorizations exclude the specific; they are hopelessly abstract. History bespeaks the need for the realignment of such terminology.

I am speaking of rethreading the fabric of democratic discourse with a new thread of the concept of rights. Parts of the civil rights and women's movements of the sixties and seventies took this discourse as their own. Much of the politics of the eighties and nineties have focused on struggle over the honest meaning of liberal democratic rights discourse. Instead of rejecting the universality of this discourse, I want to reinvent it by locating its specification in gender, race, and class. The radical subversiveness of rights discourse lies in its universal claims: anyone can claim these rights as their own. But the silent privileging of white middle- and upper-class males excludes those who are not white, male, or affluent from this source of power.

Neoconservatives are revisionist liberals. They wish to revise liberalism back to what they deem as its original core: liberty rather than equality. Neoconservatives argue that liberalism was never intended to promise equality; that, at its best, society (and government) can offer only opportunity or incentive. They argue that interpretations of liberalism that promote civil rights breed dependence and poverty. Reagan-Bush neoconservatives were preoccupied with "reverse discrimination" against white males by affirmative action programs which supposedly privilege people of color and white women.[5]

Throughout the 1980s, neoconservatives came to dominate both Republican and Democratic Party politics. Republicans became straightjacketed during Bush's tenure by the Right. A troubled relationship emerged between the rightist, evangelical, antiabortion lobby and the more centrist, neoconservative factions of the party. As a result, a rightist, moralist neoconservatism took hold. The Democratic Party, on the other hand, remains defined by a centrist neoconservatism that stands in uneasy alliance with "old-style" liberals, civil rights activists, and feminists.

The Clinton administration has begun yet another revision of liberalism. The Democratic Leadership Council (DLC), with which Bill Clinton and Al Gore are aligned, says it will provide an alternative to the kind of liberalism that dominated the Democratic Party in the 1960s. Clearly, new ideas are needed for the 1990s to cope with the global economy and with the country's fractured families. But it remains to be seen what form of liberalism will emerge. Will Clinton remain the centrist neoliberal of the election campaign? Will his administration swiftly redress the right-wing evangelical initiatives on such issues as abortion and family leave? Or will neoconservative rhetoric—endorsing less government, fewer taxes, and more governmental privatization—prove a daunting legacy that inhibits radical democratic stirrings?

At present, a neoconservative discourse of neutrality remains firmly in place: government is supposed to be neutral in order to protect "universal" rights. This discourse is used to silence specific demands related to sexual and racial equality and to justify the privatization of the state. Most neoconservatives expect individuals to create the conditions of opportunity for themselves. Privatization of the service aspect of the state has reduced government's public responsibility for private business, for families, and for individuals. The same reasoning underlies the destruction of affirmative action law: government no longer has an affirmative role in bringing about equality. The Reagan-Bush state redefined the racialized aspects of patriarchy for the 1990s through the destruction of civil rights and abortion law.

My argument challenges the dominant neoconservative view while remaining committed to universal rights. I neither want to reject the idea of a universal right nor to deny its specific meaning. Every woman has a universal human right to control her body, yet this right must be specified in terms of a woman's differing circumstances, such as her ability to get pregnant. I will work from the specific—imagining women of color—to reinvent the meaning of rights discourse. This is just as neutral a starting point for discussion as beginning with white men, and it is more honest than pretending to be universal.

LIBERAL AND SOCIALIST DEMOCRACY

Throughout the globe, current struggles to define democracy are positioned between factions of neoconservatives, old liberals, and former socialists. Liberal democrats and socialists disagree with neoconservative narrowings of democracy, but both visions of equality are based on a false universalism.

Socialist notions of equality need to specify racial and sexual equality and not reduce these concerns to economic class concerns. The liberal democratic commitment to freedom needs to specify that individual freedom must include sexual freedom as well as racial, gender and economic class equality. Rights discourse must be concretized through reference to sex (biological femaleness or maleness, and sexuality), gender (the institutionalized meanings of one's sex),[6] race (color and its meanings as defined by a racialized culture), and economic access (the economic ability to get what one needs). We must embrace the specificity and variability of the individual while recognizing the collective expression of groups within the language of equality.

Equality expresses a desired relationship between groups of people. The concept of freedom more readily focuses on individual expression and thereby cuts through the divisions of race and gender by recognizing people's differences. A concern with the diversity of individuals must be incorporated into a socialist vision of equality. And "individuality" must be deconstructed for its traditional representation of racialized maleness. The point is not to de-sex equality, but rather to allow sexual diversity without engendering or racializing it. Individual diversity requires freedom. Our similarities require equality. Radical egalitarianism must therefore recognize individuality. From this point of specificity, *I want to look through these differences to define a shared humanness.*

The concern here is not with differences per se, but rather with how we can start with differences to construct a particularized understanding of human rights that is both universal and specific. Specifying difference allows one to see individuality in a collective stance. The excesses of some postmodernism—such as the belief that there are no universals—poses problems for my analysis. Its skepticism of universals and its embrace of differences rejects any envisioning of democracy and any politics of feminism because they would represent overstated unities. Nevertheless, I intend to use the skepticism of postmodernism to radicalize democratic theory to embrace differentiated unities. I do not position my project in opposition to postmodernism, but I critique its excessive preoccupation with difference and uniqueness of context.[7] Kwame Anthony Appiah says there are several "postmodernisms." I utilize the strains which emphasize the elusiveness of boundaries, the end of metanarratives, and the rejection of the claim to exclusivity.[8]

By starting with women of color, I recognize their specificity *and* the similarities and differences between them and white women. I am not trying to create a new generalized and totalizing category in "women of color"; instead, I hope to create the exact opposite: a continual reminder of diversity. When we start the discussion of democracy with women of color, we must take notice of the racialized and sexualized bodies of women. Then reproductive rights (as necessary to the control over one's body) can be theorized as fundamental to a reenvisioned democracy—as fundamental as rights for food, shelter, and clothing. Reproductive rights are not secondary rights; they are initial and universal.

If one wonders about the promissory importance of reproductive and abortion rights for a radicalized democracy, one need only look to the United States and the assault against these rights by those who seek to deradicalize democracy. But the abortion struggle is hardly limited to U.S. politics. Abortion was a major sticking point in the unification of East and West Germany, and it continues to be a significant controversy within Poland and Hungary.

DEMOCRACY, LIBERALISM, AND SOCIALISM

The struggle over the purview of individuality and privacy rights, especially for women, is presently being contested in both socialism and liberal democracy. The struggle to achieve democracy is located somewhere in the mix between liberalism, capitalism, socialism, and feminism. An antiracist stance must be woven through this mix. But there is little agreement relative to this project. Prominent members of the Left in the United States, such as Sheldon Wolin, insist on assuming that liberal politics are conservatizing. He wrongly equates white middle- and upper-middle-class politics with a demand for rights like those guaranteed by the ERA, abortion rights, and the right to sexual preference, and he argues that these demands are one and the same with consumerism and privatism.[9] In doing so, he washes away liberalism and feminism. Christopher Lasch also discredits the democratic aspects of liberalism, and with it feminism. For Lasch, liberalism has come to represent the "tyranny of the self."[10] Feminism, then, represents this tyranny as done by women. It is difficult to distinguish leftists of this order from neoconservatives: both see feminism as a result of liberalism's excesses.

Antistatist discourse currently dominates, though differently, both in the United States and in most East European societies. In Eastern Europe, such discourse rejects the totalitarian Communist state. In the United States, it is the social welfare state of the sixties and early seventies that is being rejected. Privatization in a society defined by the capitalist market is of course different from the partial decentralization of state power in Eastern European economies. But the issues of the structure of society and the place of family life—particularly the place of woman and her relation to a state which in the past provided certain services—remain key for rethinking democracy, whether in the United States or in Eastern Europe. If democracy is to emerge in Eastern Europe, it will develop within a pluralized economy with a combination of market incentives and social planning. There will be moves away from the bureaucratic centralized planning of socialism, but no simple embrace of market capitalism.[11] A new understanding will have to emerge about what is public and what is private.

The critique of statism in Eastern Europe has particular import for women. Women's lives are often more dependent on state policies than men's are in both capitalist and socialist states. Women are most often the recipients of welfare policy, rather than its creators. They are the ones most directly affected by government support for day care, pregnancy leave, and so on. Although women often benefit from an activist service state, they can also be the targets of a paternalist, interventionist one. However, the line dividing public from private can be drawn in different places. For example, in the Nordic countries, the state is quite active, and privatization is a multifaceted concept.[12] Further privatization can mean a transfer of activities, control, and ownership from the public sector to the market, to the family, and to women. Yet privatization can also narrow the prospects of democracy for women.

FEMINISM AND DEMOCRACIES

How does one speak and write of feminism in the 1990s? There are obviously many different kinds of women. Women are located in various societies and cultures and differ by race, economic class, sexual preference, and more. The differences are endless. But there are also connections between the differences which allow me to speak of feminism. As long as one remembers that no view of gender is total and complete, it is important to call political attention to it. However differentiated gender may be, gender oppression exists.[13] The dynamics and contexts of the oppression can shift, taking on different meanings, but it is still oppression. The fact that gender is always defined through racialized economic relations does not negate its significance; it only makes clear that gender cannot be understood in isolation from the relations which define it. A more inclusive feminism would allow us to imagine a more inclusive democracy.

Feminist Slavenka Drakulic has said of Eastern Europe that new male democracies are emerging. She writes that Yugoslavia is "a country where even mother's milk is poisoned by politics."[14] She worries that many women in these countries do not see their own rights as a litmus test for democracy. They do not make enough of the fact that their economies have never been able to provide them with menstrual pads, tampons, or contraceptive devices.

Inji Aflatun, an Egyptian feminist, argued in 1949 that the enemies of women are the enemies of democracy: that Egyptian women's struggles for their political rights are part of the struggle to strengthen democracy in Egypt.[15] The Arab Women's Solidarity Association has argued for women's active participation in the political, economic, social, and cultural life of the Arab world in order to create a true democracy. Such participation requires the elimination of gender discrimination in both the public and private realms of society and a full opening up of the workplace to women.[16] Gada Samman, a Syrian feminist, has stated that "the liberated woman is a person who believes that she is as human as a man. At the same time, she acknowledges that she is a female and he is male, and that the difference between them is how, not how much. Because they are equally human, they must have equal human rights."[17]

These statements cannot be translated identically across cultures, but they do resonate with connections that allow us to see feminism more clearly. By looking at Arab women's lives, one sees, as Margot Badran and Miriam Cooke have argued, that feminism is not always a public expression. It can be the act of one woman writing to another when women are forbidden to write. An analysis of Arab, Indian, African American, South African, or Eastern European women's lives "allows us to see feminism where we had not previously thought to look." But one must be able and willing to look.[18]

Madhu Kishwar, an Indian woman, argues that although she is committed to pro-woman politics, she resists the use of the label *feminism* because of its association with Western feminism, which she sees as another Western export, one which has often been a tool of cultural imperialism.[19] But Kishwar is left without a language to express her commitment. And, in the end, she thereby allows Western imperialism to erase the continuity of the politics of gender.

I continue to use the term *feminist,* even though I recognize its troublesome history, because I need it. It is the only politics that names the problem of gender. We can make it speak through the differences to find the woman in us all. We are better off radicalizing and specifying feminism than speaking only from our differences.

I believe feminism must not only recognize the differences between women but also nurture those differences. This means that feminists must stretch beyond themselves. I am reminded of black filmmaker Bill Duke's statement about crossing boundaries: "Anybody can direct anything—but the point of view will be different." He goes on to say that he has enough humanity and anger in him to make a decent film about Jews in Nazi Germany even though "I don't have the same experience as a young boy who was rocked to sleep in the lap of a grandmother who had a tattooed number on her arm, who told him stories of the people who disappeared, the relatives she never saw again, as he drifted off with his cheek nestled next to that number."[20] Duke does not make light of the differences. But neither does he become circumscribed by them.

A DEMOCRACY BETWEEN "ISMS"

Democracy in the 1990s will be fluid: it will move freely between different economies and politics. Maybe this is the political meaning of postmodernism: that what were once thought of as clearly dichotomous and competing ideologies, discourses, and economies are now recognized as necessary pieces of each other. This realization does not erase politics or make it irrelevant; rather, it recognizes that oppositional politics are not conducive to real democracy. Oppositional politics often lead those in power to use oppressive strategies to hold the oppositions in place. Part of this process is often the limiting of dissent, privileging the viewpoint of those in power. This attempt at silencing dissent was seen in the Bush administration's charges of "political correctness" on college campuses and its wrongful attack on the Western secular model of knowledge; its call for color-blind legislation rather than preferential treatment; and its limited support for AIDS research because it was a disease of those who are "different." Even the Gulf War was made part of this process of silencing dissent and privileging the Western model: once again the message was that we should love America or leave it. Loving America meant supporting the all-American, white, heterosexual family and rescuing poor, oppressed Arab women. One glitch in this message was that many of the troops in the Gulf were women—women of color as well as white women—and these women told another story about family life.

Given recent developments throughout the world, any discussion of democracy must begin with what is missing in both socialism and liberalism. As elements of the two political systems are incorporated not only economically but also politically, we must recall the patriarchal foundations of both systems. The problem of language, especially political language, is key here. Although many argue that it is wrong to call the political systems that evolved in any of the former Eastern European states truly "communist" or "socialist," they *were* named as such, discrediting the discourses of socialism, Communism, and, indirectly, Marxism. Although the real revolution may have been against totalitarian statism, it has been named as a rejection of Communism and its variants. As a result of this naming, many on the Left have argued for modernizing Marxism via liberalism, individualism, and free markets. But others have equated this argument with an embrace of neoconservatism or neoliberalism: an acceptance of the competitive individualism necessitated by the capitalist market.[21]

The struggle toward democracy is a struggle, in some sense, over just how democratic liberalism and its discourse of rights can become. Just how much of the socialist promise of equality can liberalism incorporate without losing its commitment to individual freedom? Most neoconservatives have rejected any moves toward equality and argue that the state has no responsibility for creating equal access. On the other hand, feminists and defenders of civil rights argue that rights must become true to their democratic promise and intention. My argument here is that the radical orientation of rights discourse can be used to transform both liberalism and socialism by specifying their universal commitments to both freedom and equality in terms of sex, gender, and race. Gender, racial, and economic equality must be specified while guaranteeing sexual freedom. This argument reorients liberal democratic rights beyond liberalism and beyond democracy as we have envisioned it in either capitalism or socialism, moving us toward a new theory that has no name.

A well-known Marxist, Ralph Miliband, would agree in part with my orientation here. He acknowledges that socialists will have to build on the foundations of liberal democracy while pushing further in democratic directions. He also states that he does not reject Marxism; instead, he wants to use Marxism to highlight further the contradictions that challenge us.[22] Marxism's strength lies in such uses rather than in providing ready-made solutions. Chantal Mouffe similarly hopes to develop a "post-individualist concept of freedom" that pushes toward a radically libertarian, plural democracy. She adopts the de Tocquevillian notion of "perfect equality" and "entire freedom."[23] The challenge is to give all of these concepts concrete meaning.

Black activist and writer Manning Marable is hesitant about the enterprise of revising liberalism for socialism. For him, liberalism only tries "to humanize an inherently irrational, wasteful and inhumane system"; it "tries to reduce but not eradicate great concentrations of poverty and homelessness." Such attempts are insufficient for him when there are 3 million homeless people, 38 million people without any medical insurance, and millions living in substandard housing, poor and hungry. Given this context, he argues that we must dare to have historical imagination and dare to be Marxists.[24]

Marxism focuses on an egalitarian economy, and in this sense I am a Marxist. However, I think we must also dare to move beyond Marxism to recognize the complex interweavings of racialized sexuality and gender in current structures, and to embrace the diversity that exists within these webs. Marxism is not enough, nor is liberalism. Nor is a feminism bound by these categories. In the end, a radicalized democracy inclusive of women of color may not be enough either—but we are as yet a very long way from finding out.

My sense of postmodern politics is that theory does not create reality. At best, history will be the test of theory. For this reason, I privilege practice and everyday life as definitive of political narrative. It is this practice I turn to now.

PART 1

Stunted Imaginings

*The Problems of Patriarchal Liberalism
and Socialism*

ONE

Eastern European Male Democracies

A Problem of Unequal Equality

I begin this query wondering what kind of relationship may develop between feminism and the Eastern European democratic struggles that began in 1989. Feminism and democracy are terms which have multiple and even conflicting meanings. Be that as it may, I remain committed to the "imaginings" encompassed in the radical potential of both feminist and democratic politics.

The revolutions of 1989 in Eastern Europe have resulted in a confrontation between socialism, capitalism, and democracy. The critique of totalitarian Communist statism by liberal democratic discourse holds promise for a redefinition of liberal rights which could include a radicalized notion of women's rights. As students in Czechoslovakia and Romania have said, "There is no socialist democracy or bourgeois democracy . . . there is either democracy or there isn't."[1] The prodemocracy movements emphasized the individual and individual rights to freedom of choice in speech, thought, and life opportunities. Participants in these movements demanded plural parties, political freedom, and freedom of speech. They wanted greater freedom of expression—in the marketplace, in the universities, and in political parties. Although there was much that the democracy advocates liked about socialism—such as its universal health care and subsidized housing—their demands were for more freedom, not more socialism.

The developments in Eastern Europe thus pose spectacular challenges to our understanding of liberalism and of Marxism. Of course, it is not an accurate reading of historical political theory to view capitalism and socialism as being diametrically opposed. Liberals have previously criticized capitalism for its inequality, and Marxists have criticized socialism for being insufficiently concerned with freedom of expression. John Stuart Mill, considered the father of modern liberalism, repeatedly criticized the inequalities of capitalist economic distribution,[2] and Rosa Luxemburg endlessly called for greater freedom of expression for dissenters of the Bolshevik revolution: "Freedom is always and exclusively freedom for the one who thinks differently."[3]

Nevertheless, it was a strikingly new development for the Soviet state, through Gorbachev's attempts at *glasnost* and *perestroika*, to openly criticize the totalitarian past of "Communism" (the new, pejorative term for the old system) and to invoke aspects of a private market economy for the future. There is no political language set in place to embrace these developments as Eastern European countries, in myriad ways, try to incorporate political pluralism and individual freedom into market economies that still embrace a form of social planning. What presently exists is not completely liberal, completely capitalist, or completely socialist. This uncharted territory holds out the possibility for dislodging the patriarchal foundations of male gender privilege of capitalism (and liberalism) as well as socialism. Alternatively, patriarchy and its hierarchical sexual relations could be rethreaded.

If *really* new ground is to be broken, the insights of Western feminist theorists must refocus the discussion of democracy to include the racialized relations of sex and gender and familial structures and how these relations affect the individual and the economy. Such a refocusing does not mean the erroneous use of Western standards—or Western feminism—on Eastern European societies. Rather, it means rethinking the way democracy is being formulated, especially for women, looking specifically at how the new political structures resolve the conflict between the individual and the patriarchal, totalitarian state.

Many journalists and political analysts write that Eastern European women reject the Western style of feminism along with the enforced "statist" feminism of their previous totalitarian (often equated with Communist) regimes. Both Western liberal feminism and Communist enforced statist feminism share an emphasis on women's equality which purports to treat women like men: entry into the labor market is equated with equal rights. Both of these models obscure the fact that women are not treated equally in the market and, on the whole, occupy second-class citizenship in terms of job opportunities and pay. So neither model can seem liberating to women who are already in the market—at the bottom rungs—and who are also responsible for the care of children and the household and the maintenance of everyday life. The overburdened woman has become a vivid image in the descriptions of Eastern Europe. Less vivid, but nevertheless real, is an emerging feminist consciousness.

I turn first to the way traditional liberal and socialist theories have viewed gender, and how these conceptions continue to affect Eastern European states today. In particular, I examine legislation that purports to grant women greater equality, such as statutes regarding maternity leave, child care, and reproductive rights. I then look more closely at one country in particular: the Soviet Union. I also analyze the writings of Vaclav Havel of the old Czechoslovakia, as representative of post-totalitarian state discourses on women's role in the new democracies. Finally, I examine a few dissident feminist voices that are beginning to challenge the patriarchal orientations of the revolutions of 1989.

I center my focus on gender relations between men and women: in the family, in the economy, in the consumer market, and in the realm of reproductive rights and abortion. This involves questions of the Church and its impact on the larger culture and its ethnic/religious/racialized politics. I slice through these issues, not to obfuscate them, but to find women within them, and then draw some broad theoretical strokes.

WHAT'S NEW AND WHAT'S OLD IN DEMOCRATIC THEORY

The discussion of democracy in Eastern Europe has so far ignored both liberal feminist theory and socialist feminist theory, whether developed in the East or in the West. There is something very old about theories of democracy premised on a citizenry which is assumed to be male, and a politics which is reduced to the relations of power within the economy and the market. The fact that gender was insufficiently theorized by Marx and Lenin is problematic for socialist and democratic theory.[4] But the fact that it continues to be insufficiently recognized and theorized is problematic in a different way. The commitment to democracy for the 1990s should be informed by the feminist critiques of liberalism and socialism of the past two decades.

Liberalism and Marxism both privilege the economy as the core of society. The world of paid work defines the possibilities. Thus, the former Soviet Union as well as other Eastern European countries declared that women had equality because they were a part of the paid labor force. Liberal theory privileges the economy as well, but does so by distinguishing between the public (market) and private (family) spheres. The liberal democratic state does not declare the equality of women to be part of state discourse: her equality is not theorized as such. Rather, she has the freedom either to enter paid work or to perform unpaid work at home. Thus, socialism focuses on supposed economic equality; liberalism, on individual freedom of choice.

In neither instance is woman either really equal or really free: gender equality cannot be equated with the right to work, and individual freedom is not sufficient when women's and men's contributions are not valued similarly in the first place. In the United States as well as in Eastern European countries, most women only have the freedom to choose to work in the lowest paying sectors of the economy, and if they do so choose, they must not only work their jobs but also take the major responsibility for rearing children, buying consumer goods, and maintenance of the home. True, Lenin wanted to socialize housework—whatever that means.[5] J. S. Mill believed that although a woman should have the choice of whether she worked for wages, most women (obviously married, middle-class women) would choose not to.[6]

So where are we? Someplace between liberal and socialist visions of patriarchal society, where the tension between individual freedom and gender equality is not resolved. This place—in-between—is traversed by democratic theory. This place is where we must finally recognize the heterogeneity of power and dislocate the economy as the core of democracy. Liberals and Marxists alike assume that the essentials include food, shelter, and clothing, and that these essentials are provided for in the economy. This, then, is the first order of business: get people what they need. But societies need to reproduce themselves sexually; this is also a core need. And people like to be sexual as well. So there are at least three interconnected cores here.

Marx and Engels recognized early on in their discussions that the division of labor arising from the sex act is the *first* division of labor.[7] They also then promptly forgot about it by assuming that it became the same as the division which arises from private property. Other Marxists followed suit. Communism, the supposed "positive transcendence of private property,"[8] would emancipate women. Democracy would come to women via the transformation of the economy.

Liberal theory promises less, because liberalism does not promise emancipation to either women or men. Instead, it promises opportunity. Like socialism, it privileges the economy and denies any sexual division of labor or gender hierarchy. A woman's labor in the family—the activity of sexual reproduction and childrearing—is hidden in the political sense, because liberal theory only theorizes the relations of the market economy. Women are made absent in terms of their engendered place in the family. If they appear, they do so as workers, demanding equal pay in the labor force or equal rights before the law in the public sphere.

"MOMMY POLITICS": PROTECTIVE LEGISLATION

The kernel of women's rights in the Commonwealth of Independent States, Poland, the Czech and Slovak republics, and former East Germany has been women's right to work for pay.[9] In reality, women's pay is lower than men's, and women's domestic responsibilities are not defined as work. As part of the legacy of Marxism, gender continues to have no political or theoretical status: patriarchal gender differentiation is treated as appropriate. Hildegard Maria Nickel calls this "patriarchal equal rights policy."[10]

Sexual egalitarianism, as defined by statist doctrine, had two components. It equated women's equality with her entrance into the market, and it singled women out for "protection." Protective legislation enacted provisions such as subsidized day care and maternity leaves, which assisted women in their traditional gender roles. Thus, the institution of motherhood was enforced alongside and within the market. Woman was supposed to be treated as equal—that is, treated like a man—once this gender differentiation was put in place. This supposed equality presumed inequality in the first place. Woman was a mother first, then supposedly equal. In this instance, maternity leave served to conceal the patriarchal structure of society.[11]

The totalitarian notion of "state-enforced feminism," which was really neither feminist nor egalitarian, has, according to Ruth Rosen, discredited the discourse of sexual equality.[12] As a result, feminism itself is identified in these countries with a burdensome and deformed equality and state abuse of power. By 1948 in Czechoslovakia, for instance, women's equality was declared a fundamental law of the land, while the gendered institutions of marriage and motherhood were protected by the state.[13] This combination guaranteed women's paid maternity leave *and* their inscribed gender role as mothers.

Protective legislation has been carried out in sporadic and suspect ways. Mainly, it has set women apart as potential bearers of children.

Protective legislation is contradictory at best, not because treating men and women differently is necessarily unfair, but rather because such legislation constrains women's choices in order to ensure their domesticity. It enforces the differentiation of women from men. This is not the same as recognizing specialness in ways that allow for greater freedom of choice in the long run, after special provisions are made. The state intervenes on behalf of patriarchy, rather than affirming women's equality by creating access for them.

Protective legislation in socialist statism has created a complicated and troublesome picture. It is insufficient and problematic, yet it is sometimes better than nothing. It can provide partial relief to women in an already bad situation even as it reinforces gender discrimination. Legislation providing maternity leave and day care for children has provided much-needed assistance for women in Eastern Europe; at the same time, it has enforced domesticity. Although there is a big difference between assistance and equality, women do not want to give up the former without the assurance of the latter.

To the extent that changes toward a free market endanger maternity and child care provisions, women in Eastern Europe are reluctant to embrace them. They fear loss of their jobs. Their particular status—defined by domestic, wage, and consumer labor—defines specific problems for them. The changes toward greater democracy pose a more complicated challenge for women than for men: the free market endangers much of what has been guaranteed to women in the past, and it is not clear what it can bring them as women in the future, if it continues the patriarchal stance of the old socialism and of Western capitalism. Already assistance to Eastern European countries from the International Monetary Fund has been made contingent on the sale of state industry and the initiation of an austerity program that dramatically cuts back all social services.[14] These cutbacks will have particularly negative effects on women, who are already hard-pressed by a triple day of labor.

Such changes may be the most complicated for the women of East Germany, where the support systems for women in paid employment with children were some of the best. Although many East German feminists have critically labeled the special provisions "mommy politics," they are well aware of the import of these services for working mothers.[15] These provisions included shorter work weeks for women with two or more children; one paid day off a month for women who were over forty, were married, or had children under sixteen years of age; a year of maternity leave with pay amounting to about 80 percent of one's salary; and free day care and infant care centers.[16] East German women clearly had an array of social benefits to lose: maternity and paternity leave, comprehensive medical care, job guarantees, first-trimester abortion on demand, free contraceptives, and more.[17]

Since 1989, women of the former East Germany have been hard hit. Child care centers have closed or raised their prices. More and more women have been forced out of work and are on welfare. Single mothers are disproportionately represented among the unemployed, as are women over fifty and women with college degrees. The new social agenda and economic infrastructure are returning women to the home as the economy worsens.[18] It is right to fear that new legislation will fail to address the complicated reality of women's specific needs and universal human rights.

In Poland, where equality on the basis of gender had been guaranteed by the constitution in 1952, protective legislation was well established. By 1968 women were entitled to one year of unpaid maternity leave, which was extended to a three-year leave in 1972. The new "post-Communist" government has already limited women's entitlements. Women report continuing discrimination in government and labor. They have been hit the hardest by unemployment.[19] Those women who continue to work are in the textile, food, and pottery industries, where they hold unsafe and monotonous jobs. Almost all of these women workers remain solely responsible for household labor.

Similar events are happening throughout Eastern Europe. In Hungary, under the previous regime, women had twenty-four weeks of maternity leave at full pay, followed by a three-year leave at partial salary with a promise of job tenure. The new market economy does not promise anyone a job after a three-year absence.

When protective policies assist women in their domesticated roles, they enforce the existing gender code. Yet such policies can also lessen discrimination, as they can lessen women's responsibilities for children and domestic chores. It is in this spirit that Rosen calls for a gender democracy based on "equality with a difference," which recognizes the need for parental leave, child care, and family life supports.[20]

REPRODUCTIVE AND CONTRACEPTIVE RIGHTS

In most Eastern European countries, reproductive rights for women have remained outside the purview of equality. If women are treated like men, reproductive issues are silenced, because no man ever needs an abortion, and no man needs contraception to prevent his own pregnancy. This standard of "likeness" functions in liberal democratic as well as socialist theory. Neither recognizes reproductive rights as essential. Both systems were constructed with men (and their nonreproductive bodies) in mind. This narrow vision set the context for statist notions of equality. Such myopia has continued in the new democracies. There has been no concerted effort to address the need for sex education, the availability of contraceptives, or the fundamental right to abortion. Indeed, in several countries legislation on reproductive issues has become more restrictive.[21]

In Poland, for example, abortion was legalized in 1956 and was available without restrictions until 1990. The new government has imposed regulations for state-run hospitals requiring examination of the woman by two gynecologists and a psychologist.[22] Moreover, the government has repeatedly attempted to push anti-abortion legislation through Sejm, the Polish parliament. In May 1991, the government's legislation banning abortions was rejected; instead, lawmakers adopted a nonbinding resolution that called on the government to ban abortions by private doctors. But by spring 1993, Poland had the most restrictive law on abortion of any country in Eastern Europe. The government also ended subsidies for birth control pills in May 1991. The cost of a month's supply of pills increased from ninety cents to three dollars.[23] Reproductive rights in Poland remain a fundamental arena of conflict, both within the state and between the state and the Catholic church.

During the negotiations for German unification, abortion rights could not be agreed upon.[24] Abortion was restricted in West Germany, whereas it was unrestricted during the first trimester in the East. The parties reached a compromise that allowed both the East German and the West German laws to remain in place for two years. The abortion law subsequently passed, in June 1992, is a compromise between West Germany's restrictive and East Germany's more permissive laws. It permits abortion in the first three months of pregnancy if the woman states that she is in distress and if she has been through officially sanctioned counseling. After the first trimester, abortion can be performed only if there is a threat to the woman's life, or if the fetus has no chance for survival. Opinion polls in Germany show that 75 percent of all Germans—male and female—support the right to abortion in the first trimester.[25]

In Romania, women have started to gain some recognition of reproductive rights, especially as compared with the extreme control exer-

cised by the previous "pro-family" regime, in which the state "protected" the interests of mothers and children.[26] Under Ceausescu, abortion
and contraception were illegal, and multiple unwanted pregnancies were
a reality, as attested by the large number of children in orphanages. The
new government lifted the abortion ban in December 1989, reducing
the number of abandoned newborns in Romanian maternity wards to
a trickle.[27]

It remains to be seen whether other Eastern European countries will
expand or erode recognition of women's reproductive rights. These societies are dominated by traditional values about women's role as mother.
Such values operate as an inflexible cultural model which denies women
their right to reproductive choice and, in the end, their sexual equality.
Feminists in countries such as Sweden and Denmark have argued that
control over reproductive issues affects women's lives more profoundly
than any equality legislation could ever do. They acknowledge technological innovations like the contraceptive pill and the IUD as revolutionary for women's moves toward democracy.[28] One wonders what
the possibilities can be for women in Poland or the Commonwealth of
Independent States, where there is outright hostility to women's reproductive choices. I turn now to a more in-depth look at one of these
countries: the former Soviet Union.

A CLOSER LOOK: SOVIET SOCIETY AND THE "WOMAN QUESTION"

The Soviet state was the first government in history to declare women's
emancipation, in 1917; it wrote that emancipation into law and made
abortion legal in 1920. (Abortion was later criminalized under Stalin,
in 1936, and then reliberalized in 1955.) Article 35 of the 1977 Constitution declared equality of rights between women and men. Yet protective legislation has barred women from as many as 460 occupations, in
order to protect their maternal function and their gender roles. Motherhood, rather than parenthood, is at issue in this legislation; biologism
exists right alongside Soviet egalitarianism.[29] But there is no consistency
in this protectionism. Women have always done heavy labor in the
countryside and have been the rubbish collectors and street cleaners in
the cities.[30]

Before the dissolution of the Soviet Union, Soviet society had the
largest number of women professionals and specialists on the globe,
although few filled the top ranks; close to 90 percent of its female pop-

ulation were in the work force.[31] However, there was an average gap
of about 30 percent between men's and women's wages; women pre-
dominate in low-paid, feminized occupations, and nearly one-half of
the female work force is employed at unskilled manual labor.[32]

By the fall of 1992, economic turmoil was causing untold suffering
for Russian women. In Moscow, 70 percent of the newly unemployed
were women between the ages of 45 and 55. Women's economic degradation can be seen in the overwhelming number who have become
peddlers and prostitutes.[33]

Add to this precarious economic situation the place of abortion in
most Russian women's lives, both before and since 1989. The average
Soviet woman has six to eight abortions in her lifetime. But it is not
unheard of to have as many as eighteen.[34] Women's health care is of
key concern to women, particularly in terms of the availability of safe
abortions under humane conditions. Because of waiting lists in Soviet
hospitals, anywhere from 4 to 8 million abortions are performed ille-
gally each year.[35] A major concern of Soviet women is a more adequate
supply of reliable contraceptives. At present, diaphragms come in only
three sizes. It is almost impossible to get condoms, and there is no spermicidal cream.

The problem of safe abortions and available contraceptives reflects
more than a troubled consumer economy. *Perestroika* focuses on the
economic market, as though consumerism is ungendered. But there is a
patriarchal structure that underlies consumer products and the activity of consumerism itself. For instance, there is a particular scarcity of
labor-saving devices for the Soviet household; women do most of the
endless shopping and waiting; lines are too long, and shopping takes
too much time; children's nurseries are ill-equipped and scarce; contraceptives are almost impossible to buy. Many of these consumer issues
directly affect and reflect the sex and gender hierarchy of society. And
they in part constitute what Gorbachev calls the "decay of family life"
under the old policies. But instead of restructuring the economy to respond to the needs of women and their families, the Soviet state wants
to refocus women toward their roles at home.[36] As women are redirected toward the home, the home will not be liberalized or democra-
tized. Whatever restructuring there will be will take place in the economy.

There will most probably be an increase in the gender segregation of
the labor force and a renewed interest in woman as mother. Women
will be freed from their involuntary emancipation and will be "al-

lowed" to return to their families. This rejection of woman's emancipation may become part of the general reaction against Communism and may derive a certain legitimacy from it. The corruptness of the Communist state, which never really emancipated women, can be used to justify returning woman to her womanly duties as a form of "emancipation." But this is a vision of patriarchal democracy which harkens back to eighteenth-century France and Jean-Jacques Rousseau. In the process of rejecting totalitarian Communism, patriarchal gender relations can be rearticulated.

In Gorbachev's *Perestroika,* his plan for restructuring Soviet society, he states that women have been given ". . . the same right to work as men, equal pay for equal work, and social security. Women have been given every opportunity to get an education, to have a career, and to participate in social and political activities." He does not compare the theory with practice. For him, the problem lies elsewhere: "We have failed to pay attention to women's 'specific' rights and needs arising from their role as mother and homemaker, and their indispensable educational function as regards children." He argues that women do not have enough time for their special domestic and familial roles. He blames the slackening of family ties on ". . . making women equal with men in everything." *Perestroika* means returning women to ". . . their purely womanly mission."[37] Gorbachev proposed, beginning in 1991, an extra six months of tenured, although unpaid, maternity leave.

Soviet women have responded to these issues in a variety of ways. Surveys have shown that many rural women prefer to work and show little interest in leading domestic lives.[38] A 1990 poll showed that only 20 percent of Russian women "want to stay at home."[39] In other studies, professional women say their work and their children are the most important aspects of their lives. There are women like Tatyana Mamonova, a Russian feminist, who write openly in criticism of the sexism of Soviet culture.[40] Others, like Tatyana Tolstaya, feel that "a Soviet woman's dream is to not have to work."[41] This is the view of Soviet women which is depicted regularly by the Western press and by Francine du Plessix Gray in her much-publicized *Soviet Women, Walking the Tightrope.* She presents Soviet women as thinking they have "too much equality."[42]

The gist of the argument of *Soviet Women* is that Soviet women neither need nor want Western-style feminism. Gray clumps all Soviet women at one extreme and all Western feminists at the other; the latter are viewed as clinging to the tenet of early liberal feminism (à la Betty

Friedan) that women want the right to work and not to be relegated to the home.[43] As Gray puts it, "American women are still struggling for the freedom *to*, whereas Soviet women are now struggling for freedom *from*."[44] Actually, today there is much more similarity than difference between the two societies in this realm. Most women want some relief from their double day of labor in the United States and their triple day (including the time spent on queues) in Soviet society. Some believe the solution to their frustrations would be getting a job; others desire a better job or a job requiring fewer hours; others see a need for a reorganization of domestic labor; and still others wish for all of these things. And some women express their general disdain with their present lot as the Leningrad novelist Daniil Granin did: "*Feministka* is a strictly pejorative term in our country."[45]

A Soviet woman interviewed by Gray advises, "We must own up to our great differences and stop fearing them. . . . To differ doesn't mean to stand lower."[46] This statement is an indictment of the Soviet statist approach to equality of the sexes. For some Soviet women, *perestroika* appears to hold out a promise that they will only work if they wish to; they will no longer have to. It offers their husbands the potential to earn more money and to free their wives from the necessity of jobs. These women joke that they are all for *perestroika* if it will wake up the *lichnost*, the individualism, in their men. They say that "one of the aims of perestroika is to motivate men to work as well as women." They speak of the passivity of Soviet men and of their own resourcefulness. "Women can do everything; men can do the rest."[47] However inchoate the feelings of Soviet women are, they bespeak a tension surrounding gender relations. Gray somewhat simplistically concludes that, instead of a women's movement, Soviet society needs a men's movement. For her, women already have power because of their role in the inner emotional life of the family.

But there is a difference between being important—especially in the circumscribed world of the family—and having power. If you have power, you do not wait on queues and you do not have multiple unsafe and illegal abortions. When you have power, you take part in making the rules. Instead, the rules are made for Soviet women, and the rules treat women not as individuals but as mothers. They do not get to choose this assignment—which is different than saying that no woman would choose motherhood if left free to do so. Rather, it says that the designation of women as mothers is a political construction which deprives women of choice. Moreover, the options are constricted: the reality of motherhood in Soviet society is different from the abstract wish to have a child; the requirements of feeding, queuing, and parenting are daunting.

Whose democracy does *perestroika* envision? I do not think it is women's. Yelena Khanga, a Soviet journalist based in New York City, would agree. She deplored the total demoralization she found among women in Moscow on her visit in the fall of 1991. *Glasnost,* the cultural side of *perestroika,* had brought fashion magazines, music videos, and Western images of feminine beauty to Moscow "without Western feminist ideas about female brains and competence."[48] Women in Moscow need a feminism to make *perestroika* democratic for them, too.

HAVEL AND HIS PATRIARCHAL DEMOCRACY

Things do not look much better for the women of Eastern Europe when we examine the philosophical writings of one of the leading spokespersons of the new democracies. Vaclav Havel, playwright, former dissident, and president of Czechoslovakia (until its division), has come to represent the democratic spirit of the revolutions throughout Eastern Europe.[49] He has been a searing critic of the totalitarian state and its destruction of people's inner selves. His distrust of the state has led to his "antipolitical" stance on politics: that individuals must know and trust themselves rather than any political ideology. It is unclear, however, whether women are included in Havel's vision of a new democracy or his radical indictment of totalitarian statism.

In his latest writing, Havel prefers to speak without political labels. He no longer calls himself a socialist, although he identified as such about a decade ago. Havel says, "I stopped calling myself a socialist without changing my political opinions."[50] Now the word *socialism* seems hollowed of meaning for him. It means a market economy for Gorbachev, massacring students for Li Peng, and bulldozing his people for Ceausescu.[51] Havel sees it as obscuring, rather than illuminating, one's vision of what is possible.

Havel fears that the term *perestroika* is starting to resemble the word *socialism.* He prefers to write of "post-totalitarianism," or "anti-political politics," because he sees these as nonideological constructions. The heart of his writing is antistatist. He has a strong antagonism toward undeserved privilege and enforced inequities. He writes: "I think that everyone, as far as possible, should have the same chances."[52]

According to Havel, most Czechs and Slovaks are not hostile to so-

cialism; rather, they criticize socialism as it has been practiced for failing to live up to its principles. Whatever the term, Havel argues that
our enemy is no longer totalitarianism, but rather "our own bad quali-
ties."[53] His presidential program, therefore, focuses on bringing "spir-
ituality," "moral responsibility," "humaneness," and "humility" into
politics in order to ". . . make clear that there is something higher above
us, that our deeds do not disappear into the black hole of time, but are
recorded somewhere and judged, that we have neither the right nor a
reason to think that we understand everything and that we can do
everything."[54] His focus is on the individual as well as on a higher order
that judges us. God alone can save us.[55] There is an uneasy blend of
liberal individualism and religiosity in his "antipolitical" politics.

Havel leaves God in place as he dissolves much of modernism: ratio-
nalism, scientism, and positivism. For him, Communism was the perverse extreme of the modern construction of "universal systemic solutions." The crisis of Communism can be read as a part of the crisis of
generality, universality, and objectivity. And the answer cannot be found
in new scientific recipes or new universals.[56] The answers will be more
local and specific.

Havel is committed to economic democracy. Capitalism is no simple
answer for him: "Enormous private multinational corporations are curiously like socialist states."[57] Anonymous unaccountable bureaucracies exist in both economic systems. Instead, he believes, economic units
must be set up to renew their relationships with individuals on a continuing basis. Havel subscribes to open competition for power as the only
real guarantee of public control. Part of this process is the "rehabilitation of values like trust, openness, responsibility, solidarity, love."[58]
The economic organization of society must also be decentralized and
should ensure maximum diversity. He prefers small enterprises that respect the specific nature of different localities and different traditions
that resist the pressures of uniformity by maintaining a plurality of modes
of ownership and economic decision-making.[59] This sounds good.
However, historically, traditional patriarchal families have often existed within small business economies.

A democratic, legalistic approach is necessary but insufficient for
Havel—as are all political constructions. In the end, it is the individual,
with the help of God, who will allow the "truth" to prevail. The concept of "truth" itself appears problematic for Havel's stance, but he
believes that the truth remains open. In the end, it is not political order
for which Havel searches, but rather meaning in life for individuals. No

legal or political system can ensure this. My query remains: Are these individuals men and women, or just men?

The totalitarian state represents "special interests" for Havel. Somewhat contradictorily to his critique of modernism, he argues that the state must represent universal needs. In rejecting state totalitarianism, he argues, democratic theory needs to recognize that the universal condition is also particular and specific. Socialist theory assumed that the proletariat represented the universal need of humanity. Liberal theory assumes the universalist stance of rights. However, there are specific needs which must be recognized within the proletariat: the needs of individuals, of men and women, and of ethnic factions and religious groups. Universalism does not ensure democracy; it merely promises that democracy *can* exist.

Havel's vision of democracy focuses on and privileges the economy as the arena of democracy. Democracy requires that the relations "between man and his co-workers, between subordinates and their superiors, between man and his work" do not lose sight of the personal connection.[60] There is no mention of women and their work, and nothing to indicate even that "man" is used in the "generic" sense here. Nor does Havel's analysis include the home and the work found there, or the special relations of men and women to these spheres and to each other.

Does Havel believe that women can also construct the meanings of truth? Can we assume that Havel's critique of privilege extends to male privilege? Can we assume that when Havel argues that everyone should have equal chances in life, he includes women? Or does the birthing of children, or domestic responsibilities, define women's options differently? And why are we left to assume so much?

It is not at all clear what Havel envisions for the family or the Church. He argues that there is a higher order of religion that should constrain all politics. But religion has hardly been a democratic friend of women. This is particularly true of the Catholic church in Eastern Europe.

Havel's use of language surely tells us something. He writes only about men, naming them as "men." His metaphors are based in male preoccupations. He writes of moral "impotence" and the "castration" of culture.[61] When we explore more carefully the imagery of gender in Havel's writing, his commitment to democracy for women becomes more troublesome. One worries that Havel is not just forgetting to include women in his "post-totalitarian" thoughts—that, in fact, a post-patriarchal construction of democracy is not what he has in mind.[62]

In discussing his criticism of the Warsaw Pact and NATO, Havel says that United States troops should not be separated from their "mothers" forever. Why not speak of parents in this instance? When speaking of the difficulty of life, he states, "I only think that everything today is somehow harder and rougher, that one has to pay more dearly for things and that the dream of a freer, more meaningful life is no longer just a matter of running away from Mommy, as it were, but a tough-minded everyday confrontation with the dark powers of the New Age."[63] Woman is represented as someone men desire to escape from. He uses the category of motherhood as an inevitable construction and engenders it as such. What about fathers or the nonsexually specified "parent"? Language matters.

In his play *Temptation,* he criticizes the irrationality of bureaucracy and the sale of people's souls to the devil.[64] He establishes this critique through stereotypes of gender and sexuality. Marketa, a working-class woman, represents the pure and good in a womanhood undefiled by intellectuality. In contrast, Vilma, a professional woman, is a scientist and represents corruption. Women's choices in the play are thus restricted to the classic ones of either angel or whore. Moreover, the director of the institute, who represents evil, is homosexual. This symbolism represents an exclusionary sexual and gender politics. Women's choices are predetermined and seriously curtailed, and homosexuality is problematized. Patriarchal privilege is written all over this play.

Havel writes about his wife, Olga, that she is "someone who could respond to my own mental instability, offer sober criticism of my wildest ideas, provide private support for my public adventures."[65] In his letters to her from prison, he instructs her to be more independent in the practical areas, where she had "often complained I've suppressed your initiative."[66] In another letter, he writes: "Be calm, serene, cheerful, industrious, sociable, kind to everyone, optimistic . . . dress nicely . . . study my letters carefully and try to carry out the tasks I set you." And, in yet one more letter, he directs: "This temporary emancipation from my domination is allowing you to develop your own identity. But of course, I am happiest of all to see that you are living and acting—if I may put it this way—in my spirit."[67] Perhaps one should not make too much of these letters. After all, they are private letters written under severe stress and the constraints of prison. And yet, these letters were published with his agreement for the public to read, to let us know better who Havel is. I do not think he is a post-patriarchal democrat.

As for Olga, she has stated that although life is very difficult for Czech women with their triple work shifts, and although woman's status must change, she does not see the need to differentiate women's rights from those of old people or children. "Laws must be enacted to ease the burden of women, but there are more pressing things to be done in our society." [68]

The brief thoughts on feminism Havel records are unsettling and troubling. When a group of Italian feminists visited Prague seeking women's signatures to a petition demanding "respect of human rights, disarmament, demilitarization," and so on, Havel received them with disdain. He says he assumed the women were middle-class and thought the petition inappropriate. He explains that he does not mean to ridicule feminism, because "he knows little about it" and "assumes that it is not merely the invention of a few hysterics, bored housewives, or rejected mistresses." Yet he nonetheless believes "that in our country even though the position of women is incomparably worse than in the West, feminism seems simply 'dada.' " [69] For Havel, feminism is a foreign import. His views did not keep several Czech women from signing the petition, however.

Nor do they gibe with Alena Heitlinger's views on the status of women in Czechoslovakia or the need for feminism there. She writes that the legacy of Communism has left Czech and Slovak women particularly vulnerable under the new regime. Women continue to be marginalized politically. Economic restructuring is creating the involuntary unemployment of women. This loss of jobs is masked by a rhetoric calling for women's domesticity. [70]

As long as feminism, however it is defined, is thought of as "dada" by leaders in Eastern Europe, the struggle toward real democracy will be much more difficult. Totalitarianism and bureaucratic statism cannot be fully dismantled without addressing the unquestioned patriarchal privileging of men in the state, the economy, and the home. Democracy must be formulated for family life, as well as the market, if it is to have real meaning for everyday life. Existing liberal democratic and socialist theories of sexual equality are insufficient. Paternalist protectionist policies do not work. Neither do universalist ones.

Unfortunately, the questions that Havel's vision of democracy elicits have been put on hold. Instead, the Czech and Slovak republics have become mired in the process of privatization. Havel fears that the legacy of statist Communism may run too deep for Czechs to move truly beyond it. Racialized patriarchy may run too deep as well.

EASTERN EUROPEAN FEMINISM

Like the women in the Commonwealth of Independent States, women throughout Eastern Europe have responded in diverse ways to the post-totalitarian turmoil. Some women see staying home as new and progressive in light of the unequal burdens of the forced equality of the past. These women see the right to work as one of the old state lies that forced them into unskilled jobs, subsistence wages, and triple shifts of work. To these women, feminism sounds similar to the old Communism. In the "emerging male democracies," these women "have so many worries that the least of them is whether they are emancipated or not."[71]

Other women, who identify themselves as feminists, demand that the new governments recognize the equality of women. However, there is no easy resolution to the issues of how special legislation recognizing women's particular responsibilities should be woven into a new, radicalized vision of democracy, or how special legislation can be designed that does not relegate women to a secondary status or "mommy track." Maud Edwards argues that the institutionalized ideology of equal status and equal treatment provides no guarantee of material or real equality. In fact, such an ideology can sustain oppression by concealing it,[72] as it has in many Eastern European states.

Women's mistrust of the statist rhetoric encompassing sexual equality creates a complicated politics which defines much of the context surrounding "women's issues" in Eastern Europe. To the extent that abortion has replaced other contraceptive choices as a means of birth control, the demand for condoms or diaphragms can be seen as a liberation from repeated abortions. To the extent that pornography represents a rebellion against state coercion, it may be embraced by some as a statement of individual freedom. To the extent that the family functioned as a private sphere of resistance against the Communist state, women value the role they played in this sphere[73] and feel protective of it. An effective feminist politics must thread these concerns through a renewed critique of the patriarchal formulations of both socialism and capitalism.

Although there is little agreement over what feminism is exactly, or its appropriate role in creating post-patriarchal democracies between women in Eastern Europe and the Commonwealth of Independent States, feminist voices are emerging.[74] Shortly after the German revolution in November 1989, a manifesto was drawn up by the Lila Offensive, a Berlin women's group that is part of the Autonomous Women's Association of the German Democratic Republic (GDR). The Autonomous Women's Association is a "societal-cultural concept to ensure that women will not be cut short in the new political process."[75] The Lila Manifesto represents one of the first independent statements of women's interests in the new East Germany, and it articulates the promise that these women saw in the recent revolution. It systematically attacks the gendered formulations of what the authors term "centralized, administrative socialism."[76] The manifesto, subtitled a "working paper," indicts the conflicts between paid work and motherhood for women; the underpaid and undervalued status of jobs performed by women; and the assignment of household labor to women. The women of the Lila Offensive declare that "the women's question in the GDR has not been resolved" and that the "elimination of capitalist means of production is indeed a prerequisite, but no guarantee of the cessation of patriarchal repression."[77]

These women are anticapitalists and self-defined feminists. They view sexual equality as "one of the most basic values of a socialist society." "Feminism means for us, the protection and representation of women's interests, with the ultimate goal of achieving equality between the sexes, irrespective of lifestyle and love relations." The women of the Lila Offensive demand that women be given a more active place in political decision making at all levels; that the right to work be guaranteed to every woman and man; and that their nation be based upon the principles of antifascism, anti-imperialism, and anti-Stalinism. They specifically demand that there be no social decline for women as a result of the restructuring of the labor force and the consequent dismissals and replacements; that legislation support the compatibility of motherhood and fatherhood with employment; that social policy measures assigned one-sidedly to mothers be removed; and that the rights and duties of fatherhood be clearly spelled out. In the realm of sexual self-determination, they call for a guaranteed right to abortion and the humanization of health services, especially in terms of gynecological care.

Feminists of the Lila Offensive know that their problem is not too much equality, but rather, too little of it. They recognize that protective legislation does not in and of itself acknowledge women's rights, but rather protects gender privilege for men, unless it is committed to a sexual egalitarianism which is post-socialist and post-capitalist.

Feminist reaction to the new "emerging male democracies" continues to develop. The Yugoslav Independent Alliance of Women has been created as an independent, non–party-affiliated, and transnational women's organization. In Poland, the anti-abortion legislation sponsored by the government in 1989 created at least a dozen new groups with feminist concerns.[78] The feminist challenge in all of these countries is to address a radicalized democracy which unsettles the gendered structures of both statist socialism and "free" markets.

It is within the flux of ideas from socialism, capitalism, liberalism, and democracy that the richness of feminist theory and politics can be found. Feminist theory, even in its liberal version, recognizes the importance of individual identity within the collectivity. A feminist must recognize the collective category of women. Nevertheless, gender identity is never identical to one's individuality, and one's individuality cannot be subsumed by collectivity. The individual can never be fully conceptualized outside her community, as in liberal democratic theory, nor can she be subsumed by the community or the state, as in socialist theory. With feminism as a starting point for a new democratic theory, we begin with the tension between individuality and collectivity rather than making false starts toward one or the other.

I distinguish here between liberal individualism, which pictures an atomized and disconnected person in competition with others, and a post-patriarchal individuality that recognizes the capacities and diversity of individuals, although as a part of a community that can either enhance or constrain their development.[79] The individual is no longer seen as separate and apart from others, as in patriarchal liberalism; nor is the individual subsumed by the collective or the state, as in patriarchal socialism.

Racism and nationalism currently abound throughout Eastern Europe. Particular legacies of patriarchal privilege are being unearthed as the divestment of Communism uncovers older patriarchal traditions rooted in ethnic Slavic cultures, Catholicism, and racial conservatism with overtones of antisemitism. The human disaster produced by ethnic conflicts between Serbia and Croatia bespeaks the remains of the fascist politics of World War II. The hatred between some Hungarians and Romanians is rooted in deeply racialized and nationalistic loyalties. Gypsy women in Hungary have been singled out as scapegoats and have been coerced into undergoing sterilization. In the new Germany, Nazi Skinheads represent a growing right-wing movement which is particularly fascinated with the Ku Klux Klan (KKK) in the United States.[80] These expressions of racial and ethnic hatred pose serious threats to a non-patriarchal vision of democracy, in part because they keep gender oppression in place.

So we are left trying to imagine a democracy that is not patriarchal or torn apart by racial hatred. The Eastern European struggles toward democracy in 1989 looked hopeful and promising. Today they look much more dismal. Nationalism, racism, and sexism seem to have stunted the possibilities for democratic markets. But the story is not yet complete. In the meantime, feminists must fight for affirmative state policies which will nurture a racial and sexual equality that does not assume sameness of treatment as the standard. Feminists need to envision an activist state that does not intervene on behalf of patriarchal interests. The critique of bureaucratic statism is crucial for Western feminists as we demand greater access from our own states for abortion, for jobs, for treatment of AIDS. Let us move now to a discussion of these issues closer to home, in the United States.

PART 2

Who Needs Guns?

The Privatization of the American State

TWO

United States Politics and the Myth of Post-Racism

*The Supreme Court, Affirmative Action,
the Black Middle Class, and the New
Black Conservatives*

The revolutions of 1989 in Eastern Europe contrasted starkly with conservative developments during the same period in the United States. Even as our government was celebrating the victory of democracy abroad, our Supreme Court chose to gut existing civil rights law at home. These decisions solidified the right-wing takeover of the federal judiciary begun in the early 1980s by the Reagan Administration and orchestrated by Edwin Meese. This was a revolution of another kind, perhaps our own postmodern revolution of 1989: dispersed and inchoate. The usual political language simply no longer applies.

Beginning with the decisions of spring 1989, the Supreme Court has fundamentally changed civil rights law. Its decisions reflect and nurture the racialized gender privilege of United States culture as it enters the 1990s. This process of racializing gender is taking place within a racist framework in which people of color are devalued as not white. Although there is nothing inevitable which requires racialized meanings to be racist, it is almost impossible to imagine beyond this point in history.

As a type of politics, the system of racialized patriarchy is always in process. The sites of power shift, fluctuate, and merge. The continuing internationalization of the market and the racial diversification of the United States labor force in part explain the defensive posture of many white men. I examine here how race has become a dynamic, shifting force in renegotiating white male privilege.

This chapter and the next one discuss the politics which deny that societal racism constructs an inhibiting structural reality for people of color. In this particular neoconservative framing of race, structural racism—the system of societal, institutional, cultural, and market mechanisms that limit the choices and options of people of color—supposedly no longer exists. In this political view, race is defined by the black/white divide. "Black" stands in for multiple colors and distorts complex relations within and between different racial groups. This bipolar construction of race also distorts the complicated and various relations between these groups and white society.

Most neoconservatives blame those who are poor and "black" for not showing enough initiative themselves. The neoconservatives emphasize individual responsibility and self-help over affirmative action law. In their view, we are all individuals who are seeking opportunities according to our individual merit. Thus, equal rights mean that everyone should be given similar, color-blind treatment. Any recognition of "special" rights is viewed as unfair preference because all persons are supposedly the same. This dismissal of governmental responsibility applies to people of color and white women alike.

In the sixties and seventies, the Civil Rights and feminist movements demanded more democracy of the liberal democratic state. These movements were met with the rightist and the neoconservative assaults of the 1980s. The democratic aspects of liberalism were restricted to a more privatized notion of individual opportunity. A battle was waged by the Reagan and Bush administrations to narrow civil rights and abortion legislation.[1] Mainstream feminist and civil rights organizations were largely defined in reaction to this assault by neoconservatives and rightists.

By the end of the 1980s, the political discourse of a privatized state was firmly in place. Government was responsible for less. Individuals and their families would have to do more. In this chapter, I explore how this particular antigovernment view was institutionalized as official rhetoric through a racialized discourse that piggybacked women's issues along with it. The idea that a state should take action to affirm equality of opportunity was replaced by a classic notion of rugged individualism. The dismantling of affirmative action legislation has been the centerpiece of this process.

This individualism was positioned against established civil rights discourse in order to discredit that discourse as well as feminist demands. Such legislation is earmarked as discriminatory in reverse. It is even characterized by many neoconservatives as a new form of racism: the unfair preferential treatment of minorities. Less is said directly about white women.

The political discourse of the privatized state institutionalized this racialized, patriarchal viewpoint. Individualism, as a generalized notion (really meaning "white men"), is neutralized against the backdrop of the special interests of "black" people. The standard of "universal *man*" represents fairness. White men define their own racialized, patriarchal standpoint as neutrality.

The process of differentiating people of color from the white standard is a process of differentiating women from men, women of color from white men, women of color from white women, and men of color from white women. These relationships are silenced in most political racial talk. Racism and sexism are usually spoken of either separately or as one and the same thing in mainstream discourse. This false separation—or equation—of gender with its racialized meanings and racism with its engendered forms distorts the relations of power involved, especially for women of color.

Racialized patriarchy that reflects the complex connections between racial and sexual privilege is differentiated by gender, while gender is differentiated in and through the racialized meanings of whiteness. By "in and through," I mean that definitions of womanhood are simultaneously definitive and reflective of racist images and practices. The language reads: "single parent," "welfare mother," "woman with AIDS," and so on. Each engendered construction is illustrative of racial categorizations. We need only to speak of one to elicit the other. In official political talk, "single parents" mean black teenage girls and/or their mothers on welfare. These constructions bespeak the racialized aspects of gender.

This also happens in reverse. Anti-affirmative action talk speaks of race and also means gender. The dismissal of gender equality remains a subtext in the attack on racial equality. The open attack on racial affirmative action policies reflects the underlying racism of United States politics and the ease with which racism can be called forth. It has been easy to pit merit against entitlement programs (supposedly without merit) servicing black men and women. This focus on race allows the idea of affirmative action to be ghettoized to people of color, the people without merit. When affirmative action is specified for white women, it undermines the opposition of merit to racialized entitlement. But when white women are not named in this process, neither is their claim to affirmative action.

In much current political discourse, race stands in for gender as well. Race and gender are then treated as a political package and equated, as though when you address one, you automatically address the other. When the problem of racism is dismissed in political talk, sexism is also dismissed without ever having to deal with it directly. This reflects something of a shift from the New Right presidential politics of the early Reagan years, which were dominated by a "profamily," antiabortion, antifeminist agenda, whose subtext was racial: the disintegration of the black family. By 1988 this rhetoric, under the tutelage of Lee Atwater, had shifted to a more openly racist agenda. The texts of both racism and antifeminism trace the neoconservative rejection of liberalism and its excesses: too much equality and the "rights revolution." [2] The shifting language of the texts hides its true colors: anti–affirmative action politics are racist and antifeminist politics in drag.

The attack on "rights" legislation (and, less so, on abortion) provided the Bush administration with a needed deceptive rhetoric. It justified the dismantling of affirmative action law as the only fair thing to do. At the same time, it reconstituted the state and its responsibilities within a highly privatized and moralist discourse.

RACISM AND U.S. POLITICS

More often than not, the 1964 Civil Rights Act was treated by the Reagan and Bush administrations as the problem rather than as the solution to racial inequality. Affirmative action policies were blamed for creating a new racism, one that denied white men a fair chance to compete and one that crippled blacks, particularly black men, from striving to achieve on their own merit. Racism, however, both predates and postdates affirmative action. It existed long before affirmative action law. It was not caused by it. The Civil Rights Act of 1964 was enacted because of the racist nature of U.S. law and social relations. A black slave was considered three-fifths of a person in 1787; in 1857, persons of African descent were found to be an inferior and unequal class of beings; not until the Emancipation Proclamation were slaves legally freed; our Constitution needed the 13th amendment to prohibit slavery; as late as 1896, the Court found that racial segregation did not jeopardize equal protection under the law; and not until 1954, in *Brown v. Board of Education,* was segregation in the public schools found to be unconstitutional. [3] At its best, affirmative action has sought to straitjacket racism, not remove it. To say that affirmative action created a new racism is to rewrite history and turn civil rights against itself.

Take the differential treatment of whites and people of color by the courts themselves. The 1991 report of the New York State Judicial Commission on Minorities states that the New York Court system suffers from unequal access, disparate treatment, and frustrated opportunities for most minorities. The report documents two justice systems at work in New York State: one for whites and a harsher one for minorities and the poor.[4]

As the report describes in detail, a system of ghetto courts and assembly-line justice has resulted in a prison population in New York State that is 82 percent African American or Hispanic; in New York City, this population makes up 90 percent of the inmates. Because of the frequency of all-white juries, blacks receive sentences of incarceration for crimes that whites are not jailed for. The report argues that racial discrimination accounts in part for this overrepresentation: whites are released more readily on bail, whereas minority defendants are given harsh sentences such as incarceration rather than fines.[5] The *New York Times* describes the court system as "infested with racism."[6]

Most damning for people of color are recent changes in the law that require documentation of intent to discriminate, because most of the racial discrimination found in the courts is not overt. According to U.S. Justice Department statistics of December 1990, 40 percent of those on death row are black, whereas blacks make up only about 12 percent of the population. Yet the discrepancy is said to be racially neutral in intent.

A recent study documents the reality of racial segregation in school systems and residential living patterns. Atlanta, often considered a racially progressive city by city planners, remained in 1992 a separate and unequal city. Serious racial barriers exist for both poor and middle-class blacks. The black middle class is severely threatened by continued government cutbacks that directly affect the jobs they hold. Racism continues to define the ladder of opportunity.[7]

Andrew Hacker, a white professor of sociology at Queens College, suggests that there are really two nations in the United States: one black and one white. Unequal and separate, the two nations are marked by pervasive differences.[8] Orlando Patterson, an African American professor of sociology at Harvard University, takes issue with Hacker's description. He feels Hacker wrongly clumps African American and white populations in separate, homogeneous groupings that do not reflect in-

ternal differences. Patterson acknowledges that racism remains a horrible blight on this society, but he also thinks that the plight of the black
poor is identical to that of the white poor.[9] Thus, racism appears to
play no specific role for him. But we will return to this discussion later.

The disjuncture between political discourses that equate the end of
structural racism with the ending of legalized slavery in the last century,
and the reality of a racially divided society, has led to the crisis surrounding race today. In the last few years the newspapers have been
filled with descriptions of racially motivated acts of violence: the brutal
Central Park rape of a white woman by black teenagers that drew national attention; the horrific murders of black youths by white gangs in
Howard Beach and Bensonhurst, New York; the rape trial at St. John's
University where three white lacrosse players were acquitted of all charges
of sexual assault against a black woman who was a fellow student; the
riots in Crown Heights after black children were killed by a white Jew
driving a car and the resulting violence; the cross burnings in Dubuque,
Iowa, and the activities of the National Association for the Advancement of White People (NAAWP); the candidacy of David Duke, former
member of the Ku Klux Klan, for Louisiana governor, with hopes for a
presidential bid; the videotaped beating of Rodney King, a black man,
by white police officers in Los Angeles; and the violent aftermath in Los
Angeles of the acquittal of the police officers responsible for the beating.
In New York City alone, police logged twenty-two racial bias incidents
in the first eleven days of 1992. However the system of racism has
changed, it continues to divide people and affect lives.

The meanings tied to race and racism do change. Politics is the struggle to define racialized meanings, which are cultural, economic, and
historical. Given the present crises of family structure and of the economy, the conflicts surrounding the meanings of race have increased.
Thus, race is "an unstable and decentered complex of social meanings"
that are always being negotiated.[10] The system of racism should therefore be understood as dynamic and in flux.

The racism of legalized slavery was significantly different from the
racism of the 1990s. However, the changes do not bespeak the demise
of racism, but rather its reformulation. There remain structural elements of racial privilege that deny individual people of color opportunities similar to those available to whites *even though* there have been
compelling changes. The reality of a black middle class today constructs
a newer, more complex racism: blacks who have attained new economic privilege have done so while poverty has continued to dominate

many African Americans' lives. Such developments have created conflicting class interests within the African American community rather
than dismantling racism itself. Economic diversity within the African
American community does not deny the reality of racism; rather, it par-
titions racism according to a system of economic privilege. In fact, much
of the economic change for some African Americans has resulted from
legal strategies that have increased economic opportunity without dislodging racial inequality.

It is not at all clear that the economic gains of individual blacks can
be maintained or any new gains be initiated without civil rights legislation to counter the racially structured inequities that remain in place.
For example, even though there is a law encouraging the involvement
of minority-owned concerns in managing the assets seized from failed
savings and loans associations, the federal contracts have gone almost
entirely to companies owned by whites.[11] No wonder the chairman of
the United States Commission on Civil Rights said in 1991 that "the
climate is anything but positive for civil rights right now."[12] There is
no guarantee that a new administration will have much effect on the
structure of racism.

The contradictions abound. On the one hand, the "old" racist relations of slavery are dismissed as anachronistic description. On the other
hand, society is rife with an engendered racist violence. There is endless
talk regarding the politics of race, but little action.

In 1991 the cover of the May 6 issue of *Newsweek* announced "The
New Politics of Race." In the same month, the *Atlantic Monthly*'s cover
story was "When the Official Subject Is Presidential Politics, Taxes,
Welfare, Crime, Rights, or Values . . . the Real Subject Is RACE."[13]
This article excerpted sections of Thomas Byrne and Mary D. Edsall's
highly publicized book *Chain Reaction: The Impact of Race, Rights,
and Taxes on American Politics*, which argues that politics is race-laden
and race-driven but is (silently) coded through the non–race-specific
language of rights, taxes, crime, and drugs.

The Edsalls date the beginnings of this process from the 1964 presidential election between Lyndon Johnson and Barry Goldwater, when
the Republican party ran for the last time on an explicitly anti–civil
rights platform.[14] They trace Richard Nixon's and George Wallace's
parts in staking out a conservative politics on racial issues. Reagan further "coded" the issue of race by attacking "policies targeted toward
Blacks and other minorities without reference to race." The Edsalls argue that the use of a race-free political language is at the heart of a new

"conservative egalitarianism," which assumes a meritocratic, antidiscrimination, equality rhetoric.[15] This newer rhetoric rejects the civil rights agenda as one of unfair entitlement and "special" interests.

The Edsalls' argument concludes with the following analysis of the political scene in 1991. The issues of race and taxes had overlapped, pitting taxpayers against tax dollar recipients to create a middle-class, antigovernment stance. Because many of the costs of racial equality had been borne mainly by lower–middle-class and low-income whites, they had become hostile to the programs which they saw as allowing others to achieve while they did not. The resentment of this constituency appeared to have led to the disintegration of the liberal coalition on which the Democratic party depended. In its place stood a different coalition, built on the shared opposition of the white working poor and the affluent toward federal regulation and increased taxes.[16] Of course, this depiction was written before the 1992 election, when the original coalition was realigned.

It is significant that the Edsalls write of race rather than of racism.[17] *Race,* in and of itself, does not elicit the idea of powerful oppression. *Racism* does. Whereas individuals are identified by race, racism has a structure and politics to it. The Edsalls allow the subtext of "race" to be a stand-in for too much, even for racism itself. They do not examine why this racial coding occurs.

The "rights revolution" is carefully (although inaccurately) analyzed by the Edsalls only in terms of race, when it is equally about sexual and gender equality. Their focus on race disconnects and misrepresents the interconnections between racism and sexism: how racism and sexism implicate each other in racially coded talk. They never ask why the imagery of Willie Horton, in particular, was used in terms other than just race. After all, Horton was not just black. He was a black man who raped a white woman. The problematic imagery is not just about race but also derives from a racialized patriarchy: white womanhood must be protected by white men. Such imagery nurtures a racism embedded in a protectionist sexuality: white women need white men to protect them. This protectionist view undermines the demand for white women's rights. Racism is used here silently to subvert the white women's movement. And women of color are completely dismissed, by both race and gender.

By ignoring the issue of gender in the rights revolution, the Edsalls inadvertently authorize the ghettoization of rights discourse to race. This ghettoization has been brought about by, for example, identifying affirmative action only with blacks, especially black men. When racism stands in for white patriarchal privilege, the politics of racism and sexism, of racialized patriarchy, are obfuscated. Both people of color and white women are the losers. And the potential for affirmative action to assist a *majority* of the population—if one includes all people of color and white women—is also lost.

The United States work force has become more diverse. The economy is shrinking. The number of good, paying jobs is decreasing. By the turn of the century, more than three-fourths of new entrants to the work force will be female and/or persons of color. Affirmative action has been particularly effective in helping blacks bypass the social networks that close them out of service industry jobs.[18] This makes affirmative action policy all the more subversive to white male interests. In addition, the success of the ghettoized rhetoric surrounding affirmative action has turned many people against it. Race has become the "privileged sign of the multicultural threat."[19] Equating affirmative action with racial preference, 60 percent of the respondents in a CBS News poll in November 1991 said they did not think preference should be given to black job applicants. Such opinions reflect the success of racializing the issues of racial and gender equality.

THE RACIAL POLITICS OF AFFIRMATIVE ACTION

To affirm means to be positive, to be active, and to intervene on behalf of. Affirmative action, as the term is applied to the body of law based on Title VII of the Civil Rights Act of 1964, was conceived to address racial and gender discrimination and to allow for greater opportunity for people of color and white women. But affirmative action has become a political football with a myriad of meanings within public discourse, ranging from hiring goals to quotas, to statistical guidelines, to preferential treatment, to special preferences. Opponents of affirmative action claim that it is preferential treatment, that it excludes considerations of merit. This view of affirmative action as unfair preference was first given voice in the Bakke case (1978). Bakke challenged the special admissions program of the medical school of the University of California at Davis, which assured the admission of a certain number of black and other minority applicants. Bakke's lawyers argued that his rights as a white male were violated because his grades had been higher than those of some of the candidates admitted under this program.[20]

Law professor Michel Rosenfeld has defended affirmative action policy against the image of the "innocent white male." He argues that the policy does not violate equality of opportunity. It takes "nothing away from them [white men] that they have rightfully earned or should be entitled to keep." Nor is it likely to cause a white man any greater harm than would come from a sudden, unwelcome increase in the size of the pool of applicants against whom he is competing. Whereas affirmative action means a somewhat increased chance of failure for white males, it increases the chance of success for people of color from near-zero to an almost even chance. The opportunities are not equivalent. Affirmative action is meant to be inclusionary in the end, whereas racism and sexism are inherently exclusionary.[21]

Affirmative action law has evolved over almost two decades. Initially, governmental affirmative action guidelines required that job vacancies be advertised publicly; that job announcements clearly state criteria related to job performance; and that gender, race, and ethnicity be irrelevant to hiring decisions—unless they were legitimate occupational requirements. Title VII required a commitment to recruiting qualified people of color and white women but prohibited the use of quotas or the lowering of standards. Preferential treatment meant only that race or gender counted as additional qualifications if everything else was equal. Hiring was to be guided not by quotas but by goals and timetables to ensure a more diverse work force.[22]

Over the years, affirmative action has come to mean different things and has been implemented in different ways. Some programs include preferential treatment; others do not. Most use goals and timetables, and a few impose quotas. Most do not adjust test scores, but a few do. Some guidelines state that the "basically qualified" should be hired, even if they are not the "best," because "best" is often defined by and through a discriminatory lens. Other programs have adopted aggressive recruiting policies that give a person of color or a white woman preference at the start. Many affirmative action programs focus on needed education and training programs. Others focus on hiring.[23]

Defenders of affirmative action, such as Eleanor Holmes Norton, claim that it allows those with skills to get jobs from which they otherwise would be excluded in spite of their skills. Thus, it gives people opportunities to be considered where formerly they were excluded.[24] Rosenfeld argues that affirmative action creates a real equality of opportunity where it did not exist. Unassisted, superficial equality of opportunity perpetuates existing discrimination.[25]

Even with the assistance of affirmative action, leftover discrimination is difficult to dislodge. As late as November 1991, Yale University felt the need to adopt a policy for all university departments that "a woman or minority candidate should be deemed better qualified," testifying to the limited effect affirmative action has obviously had so far at Yale.[26] Elsewhere, too, affirmative action law has been implemented with varying effectiveness. Although it has made some real differences in many people's lives, it has had little impact on many others who should have benefited from it. It has done both more and less than is often said.

The subversiveness of affirmative action policy is inherent in its initial formulation. It recognizes groups of people as discriminated against and requires that the structure account for this imbalance so that they can act on individual opportunities. The need for such a policy reflects the inadequacy of liberal individualism, the idea that individuals are entirely accountable for themselves.

AFFIRMATIVE ACTION AND THE BLACK MIDDLE CLASS

Middle-class occupational opportunities for blacks have been created in large part either in government itself or with governmental support and pressure. It was unusual before 1965 to find blacks in professional jobs outside the government and African American business. By the mid-seventies, affirmative action policy had assisted blacks in entering new occupational territory. Most professional jobs held by blacks in both the public and the private sector have depended on federal policy rather than on economic factors.[27] William Domhoff and Richard Zweigenhaft have documented what is possible when black Americans are given a chance.[28] They studied the ABC (A Better Chance) program in its heyday, from 1964 to 1975, to judge the effects of an aggressive educational program for poor blacks who were provided with elite private school education through the assistance of the Office of Economic Opportunity.

Domhoff and Zweigenhaft found that an outstanding number of these students emerged from the ABC program well-educated and psychologically intact. Over 94 percent of them graduated from their prep schools and attended college. Many of them continue to flourish. The real question is what remains for young blacks today. Since Reagan first took office, there has been a drop of over 20 percent in federal programs for education, job training, and social services related to employment.

If African Americans have moved into the middle class due to federal legislation and federal programs, they can easily be kept from such advancement without it. The faltering economy as well as the revisions in civil rights law have created a crisis for blacks who hope to improve their economic class standing and even for those who just hope to hold onto their present middle-class status. Given their positioning in government jobs, African Americans are disproportionately hurt by governmental privatization and resultant cutbacks in jobs and services.[29] The erosion of support for affirmative action has exacerbated this situation.

The 1989 study *A Common Destiny: Blacks and American Society,* conducted by the National Research Council, found that most African Americans, even of the middle class, continue to live in segregated communities and to receive low-quality, segregated schooling.[30] Most African Americans continue to live in poverty, with limited opportunity.

The most significant economic gains for African Americans took place before 1980. Since then, blacks have lost ground. Even with the assistance of affirmative action legislation, over one-third of the black population is locked into poverty. The number of affluent blacks has skyrocketed, but the wealth of African American households is still only one-tenth that of white households. In 1987, the income of a typical black family was $18,098, just 56.1 percent of a typical white family's income. This was the lowest relative percentage since the 1960s. In 1989, 25 percent of black families had incomes below $10 thousand. In the same year, the national median household income for white families was $31,435; for black families, it was $19,758. In 1990, more than one black family in nine earned less than $5 thousand a year. Black babies die at twice the rate of white babies. The homicide death rate is six times higher for blacks than for whites. Blacks make up only 12 percent of the population, but accounted for 31 percent of all new AIDS cases as of 1989.[31] Although black poverty is not new, the extreme differences between rich and poor within the African American community are new. Poor families are getting poorer, whereas families at the top end of the scale are getting wealthier. The growing class diversity within the black community charts new political territory.

This is the context in which the Supreme Court's decisions since 1989 must be understood. Laws never tell the whole story. Yet they matter. They allow and sometimes even instigate change. The legal dismantling of slavery mattered. The civil rights legislation and affirmative action laws of the 1960s also mattered. The Supreme Court's recent decisions matter, too. But this time they move in a different direction. They both reflect and originate formulations of a new racism.

NARROWING AND REVERSING CIVIL RIGHTS LAW

The neoconservative Supreme Court's decisions beginning in the spring of 1989 have made quite clear that race and sex, as collective categories, have been denied; and racial and sexual discrimination, defined as structural and historical realities, have been erased. The Court's decisions reject the idea of racism as an institutionalized aspect of society. Statistical evidence of racial or sexual inequality is no longer acceptable as proof of unfair treatment of groups or classes of people. Discrimination can be proved only by an individual, in the terms of a specific case. Equality doctrine has been refocused: civil rights legislation has been narrowed to the privacy stance of abortion rights.[32] Concerns have been redirected toward the problem of "reverse discrimination" against the white male and against the fetus.

Based on the Court's decisions, the government no longer has any responsibility to create access if there is no clear proof of prohibition. That is, so long as a black is not officially restricted from advancement in her job, it is presumed that her lack of promotion is not due to racial discrimination. There must be some other, individual reason. This narrow, individualist framework has always defined abortion law, which is based on the most individualist notions of liberty. However, it represents a significantly different reading of civil rights legislation.

Along with this shifting of focus from class to individual is the full-blown rejection of the right to equality of opportunity in the market. An individual's right to opportunity is no longer to be confused with equality of opportunity. The former is what many neoconservatives view as the proper interpretation of law. Individuals compete as individuals, not as members of (discriminated) classes. The burden of proof is on the individual to prove that she acted on whatever opportunities existed, regardless of the barriers that hampered her attempts. The concern with equal *availability* has been lost. Because the Court does not recognize any historical or structural constraints limiting individuals or their opportunities, it is left to individuals to act on their own behalf. As a result, the Court is always able to find reasons for differential treatment of an individual other than discrimination: individuals will always have other specifics to consider in addition to their race and gender because they are individuals at the same time that they are members of racial and sexual classes.

The Supreme Court has put civil rights law in jeopardy. In the 1989 case *Croson v. City of Richmond,* it declared for the first time that government programs that give African Americans or members of other racial minorities a preference over whites must be scrutinized by the same strict constitutional standard that applies to discrimination against blacks.[33] The Court's findings reject race-based measures that are "differently" devised in order to address the issue of past discrimination. Discrimination against whites now has the same legal status as discrimination against minorities.

Justice O'Connor, writing the decision for the Court, rejected the generalized, statistical proof of racial discrimination as justification for the Richmond set-aside program, which designated that 30 percent of the dollar amount of each contract was reserved for one or more minority business enterprises. Although the program was said to be remedial in purpose, O'Connor stated that there was no "direct evidence of discrimination"[34] and that the plan was therefore not narrowly tailored to remedy particular discrimination. The "generalized assertion of past discrimination" in the construction industry was not enough reason to design a racial quota. She argued that there were no clear facts proving discrimination, but only "broad-brush assumptions of historical discrimination."[35] She concluded that "societal discrimination does not suffice"[36] as sufficient justification for such a program, even though in a city whose population is 50 percent black only 0.67 percent of Richmond's prime construction contracts had been awarded to minority businesses before the program was instituted.

Justice Scalia not only concurred with this opinion, but further stated that the set-aside program represented "unlawful racial classification." He argued that we need to focus on "actual victims of discrimination," not broad categories of persons. The issue should not be race, but only whether an individual was wronged.[37] He argued that classifications of race only aggravate the problem; they are not the solution.[38] Justice Kennedy, in a separate concurring statement, considered the city's plan as itself unconstitutional preference.

Justice Marshall, in a dissent, argued that Richmond had a compelling interest in the set-aside program, "to prevent the city's own spending decisions from reinforcing and perpetuating the exclusionary effects of past discrimination."[39] He also rejected the claim that Richmond relied on "generalized societal discrimination as its justification" and concluded that the city had showed "localized, industry-specific findings."[40] He also noted that the 30 percent assigned to public set-asides translated to only 3 percent of Richmond's overall area contracts.

The Court's decision rejected earlier conceptions that treated discrimination as an historical and societal reality. Although it is important not to overstate the radical implications of pre-Rehnquist civil rights law—affirmative action was always a limited doctrine—even this limited doctrine has come under complete assault.

Racial discrimination has now been narrowed to mean only specific and factually proven discriminatory action against an individual. The understanding of race as a structural element of society has been replaced with a view of disparate individuals. The ability to use racial categories to address prior discrimination has been destroyed: there are no categories as such—hence, no institutional discrimination. Even the recognition of race as a category unfairly distinguishes the person of color from a white person.

Wards Cove Packing Co. v. Atonio, another case reviewed during the Court's 1989 term, further limited the use of statistical evidence of discrimination and narrowed the ability of individuals to prove discrimination.[41] It challenged a 1971 decision, *Griggs v. Duke Power,* which construed Title VII as proscribing "not only overt discrimination but also practices which are fair in form but discriminatory in practice."[42] *Griggs* also determined that the burden of proof was on the employer to justify discriminatory policies as necessary to the employer's business. If a qualification or job requirement had an adverse impact on minorities, the employer had to show that it was a business necessity. This applied to overt discrimination as well as supposedly neutral practices which appeared fair but in fact were not.[43] The Wards Cove case shifted the onus to the employee, who must show that the policy cannot be justified as necessary for the employer.

In the case presented to the Court, a worker argued that the unskilled cannery jobs at Wards Cove were filled by nonwhites, Filipinos, and Alaska natives. In contrast, the noncannery jobs, which were skilled, were filled by white workers, who lived in separate dormitories and ate in separate mess halls. The cannery workers argued that it was the hiring/promotion practices of Wards Cove that were responsible for the racial stratification of the work force. Wards Cove claimed that its practices were not discriminatory and that the stratification occurred because the union, which supplied most of the cannery jobs, was predominantly a nonwhite union.

The Court found that statistical evidence of a high percentage of nonwhite workers in cannery jobs does not make for a prima facie disparate-impact case. One needs to show specific causation; statistical disparities are not enough. It must be shown how "each challenged practice has a significantly disparate impact on employment opportunities for whites and nonwhites." The Court concluded that the "racial composition of the qualified population in the relevant labor market" was the critical factor. A lack of nonwhites in skilled jobs can reflect a lack of qualified worker-applicants. "As long as there are no barriers or practices deterring qualified nonwhites from applying . . . the employer's selection mechanism probably does not have a disparate impact on minorities."[44] Thus, racial imbalance in a segment of an employer's work force does not necessarily mean that there have been discriminatory practices. The burden of proof no longer rests with the employer.

Given this frame of reference, the Court found that it is "essential that the practices identified by the cannery workers be linked causally with the demonstrated adverse impact." In writing for the Court, Justice White relied on an earlier decision by Justice O'Connor, *Watson v. Fort Worth Bank & Trust,* which claimed the existence of many "innocent causes that may lead to statistical imbalances in the composition of their work forces."[45] Evident in this reasoning is the presumption of nondiscrimination, as well as a nonstructural view of race.

Justice Stevens, writing for the dissent, reinvoked much of the decision in *Griggs,* where Title VII was used to achieve equality of opportunity in practice—not just in theory—by removing past barriers to equal employment opportunity. He criticized the Court for shifting the burden of proof of discriminatory practices to the employee by way of a "newly articulated preference for individualized proof of causation."[46] Justice Blackmun, also in dissent (with Brennan and Marshall concurring), wrote that overt and institutionalized discrimination was being legitimated in this decision and that the Court's new agenda seemed to be redressing the problem of reverse discrimination against white men. "One wonders whether the majority still believes that race discrimination—or, more accurately, race discrimination against nonwhites—is a problem in our society, or even remembers that it ever was."[47]

A neoconservative view of discrimination finally prevailed in this case. In this view, discrimination can only be against an individual, not groups of individuals, as would be identifiable through statistical evidence. Only specific actions against specific individuals are subject to scrutiny. The problem of discrimination is now viewed in reverse. The job market merely reflects the labor market and the individual abilities it takes to succeed. As long as no clearly articulated discriminatory guidelines exist, discrimination does not exist as far as the judicial system is concerned. Discrimination must be an overt, easily identifiable phenomenon.

President Bush reinforced the Court's decision in Wards Cove when he supported the idea that a high school education should be considered a job requirement even if the job does not necessitate the degree. He argued that such a requirement would encourage people to complete their high school education. He ignored the disparate impact such a policy would have on minorities.

The case of *Patterson v. McLean Credit Union* further gutted civil rights legislation.[48] Patterson, a black woman who had been a bank teller and file coordinator from 1972 until 1992, charged her employer with harassment, the assignment of demeaning tasks, overwork, racial slurs, unnecessary public criticism, and lack of promotion and of any possibility of advancement. In its decision on *Patterson,* the Court upheld its 1976 precedent, *Runyon v. McCrary,* which applied a reconstruction-era civil rights law to bar discrimination in private employment. In *Runyon,* the Court had prohibited private schools from excluding, solely on the basis of race, children who were otherwise qualified for admission. The present Court said that that law applied only to the initial hiring state and could not be used to challenge racially biased treatment on the job. This interpretation narrowed and weakened the meaning of Section 1981 of the Civil Rights Statutes.[49]

The employer's conduct was viewed by the Court as not precluding the "right to make and enforce a contract"; it was conduct that occurred after the formation of a contract.[50] The difference between one's right to enter a contract and one's rights in the contract are key here. Neoconservatives on the Court found that an individual has the right to the opportunity to enter a contract, but not to equal treatment in the contract. The difference is between having "opportunity" and having meaningful equality. For the Court, racial harassment on the job stands outside the purview of one's rights to enter a contract. Racial harassment "impairs neither the right to make nor the right to enforce a contract."[51] Such a narrow reading makes the law almost meaningless. One is left to ponder what a contract means if it does not pertain to the actual conditions of the job itself. Discrimination on the job violates the idea of a contract if a contract is viewed as a process that both initiates and regulates a job. Patterson had a right to the job, but no rights on the job—to fair treatment, promotion, or any of the other rights guaranteed under Section 1981.

Justice Brennan, in the dissent, criticized the "cramped reading" of the Civil Rights Statutes and argued against this narrowing of its scope. The language of 1981 "quite naturally read as extending to cover post-formation conduct that demonstrates that the contract was not really made on equal terms at all." Patterson was denied the right to make a contract on an equal basis, and this denied her right to enter into a contract like a white citizen.[52] The issue is equality: the equal right to make a contract with the same protections that would be guaranteed to a white citizen, including freedom from racial harassment. It is not just about having the right to make a contract. Patterson did not enter her contract on an equal footing with white employees.

Justice Stevens also dissented from the Court on its narrow and literal reading of Section 1981. He stated that this interpretation of the meaning of "to make a contract" was wrongheaded. It was part of the neoconservative redefinition of civil rights law as encompassing only the opportunities afforded to individuals. In this view, the law protects only individual opportunity to enter a contract, not equality of treatment.

A look at *Martin v. Wilks* clarifies how these redefinitions and narrowings of discrimination law have dismantled the substance of affirmative action. In this case, white firefighters in Birmingham, Alabama, challenged a decree in which the fire department had settled a discrimination suit by agreeing to hire and promote more African Americans. The Court found in favor of the white firefighters that persons cannot be deprived of their legal rights in proceedings to which they are not a party.[53] This finding allows challenges to affirmative action policy by any persons who have not been party to these kinds of proceedings.

This decision was a major setback for affirmative action procedures in hiring and empowered the proponents of reverse discrimination. Whereas the fire department agreement was put in place to assuage former racial discrimination against blacks due to unequal access, the *Martin* decision puts access of individual whites on equal footing with that of individual African Americans. Because it does not recognize structural and historical racism, the Court has effectively espoused a catch-22: the law should treat blacks and whites the same, yet they have never been treated the same or had access to the same opportunities. Even to name race as a problem is to privilege blacks against whites. Therefore, to be fair to whites, one must treat blacks as individuals before the law, like whites. The problem is that the law is already racialized by extralegal practices found within the society and culture.

In the last racial discrimination case of the spring term, *Jett v. Dallas Independent School District,* the Court gutted the prior interpretation of the Civil Rights Act of 1866, the precursor to Section 1981, which was discussed in *Patterson.* By another 5–4 decision, the Court determined that Section 1981 does not permit damages against those who violate its terms and therefore could not be used to bring damage suits against local governments for acts of racial discrimination. Jett, a white male teacher, athletic director, and coach at a predominantly black school, was dismissed and reassigned by his principal, Todd, a black man, after repeated clashes over school policy. Jett charged racial discrimination. The Court ruled that he had no civil redress, and, in doing so, denied governmental responsibility for ensuring equal treatment.[54]

A more recent ruling that echoes the tenor of the 1989 decisions is the 5–3 opinion of the Court in January 1991 that formerly segregated school districts can stop court-ordered busing once they have taken all steps necessary to eliminate the "legacy" of segregation. According to this ruling, housing patterns do not necessarily support a continued need for busing, so long as they reflect private choice and are not part of the "vestiges" of former segregation.[55] How one determines when the legacy of segregation ends and choice begins is not delineated by the Court. Instead, the ruling presumes that societal, structural segregation no longer exists.

The strain of neoconservative jurisprudence established in the spring of 1989 does not reject outright the language of equality. Instead, it narrows and redefines the contours of what equality—and therefore discrimination—can possibly mean. One must prove discrimination before the time to challenge it runs out; one cannot prove discrimination after the contract is signed; and one cannot prove bias if it is not the determining factor of one's treatment. The Court eliminated all redress for subtle and covert forms of racial discrimination at the very time when more and more discrimination is operating in this form. General practice, indirect effects, and numerical differences no longer count. One must show a specific practice, with direct effects for one's individual outcome.

In short order, the effects of the Court's decisions were felt by working people of color. According to Anthony Robinson, president of Minority Business Enterprises Legal Defense and Education Fund, the decision on the Richmond case was devastating for African American and

Hispanic contractors, resulting in a large loss of income. One black contractor in Atlanta, Georgia, says that the Richmond decision cost him $8 million in contracts on work that was already in progress.[56]

Such results confirm former Harvard law professor Derrick Bell's belief that equal protection doctrine cannot sufficiently address issues of racial discrimination. It has not served to protect people of color against policies that are racially neutral but nevertheless burdensome in effect. He also argues that considering race as a "suspect classification" in the law provides no protection at all unless the unequal treatment is completely blatant and arbitrary. Proving intent of discrimination has almost always been impossible to do, yet this is the only form of discrimination the Court recognizes today.[57]

In contrast to the Court's 1989 decisions, in June 1990 it reaffirmed the role of the federal government in devising programs that give minorities preference when competing for government benefits. The 5–4 decision in *Metro Broadcasting v. FCC* affirmed the power of Congress to use "benign race-conscious measures," even if the measures were not "remedial."[58] The decision upheld two Federal Communications Commission programs aimed at increasing minority ownership of broadcast licenses. The decision gives the federal government more leeway than state and local governments have in designing affirmative action programs that are not limited to remedial actions for past discrimination. In this instance, the Court found affirmative action was justified in order to increase the number of radio and TV stations owned by minorities so as to create greater diversity in programming. Justice Kennedy dissented from the decision: "I cannot agree with the Court that the Constitution permits the government to discriminate among its citizens on the basis of race in order to serve interests so trivial as 'broadcast diversity.' "[59] This decision stands as an exception to the Court's general trend, although the Court made clear that it was simply deferring, somewhat grudgingly, to Congressional guidelines. In this decision the Court denied the Bush administration's urging not to reopen the affirmative action debate.

Otherwise, post-1989 decisions have continued to narrow civil rights doctrine. In 1992, in an important ruling on the federal Voting Rights Act, the Court took a restrictive view of the 1965 law. It determined that the Voting Rights Act did not apply to the reorganization of voting districts in this case. "The Voting Rights Act is not an all-purpose anti-discrimination statute."[60] The Court has also lifted curbs on formerly segregated schools by providing standards for the termination of federal court control. Justice Scalia reiterated the position that intent and causation, not mere racial disparity, must be shown in order to claim segregation.[61]

REDEFINING SEX DISCRIMINATION STANDARDS

It is easy to lose sight of the effects on women of color and white women of the Court's decisions narrowing the reading of civil rights. The Court's decision in *Price Waterhouse v. Hopkins* specifically addressed the issue of sex discrimination.[62] Hopkins alleged that she was not promoted to partner status in the Price Waterhouse accounting firm because of gender bias. At the time she was being reviewed for partner status, there were 662 partners, 7 of whom were women. Of the 88 persons proposed for partner that year, only one, Hopkins, was a woman. Forty-seven of these candidates made partner; 20 were held over for reconsideration, as Hopkins was. The main reason given for denying her partnership was her inability to work with the staff. She was said to be "difficult" and "impatient." Hopkins was advised by the firm to improve her relations with the staff and to work on her interpersonal skills and style. She was also counseled to try to look more feminine, such as by improving her hairstyle.[63]

The Court found that an inappropriate standard of proof was used by the lower courts, who had required Price Waterhouse to show by clear and convincing evidence that "even if it had not taken gender into account, it would have come to the same decision." The Court lessened the standard by which defendants must prove that they had not been discriminatory: all the firm needed to show was a preponderance of the evidence. This court ruling makes it more difficult to prove discrimination. But this is not all that is troublesome with the Court's finding; equally problematic is the way that the court distinguished between discrimination and reasons "other" than discriminatory ones.

Although the Court found that an employer cannot take gender into account in making employment decisions, the employer is "free to decide against a woman for other reasons." The plaintiff must show that the employer "actually relied on her gender in making the decision."[64] The Court required Price Waterhouse to prove that the refusal to promote Hopkins was based on "legitimate" and not discriminatory reasons. The issue here is "intentional" discrimination: the employer is allowed not to hire or promote an individual, even if gender stereotyping is involved, if, as in the case of Price Waterhouse, the decision is based on "other" reasons. On the one hand, the Court says gender must be irrelevant to employment decisions; on the other hand, the Court says gender can be an issue, so long as it is not the decisive one: "We conclude that the preservation of this freedom [of the employer to choose] means that an employer shall not be liable if it can prove that, even if it had not taken gender into account, it would have come to the same decision regarding a particular person."[65]

This appears problematic at best. If sex stereotyping plays a part in a decision, in what sense can it be found to be irrelevant or not decisive? The stereotyping sets the context for interpreting so-called "other" issues. Moreover, it is unclear whether one could ever prove that gender bias was the crucial element in a decision if such a bias can be deemed irrelevant in certain circumstances. Justice Kennedy argues in his dissent that sex stereotyping is different from discrimination. According to Kennedy, Title VII does not outlaw sex stereotyping, nor does it "support the creation of a duty to sensitize." Title VII cannot be expected to "root out sexist thoughts."[66]

The Court chose to interpret the problem of sex discrimination within narrow confines: gender bias can exist without being deemed the reason for a particular action. It becomes almost impossible to prove that discrimination is the reason for a particular decision because other reasons will always exist and because it is almost impossible to prove discriminatory intent. Hopkins was described as difficult and impatient. But given the makeup of her firm, her male colleagues and the female staff judge her by a different set of standards—tied to sexual stereotypes and gender bias. Women associates such as Hopkins are expected to be either nicer (because they are women) or more difficult (because they are women with a male demeanor) than the male associates. One cannot prove bias within this set of standards.

The Court remanded the Hopkins case to the trial court for further proceedings. On remand, Price Waterhouse was found discriminatory in its treatment of Hopkins. The United States District Court for Washington, D.C., complained that the "Court has been provided with no guidance to enable it to differentiate between all sexually stereotyped comments and comments not influenced by stereotyping" and that "Price Waterhouse has made no effort to suggest guidelines for identifying sexual stereotyping."[67] As a result, the district court found that it was impossible to distinguish "comments tainted by distinct sexism from those free of sexism."[68]

The Hopkins case was a clear instance of discrimination. But neoconservative jurisprudence has left potential plaintiffs with cases that are less clear little room to maneuver: they must prove actual intent to discriminate against them as individuals. Statistical evidence of discrimination cannot be used. And if other reasons can be shown as determining the employer's decision, discrimination is irrelevant. This revised and narrowed standard is evident in the outcome of a suit brought against the State of California by women state employees in October 1989. In this case, sixty thousand past and present women state employees charged California with deliberate sex discrimination in setting salaries. The United States District Court of California found that there was no intentional gender-based discrimination: "that the policy makers based pay differentials on prevailing rates, not on gender."[69] Market forces were presumed to be "other" than sexually discriminatory. The difference in wage structure was unintentional discrimination.

The Court's requirement of intentional discrimination has further ramifications for women who suffer unintentional discrimination all the time in terms of juggling family responsibilities with their jobs. If the Court continues to move more and more to a standard of intentional discrimination, it will bury ever more deeply the complicated jeopardy of women or of any wage-earning parent who is also responsible for children and home.[70] The structural aspects of racialized patriarchy are legally denuded.

One other case in the 1989 term dealt directly with sexual discrimination. *Lorrance v. ATT* again limited the effect of Title VII by reinterpreting the legal definition of actionable sex discrimination.[71] The women testers involved in the suit argued that changes in 1979 in the rules governing the tester seniority system were made in order to "protect incumbent male testers" and to discourage women from moving into the traditionally male tester jobs. It was claimed that the seniority system was sexually discriminatory in its differential impact and that it had its "genesis in [sex] discrimination," in that it intentionally discriminated against women and altered their contractual rights.[72] In this case, the Court found that the women's charges had not been filed within the required period. It stated that although a "facially discriminatory seniority system can be challenged at any time, . . . a facially neutral system, if it is adopted with unlawful discriminatory motive, can be challenged within the prescribed period after adoption,"[73] but not after.

The dissenting justices saw it differently. Justice Marshall wrote that there was no way that the employees could have reasonably expected that they would be demoted or otherwise concretely harmed by the new system at the time of its adoption. He criticized the Court's decision for requiring employees to sue "anticipatorily," significantly diminishing the applicability of Title VII to seniority systems.[74] This redefinition of the applicability of Title VII attacks the heart of civil rights legislation. Without denuding the actual law, it greatly limits its practical use. The discourse of "equality" legislation—and civil rights law—has been whittled away, leaving it almost impossible to resolve or even name discrimination. It is now up to the individual to prove her case. She is on her own. The government has no affirmative role to play.

These Court decisions have authorized and sanctioned the narrowing of racial and sexual discrimination law. The legal system has become more and more inhospitable to racial and sexual discrimination cases. Not surprisingly, age discrimination cases, which are primarily the preserve of middle-aged white males, have much greater success.[75] According to the Equal Employment Opportunity Commission, litigation of this sort increased 250 percent between 1985 and 1990.

EQUALITY OF TREATMENT AND THE PREGNANT WOMAN

Sexual discrimination cases are complicated because they push the bias of racialized patriarchy as far as the current interpretation of the law will allow. Equality—specifically meaning likeness of treatment of men and women—was not initially structured into the law. Such a notion of equality remains highly contested because elements of the inequality of racialized patriarchy *are* part of the structure of the law. Within this context of inequality, an "equality" requiring sameness of treatment is both a radical critique of discriminatory practices and an insufficient revision. The reality of pregnancy underscores this dilemma. If you are a pregnant woman, being treated the same as a man may mean that you are not being treated fairly. If you are an African American, being treated the same as a white person may not be fair, given the differential opportunity structure. The Court remains resistant to rethinking and reconceptualizing these issues. It remains straitjacketed by the white male standard.

The 1991 case *International Union v. Johnson Controls, Inc.* allows one to see how complicated the issue of sexual equality is when one recognizes the issue of pregnancy. In 1982, Johnson Controls instituted a "fetal protection policy" that barred all women except those with medically documented infertility from jobs involving actual or potential lead exposure exceeding the Occupational Safety and Health Administration's guidelines. The Court held that the policy was discriminatory on its face because the employer did not sufficiently establish that gender was a bona fide occupational qualification. The Court also found that requiring females but not males to prove their infertility was unfair, because lead exposure was also harmful to male reproductive systems. If fertile men were allowed to choose whether to risk their reproductive health for a particular job, the same should be true for women. Likewise, it should be up to a woman to decide whether her reproductive role was more important than her economic role. According to the Pregnancy Disability Act (PDA), pregnancy cannot be used to deny a woman a job unless it makes her unable to perform the job.[76] In sum, the Court found that fetal protection policies are a form of sex discrimination.

There are multiple ways to read this decision. One could say that it represents a victory for feminists: women are now free to choose how to act on their reproductive rights, just as men are. Women have the same rights to jobs as men have, whether pregnant or not. But women are actually the ones who get pregnant and gestate fetuses. So there is not complete identity, and sameness of treatment is not enough. A better solution would require that the workplace be safe for females who may be pregnant. Otherwise, the employer should provide a pregnant woman with the equivalent wages of the desired, but dangerous, job while she performs her work elsewhere.

Sheer sameness of treatment—for pregnant women or for persons of color—is not the same as equal treatment. Affirmative action law is being destroyed on the basis of this wrongheaded equation of sameness with equality. Sameness of treatment will not do as a standard of fairness. People of color are not the "same" as whites. Slavery has defined a history which makes "blackness" within white society different, lesser than. A culture of black resistance and subjugation is positioned against whiteness. Difference is institutionalized in structures and arrangements that stand outside the individual. An African American is never just an autonomous self as envisioned by bourgeois and liberal individualists, and never merely a "victim" of structural inequity. He or she is both.

Law, as the authorized discourse of the state, tells one plenty about the privileges and power relations of society, often through a series of tricky silences. Here, white men are the standard, so anyone else or any other group must be specified as "different" in order to have their interests recognized. And their interests are often recognized only to the degree that their interests can be treated like white men's interests. Questions of racial equality and pregnancy pose the toughest dilemmas.

Differences caused by discrimination—or the lifelong struggle against it—must first be taken into account if equality is to be achieved. Even then, equality need not mean identity. Affirmative action legislation is as close as United States politics has come to accepting this reality. The dismantling of this policy leaves us with the inequalities of racialized patriarchy that underpin a crass liberal individualism.

A NEW BLACK CONSERVATISM

Curiously, the dismantling of affirmative action law has been supported by a group of African American men that I hesitantly term "new black conservatives." They are not exactly or simply conservative, nor are they all alike. Yet they and their writings have created justification for a backlash against affirmative action. They have done so while actively identifying as African American men. Of course, black conservatism is not wholly new; one need only remember Booker T. Washington, Marcus Garvey, and, more recently, Thomas Sowell.

Three key actors here, even though their politics differ considerably, are William Wilson, Stephen Carter, and Shelby Steele. I call them new black conservatives to differentiate them from the white proponents of neoconservative politics. I do not name them simply neoconservatives because their concerns are in large part defined by their experiences as African American men. They have nevertheless espoused and identified with much of the self-help neoconservative rhetoric, while disclaiming the neoconservative label for themselves.

The new black conservatives applaud individual choice and standing on one's own and are critical of affirmative action for the stigma of race that they think it creates. They want to be thought of as able-bodied and meritorious individuals. They do not reject civil rights legislation in its entirety, but they do reject race-specified affirmative action. This is because the new black conservatives reject the idea of a collective experience of racism that affects all African Americans in similar fashion. Instead, they focus on economic class differences within the African American community. For them, there is no collective experience of racism, because poor and middle-class blacks are defined by their economic class interests more than by their race.

WILLIAM WILSON ON CLASS VERSUS RACE

William Wilson is the most articulate proponent of the view that economic class is more definitive than race in defining the opportunities of individual blacks today. In his highly acknowledged book *The Declining Significance of Race,* he argues that the life chances of blacks have more to do with economic-class position than with their encounters with racism. He distinguishes between the black middle class and the black underclass. For him, it is the latter that suffers racially. "The black experience has moved historically from economic racial oppression experienced by virtually all blacks to economic subordination for the black underclass." [77]

Wilson traces the process of the economic development of blacks from slavery to after World War II as moving from a homogenized economic slave status to the differentiated economic classes of the present. He argues that economic diversity within the black community denies the significance of racism. He distinguishes between historical racial subjugation and contemporary racism. The latter does not exist, at least for blacks outside the underclass.

The problem with Wilson's argument is that if racism exists for blacks of the underclass, it exists for many black men and women. It is not clear how racism can exist for one black but not another, especially if one's class is not evident as one walks down the street. So why try to sever racial oppression from its economic meanings? Why deny the structural realities of racism that confront all individual blacks, no matter how differently?

Wilson's definition of racism sheds a modicum of light on his underlying assumptions. He defines racism in a later book, *The Truly Disadvantaged,* as the "conscious refusal of whites to accept blacks as equal human beings and their willful, systematic effort to deny blacks equality of opportunity." [78] This is a narrow reading of racism, much like the Supreme Court decisions of 1989: discrimination has to be conscious, intentional, and clearly directed to a specific individual.

Because Wilson rejects the problematizing of racism, he rejects race-specific legislation. He argues that one "does not have to 'trot out' the concept of racism to demonstrate . . . that blacks have been severely hurt by deindustrialization." The etiology of the black underclass has "little or nothing to do with race," but is tied to broader issues of economic organization. He argues for universal economic programs that move beyond race-specific public policy.[79] He thinks that the way to address the problems of the ghetto underclass is to get at the broader problems of the economy.[80]

I would argue that legislation needs to do both: it needs to address the way the economy continues to institute racialized policy. We need to deal with both the economic *and* the racial aspects of the ghetto underclass. And we must weave gender through these concerns. By disconnecting these relations, one is left with nonspecified policies that silently continue to privilege white men.

Wilson himself may be changing his mind about the "significance of race." In a recent interview, speaking of his latest research, he says more about racial attitudes, racial prejudice, family structures, and social networks than about economic forces. He "would even go so far as to argue that for some black males, those with little education and few skills, race has become even more important in the past two decades."[81]

Nevertheless, Wilson supports "universal" programs that apply to everyone. But there is no such group as "everyone." Speaking of "everyone" is like speaking of the "individual": existing privilege remains intact. The only way one moves toward a truer universality is to specify the existing system of oppression. Specific needs of the underclass will not be addressed sufficiently by general programs of full employment or health care legislation, because the specificity of the needs of different races or genders is sidelined by the very generality of the programs. One's starting point for public policy, given the existing discriminatory practices of society, must be the problem of racialized patriarchy.

STEPHEN CARTER ON RACISM

Stephen Carter provides a personal accounting of and attack on affirmative action. Carter, like Wilson, argues that the term *racism* would be accurate only if all black people were similarly situated. If racism were systemic, it would have to touch him in the same way as it affects "those who mug." Instead, as a middle-class black, his "experience of the worst forms of privation is entirely vicarious." Although he has scars from a rejecting white world, "they are not the scars of disadvantage."[82] Racism appears to be one and the same as poverty for Carter: because he is not poor, he cannot know racism or the *same* racism as a black who is poor. He thinks racism exists only for poor blacks. And, like Wilson, he does not clarify how racism—which politicizes color—affects some blacks but not others.

For Carter, racism is a homogeneous category, and African Americans are economically diverse. He argues in somewhat backward fashion: because there are middle-class blacks, racism does not exist for them. He assumes that the middle-class status of some blacks subverts the racialized culture of racism. I would argue that although they may be middle class, they remain African Americans, subject to racialized politics.

As for the politics of racism, Carter insists that people who oppose "some part of the traditional civil rights agenda" are not necessarily racists. "True racists [are] people who really *do* mean black people ill." Racism seems to describe a historical past for Carter. It is not very much a part of the present. Yet, although racism is receding for the black middle class, it "continues to operate with awesome force in the lives of many of the worst off members of our community."[83] So although racism does not affect anyone now living and it is receding, it does affect poor blacks. This is a confusing argument.

Having dismissed the problem of racism, Carter addresses affirmative action. His major criticism is that it has done him an injustice. Affirmative action has denied him recognition of his merit because he has been treated in terms of his race. He did not need the assistance, yet he is judged as though he did. For him, affirmative action works to deny its beneficiaries the opportunity to show what they can do without it. There is no way to distinguish which people of color needed affirmative action and which did not. Even though he acknowledges that much progress has come from affirmative action, he attacks it for the stigma it creates, especially for "gifted" blacks like himself.[84]

Carter misnames the problem. Affirmative action calls attention to race in an effort to neutralize racially discriminatory practices. But the stigma of race is already in place. Affirmative action does not create it. So the problem is racism as it threads through civil rights policy, not the policies themselves.

The depiction of affirmative action as making up for inadequacy reflects a racialized culture. The belief that preferential treatment replaces individual merit is not inherent to affirmative action policy. Such charges are not made about preferential treatment for veterans or alumni children. These kinds of affirmative policies are not characterized as nonmeritorious.

Although Carter supported the initial affirmative action programs that provided opportunity for developing talent, he rejects the use of such programs today. He says that they wrongly focus on diversity. He

rejects the idea that "there is a black way to be," which he says under-
pins the diversity approach: hiring a black to represent the black point
of view. He prefers to be seen as just another intellectual, cherishing his
freedom to think for himself, rather than as a black. But Carter says
that he can never escape the assumption "that black people cannot
compete intellectually with white people." By his own admission, his
generation has an obsessive concern with proving themselves in the white
man's world. Affirmative action makes it impossible to "compete on
the same playing field with people who are white."[85] Again the enemy
seems misplaced.

It is unclear how this hostility to affirmative action squares with
Carter's support for educational funding in the inner city, or his en-
dorsement of the Civil Rights Act of 1990–91, or his belief that the
death penalty is implemented in race-conscious ways, or his view that
racial preferences are generally constitutional.

SHELBY STEELE: RACISM VERSUS "RACIAL ANXIETY"

Shelby Steele, like Wilson and Carter, rejects the "monolithic form of
racial identification" of the 1960s and applauds individuality over group
identity. He argues that the real problem facing blacks today is self-
doubt rather than discrimination. For him, as for Carter, racial preference policies enlarge self-doubt. Affirmative action should enforce equal
opportunity, not racial preference, which he equates with the lowering
of standards. Racial preference encourages dependency and an expec-
tation of entitlement. He calls for a de-raced policy.[86]

Steele believes that blacks have greater opportunities than they did
before the 1960s, and that they have simply been ineffective in taking
advantage of these greater opportunities. The problem is not a lack of
opportunity, which is "raceless" in character, but the fact that blacks
reenact their victim status. Blacks have chosen to believe in their infe-
riority. And Steele blames them, because "choice lives in even the most
blighted circumstances." In the end, Steele reduces the problems of African Americans to their fear of success or fear of failure. This "racial
anxiety," defined as self-doubt, keeps blacks from taking advantage of
opportunities. This problem is "as strong or stronger than the racial
discrimination we still face."[87]

Steele adopts the discourse of liberal individualism and conservatizes
it against the demands of the civil rights and black liberation movements. He says blacks need to rely on individual efforts, not social pro-

grams; that they need to recognize the diversity that exists in the race, and not treat all persons as similarly discriminated against; and that blacks should expect only the chance to compete, because nothing is guaranteed. "It is only an opportunity, not a deliverance." [88]

Steele's analysis, much like Wilson's and Carter's, seems to be directed specifically to black men. Steele urges black men to try harder and to act on their existing opportunities. One is left to wonder what he thinks about what black women should do. Does he assume that they should support the black man in his quest? He does not say.

One is left to wonder why black men, not black women, have led the assault against affirmative action programs and their specification of race. Why do they so longingly embrace the language of universalism and neutrality and use these terms as a basis for developing "fair" policies? Julianne Malveaux, an African American woman economist and columnist, has called attention to the fact that many of these men are the beneficiaries of the very programs they now criticize. She wonders whether "they are playing a masculinist game to prove they can fight the good fight with white men." Malveaux says that the black males' bashing of affirmative action might just be their "hankering for a 'fair fight' on a 'level playing field.'" These high achievers "may feel diminished by the notion they got where they are because of affirmative action." [89]

Malveaux argues that while white men are trying to protect their privileges, black men are trying to prove they can get the privileges on their own. On the other hand, black women, defined by intimate networks of familial and social obligations, do not embrace this rugged male individualism. Their experience of racialized gender oppression stands counter to the simplistic oppositions of race and class and its silencing of gender.

The critique of affirmative action by new black conservatives embodies unique descriptions of having grown up as black, male, and middle-class—as affirmative action babies. It denies the old racism and supplants it with mythical patriarchal individualism. It is a position unique to a post–civil rights era, and it legitimates a new kind of racialized patriarchy.

The "New Racism" and Its Multiple Faces

The Civil Rights Act of 1990–91, the Clarence Thomas Hearings, the Gulf War, and "Political Correctness"

For the time being, hold onto the idea that white male privilege is constructed in and through a racism that differentiates people of color as "less than" at the same time as it constructs racialized gender privilege. I will continue to uncover the racist and engendered priorities of the post–civil rights rhetoric that gained authority through the Reagan and Bush years. As we examine the process of racializing patriarchy through the 1980s, it helps to remember that white males feel under siege in a multicultural workforce.

Under discussion are the controversy over the Civil Rights Act of 1990–91, the Clarence Thomas Supreme Court confirmation hearings, the orchestration of the Gulf War, and the right-wing caricaturing of the civil rights agenda as "politically correct" (PC). Also discussed is the 1992 presidential election, with these developments as its backdrop. These events map a complicated series of connections which are neither linear nor simply causal.

The politics of the last decade appear inchoate and inexplicable on the one hand, and self-conscious and deliberate on the other. This mix reflects the special inability of the predominantly white male Bush administration to address the overwhelming challenges affecting American society, including the increasingly complex internationalization of the market; the upheavals in Eastern Europe; the growing inequity between rich and poor; the prevalence of single-parent families; multiracial demographic shifts; abortion; and AIDS. The incompetence of these officials stemmed in large part from their vested interests in an outdated status quo.

The Gulf War initially worked to silence dissent. At the time of the war, dissent was effectively muted through a fervent yellow-ribbon patriotism. The war was also used to discredit the sixties' civil rights agenda by calling attention to the large numbers of "women and minorities" who were fighting. The military was presented as a showcase of equal opportunity employment, distracting us from the first world / third world divide of the war itself.

The Gulf War was effectively used to silence at last the antiwar sentiment of the seventies. The American public seemed to accept the Bush administration's line that the anti–Vietnam war movement had been unfair to those who had fought that war. This time around, "we" should support "our" troops, even if we did not support the government's decision to attack Iraq. Although the distinction between support for the troops and support for the government's decision is an appropriate one, no significant antiwar stance was maintained once the air war began. The support of United States troops was quickly translated into and interpreted as support for the war.

In fact, it was against the backdrop of the Gulf War that President Bush made his first public statement criticizing "political correctness" on college campuses. Shortly after the United States withdrew from the Gulf region, Bush argued that a new intolerance was growing that was silencing freedom of speech for those who thought differently—that is, for those who did not support the "rights" agenda. He did not mention, of course, the curtailment of the press's freedom of speech—or of information, for that matter—during the Gulf War. The freedom of speech he was concerned with was the one that protects white men's privilege. Let us examine more closely the opportunism of the Bush administration's preoccupation with white male privilege and the politics of "reverse discrimination."

THE BUSH ADMINISTRATION:
AFFIRMATIVE AMBIVALENCE

While running for the Senate in 1964, Bush campaigned against the Civil Rights Act of 1964 and has had an ambivalent relationship to it ever since. At the time that he spoke out against the Civil Rights Act, he also held that the Republican Party should not be a home for segregationists. In 1970 he supported the "Philadelphia Plan," which was the first federal program that mandated the hiring of blacks.[1] But this support came after the assassination of Martin Luther King. Civil rights legislation had become more politically viable at this point, and less of a political risk for Bush.[2] He has somewhat inconsistently opposed federal civil rights legislation since then, based on his belief that individual "good will" was sufficient to guarantee equality. His reluctant signing of the Civil Rights Act of 1990–91 reflects this position.

In 1988, when running for president, Bush received only 10 percent of the black vote. In opinion polls, Bush received his lowest marks from the public on domestic and civil rights issues. In June 1991, in a *USA Weekend* survey of its readers, only 5 percent of respondents thought Bush was effective in protecting civil rights.[3] This public opinion reflects Bush's contradictions and unease surrounding the issue of race. The racist motivation for the Willie Horton image in the 1988 campaign is now well recognized. But Bush's appointment of the first black chairman of the Joint Chiefs of Staff, General Colin Powell, is used to soften this racist image. So is Bush's long-standing support of the United Negro College Fund. On the other hand, Bush fought the Civil Rights Act of 1990–91 on the basis of rejecting quotas. Then he turned around and appointed Clarence Thomas to replace Thurgood Marshall on the Supreme Court, seemingly supporting quotas by replacing one black with another. His administration appeared hostile and inept on the issue of race, and its mistakes were not without consequence.

If the Thomas hearings had gone better for the Bush administration, and if former Ku Klux Klan spokesperson David Duke had not garnered such a large national hearing in the Louisiana governor's race— with an appeal that sounded similar to the Republican line on affirmative action—it is not at all clear that Bush would have signed the 1990– 91 Civil Rights Act. These unexpected events placed Bush in a tough political position. His own opportunist inconsistencies, as well as the bitter conflict over racial "rights" which ran deep in his administration, threatened to snap the tightrope he had been walking. His balancing act between speaking on behalf of those (white men) whom he saw as suffering from affirmative action law (so-called quotas) and looking like a racist himself was becoming more precarious. The tension over "race" and "rights" in his administration was palpable.

This internal conflict first became evident in December 1990, when Michael Williams, assistant education secretary for civil rights and a black man, issued the statement that colleges and universities receiving federal money could not legally grant scholarships based solely on race.[4] Such scholarships were said to be in violation of Title VI of the Civil Rights Act of 1964. The official statement caused much confusion and upset among civil rights groups and was quickly revised to say that racially based scholarships were acceptable so long as the money came from private donations designated for that purpose or from federal programs set up to aid minority students. Only money from general operating budgets was off limits.[5] Nevertheless, the guidelines distinguishing usable government and private funding remained unclear to everyone involved. This lack of clarity resulted from the dilemma that the Bush administration was not free to dismantle civil rights law, yet could not live with it. Factions in the administration were unable to find a middle ground that could work for them.

In December 1991, education secretary Lamar Alexander was still revising Williams's initial position. He said that race-exclusive scholarships were illegal because they were discriminatory, but qualified this statement as meaning that race could not be the *only* factor in granting scholarships.[6] One could mention race as a factor, but there should be no obligatory condition connected to it. On the other hand, Alexander said he was not challenging the existing forty-five thousand race-based scholarships then available.[7] These revised guidelines appeared to clarify little, if anything. He said they were meant to be race neutral, and were not meant to deprive minority students of opportunities for scholarships. But these contradictory statements left the issue no clearer than before.

Although the legality of race-based scholarships is still under review at the time of this writing, the Clinton administration has spoken in favor of them. The new secretary of education, Richard Riley, has said he considers race-based scholarships to be a "valuable tool" for providing equal opportunity.[8]

Reiterating the Court's 1989 decisions, the Bush administration further declared that the law had no obligation to correct historic inequities faced by women and minorities in employment.[9] Solicitor General Kenneth W. Starr, in a major desegregation case, stated in the government's July 1991 brief that there was no "independent obligation flowing from the constitution to correct disparities" between the historically black and historically white colleges in Mississippi. This position did not sit well with many outside the administration. Bush intervened to quell the upset created. By October 1991, the administration's position was reversed; its new brief declared that "eliminating disparities in financing is part of the state's duty to provide equal educational opportunity."[10]

One of the more public revelations of the conflict over race policy within the Bush administration occurred on the day of the signing of the 1990–91 Civil Rights Act. On that day, legal counsel C. Boyden Gray announced his intention to phase out affirmative action hiring policies that used racial preferences, which he considered "unfair." Such an action would have meant the reversal of regulatory policies that had been in place since 1965.[11] It stood in stark contrast to the spirit of the Civil Rights Act that Bush had just signed. So, in the eleventh hour, Bush reversed Gray's announcement: "I say again, today, that I support affirmative action"; he affirmed the necessity of ending barriers.[12] There was clearly a war going on here.

THE CIVIL RIGHTS ACT OF 1990–91

In an attempt to reverse the Court's 1989 civil rights rulings, which gutted established discrimination law, Congress initiated the Civil Rights Act of 1990–91, sponsored by Senator Edward Kennedy and Representative Augustus Hawkins. The act was meant to restore civil rights protection, extend federal law to determine unlawful discrimination and compensate victims of such discrimination, and provide additional protection against unlawful discrimination.[13]

President Bush treated the legislation as a "quota" bill, although there was no mention in the bill of the use of quotas. In arguing against the bill, Bush continually stated that "group preferences" are unnecessary, and that what was needed instead was color-blind legislation. It is astonishing how much was said about quotas when the legislation addressed only the impact on hiring of employment practices and educational requirements. Bush argued that this language was equivalent to quotas: in order not to be charged with discrimination, businesses would hire racially, by numbers, rather than according to merit. Section 211 of the House bill made explicit that quotas were an "unlawful employment practice" and stated explicitly that "no provision of the legislation expressly, directly, implicitly, or indirectly requires or encourages such a result."[14]

Quotas were used as a smoke screen to make the very issue of remedying discrimination look unfair. Bush endorsed a diffused notion of discrimination—one that denied the group categories of race and gender.[15] He stated that we must not think of ourselves as colors or numbers; that we must be measured by merit, not by creed or sex or color; that government's responsibility is to enhance, not redistribute, opportunity; and that public policy must enhance opportunity, not ensure racial success.[16] From his stance of a color-blind neutrality, he denied sex discrimination altogether and covered over racial discrimination by definitional fiat.

Bush also sought a narrowing of the definition of discrimination to include only "intentional" discrimination, which would be more in keeping with the Supreme Court's 1989 decisions. Bush wanted to keep unintentional discriminatory policies defensible, particularly if they could be shown to be "necessary" to do business. Instead, the 1990–91 Civil Rights Act restored the burden of proof to the employer in disparate-impact cases. Employers now must prove that a practice is essential to their business; the plaintiff no longer has to prove that it is not.[17]

This legislation should make it easier to sue in job discrimination cases. It should also make it easier to win a suit against unfair job qualifications that have disparate impact on persons of different race and/or gender. It makes it possible to get cash damages for sex discrimination cases, although the cap on such damages is lower than on race cases. The act does not, however, address the Supreme Court's ruling in *Croson v. City of Richmond,* which declared unconstitutional an ordinance that set aside 30 percent of public works contracts for minority contractors. It remains to be seen what effect the new law will have, given the significant skepticism and hostility expressed toward it.

There had been little substantive revision of the 1990–91 act when at last Bush approved it. Although Bush said he had signed the revised bill because it finally bolstered equality, this justification did not square with the facts. He gave in on the amount of compensatory and punitive damages allowed plaintiffs and compromised on letting existing affirmative action policies stand, even if certain current workers had not been party to such agreements.[18]

Then why did Bush sign? What had changed? Bush's positioning within the discourse of the "new racism" had changed. By October 1991, Bush had no choice but to endorse the 1990–91 Civil Rights Act. He had begun to step over the delicate line of acceptable public racial talk, which in part attests to the continuing saliency of civil rights discourse. He needed to disassociate himself from his anti–civil rights position and his apparent insensitivity to minorities.

It is important to note that Bush chose to represent the Civil Rights

Act of 1990–91 as "special legislation" for blacks, even though it is entitled "Civil Rights and Women's Equity in Employment Act." The false separation of the civil rights of people of color from the rights of women has ghettoized civil rights into a racial issue. Viewing it as a racial issue misrepresents the specific sex and gender concerns of women of color and disconnects these from the concerns of white women. It is more difficult to caricature civil rights as "special interest" legislation when it is recognized as including the interests of white women workers along with those of people of color. It then has majority status.

THE LOS ANGELES RIOTS AND MURPHY BROWN

The rioting in Los Angeles in May 1992 was sparked by the acquittal of several white police officers who had excessively and brutally beaten Rodney King, a black man. What made this case so explosive was that the beating was videotaped by an observer and shown repeatedly on TV news programs throughout the country. Hardly anyone could fathom an acquittal—not even Daryl Gates, then Los Angeles police chief, which might explain why he was so unprepared for the rioting that ensued after the verdict.

The acquittal had racism written all over it in the eyes of people of color, especially inner-city blacks. Several white jurors said race had nothing to do with it. They claimed that King was out of control, and the police had to protect themselves. It is difficult, however, to forget that there was only one of him—and he was on the ground—while there were at least four police officers at any given moment, upright and flailing batons.

Life in the inner city is dismal, a dead end for most people living there, who are looking for a way out of the drugs, the crime, and the unemployment. The Los Angeles acquittal sparked a rage that had festered within the system of racism. The riots that followed were understandable, yet made no sense. They were horrifically self-destructive. They were violent. They were anarchic. For some, they were a cry for help. For others, they were a sign of desperation. Whatever their meanings, the riots dumped the issue of racism—not just race—in Bush's lap.

This "multi-ethnic urban riot" was an outpouring of black rage and of the desperation of the Los Angeles Hispanic community. There were 58 deaths, almost 2,400 injuries, over 5,000 fires, more than 16,000 arrests, and damage of at least $785 million. The Korean immigrant community felt much of the damage. And Los Angeles appeared to be a rigidly segregated and hostile city.[19]

According to African American cultural critic Cornel West, the Los Angeles riots were not simply either a race or a class rebellion. He instead depicts the riots as an enormous upheaval which was multiracial, cross-class, and largely male. Only 36 percent of those arrested were black. For West, race was a visible catalyst, not the underlying cause. "What we witnessed in Los Angeles was the consequence of a lethal linkage of economic decline, cultural decay, and political lethargy in American life."[20]

It is interesting to see how Bush chose to extricate himself from the aftermath of Los Angeles. First he tried blaming the riots on Democratic social welfare policies of the 1960s. He said these policies had created a culture of dependency and a crisis in family life which had caused poverty and the decay of the inner city. This well-worn neoconservative rhetoric did not work. People asked which policies? With what effect? Bush then shifted gears and said it made no sense to cast blame, that instead we must come up with better policies than the programs of the Great Society, which had required an overage of government spending.[21]

His next attempt at neutralizing the riots rerouted the earlier blaming posture and refocused the neoconservative rhetoric to a right-wing family values campaign. Bush had already used the restoration of "family values" as a theme of his 1992 election campaign—with little success. After the Los Angeles riots, he picked it up again. During a commencement speech at Notre Dame, Bush called for the rebuilding of strong families as an alternative to dependence on government social service programs.[22] He argued that we must start with a set of principles and policies that foster personal responsibility, choice, and competition where government once played a role. His rhetoric offered family values and a privatized role for the state to resolve the crises of inner cities.

Enter Vice-President Dan Quayle. Like Bush, he said that the Los Angeles riots were the result of a "poverty of values." Note that actual poverty is sidelined by the focus on values. Quayle affirmed that the lawless anarchy in Los Angeles had stemmed from a breakdown of family structure and personal responsibility in which the urban poor have lost their moral fiber. To make his point regarding the importance of creating stable two-parent families, Quayle criticized the TV character Murphy Brown for celebrating single motherhood and devaluing the importance of fathers.

Here we have moved from the racist verdict in the King trial to the ensuing Los Angeles riots and poverty-stricken African American and Hispanic inner cities, and from there to a discussion of family values and single mothers.[23] Murphy Brown, a white upper-class TV character who chose to birth a child without a husband, was used by Quayle to invoke a notion of families in crisis. We would seem to have moved from race to gender, but not really. In this instance, the character Murphy Brown (an upper-class white woman) stands in for single motherhood (poor women of color). Discussion of family issues and single mothers allowed the Bush administration to sidestep the problem of racism by talking about gendered family issues instead. Single motherhood is *already* encoded racially. Because the imagery of black single and often teenage mothers was already in place for Quayle, he did not have to speak of race. So he said little, if anything, concerning the racialized reality of single motherhood. Instead, he talked about family, which also meant race. He said, "I believe that children should have the benefit of being born into families with a mother and a father who will give them love and care."[24] This sounds simple enough, but it isn't.

It is incredible how messy the family values theme quickly became for the Bush administration. There are too many single mothers today for it to work as smoothly as once it might have. It also caught Bush and Quayle in their own antiabortion rhetoric. As all the news media were quick to ask, why criticize Murphy Brown? At least she did not have an abortion. Eventually, White House spokesman Marlin Fitzwater was forced to switch gears and praise the Murphy Brown show for exhibiting "pro-life" values. The following statement, which sums up the incoherence of Bush administration policy in this realm, was made by Diane English, the creator and producer of Murphy Brown: "If the Vice-President thinks it's disgraceful for an unmarried woman to bear a child, and if he believes that a woman cannot adequately raise a child without a father, then he'd better make sure abortion remains safe and legal."[25]

The promotion of marriage and of heterosexual two-parent families constituted the Bush administration's antipoverty inner-city program. Their domestic policy seemed to suggest that the problems of unemployment and underemployment, especially of people of color, would be best addressed by marriage. This hardly seems like a serious policy formulation.

This lack of credibility underlines much of the Bush administration's policies on the racialized aspects of American life. The nomination of

Clarence Thomas, a black man, to the Supreme Court bespeaks a similar incoherence.

THE CLARENCE THOMAS CONFIRMATION HEARINGS

If the Los Angeles riots remind us of an old racism deeply connected to the poverty of African Americans and, more recently, of Hispanics and Koreans, the Thomas hearings are a window into the newer, more complicated racism defined in and through a black middle class. Bush's nomination of Clarence Thomas was dishonest. Even though Bush denied that he chose Thomas because of his race, it seemed clear that a man with Thomas's mediocre legal record would not have been chosen otherwise. Bush's nominee was a pawn to appease those within both the Republican and Democratic parties who thought a black should be chosen to replace Thurgood Marshall. And he found a black man who could also pass the right-wing litmus test: he had repeatedly spoken against the right to abortion and was extremely critical of affirmative action policy. As a Reagan-Bush neoconservative, he supported "self-help" as the best palliative against racism. There were numerous qualified African Americans from which to choose, but they were not rightist neoconservatives. And there were numerous neoconservatives from which to choose, but they were not black or sufficiently right-wing.

The Thomas nomination once again trapped the Bush administration in its own contradictory politics. Official administration discourse mandated that policy initiatives be color-blind. It also maintained that affirmative action wrongly brings attention to race rather than individual merit. Yet Bush appointed a black man to replace a black man. Then he denied the importance of color and said he chose Thomas for his merit, when it was perfectly clear that merit was not the deciding factor. To make matters worse, the black man, who was not spectacularly meritorious, was a benefactor of affirmative action programs at Yale Law School, but now argues that such programs create more problems than they solve. It is the very affirmative action that the administration and Thomas himself assail that gained him his nomination to the Supreme Court. This looks disingenuous at best.

Thomas had distinguished himself during the Reagan administration as an African American who supported an anti–civil rights approach to racial equality.[26] He favored the adoption of color-blind legislation: "I firmly insist that the constitution be interpreted in a color-blind fashion. It is futile to talk of a color-blind society unless this constitutional principle is first established. Hence, I emphasize black self-help, as opposed to racial quotas and other race-conscious legal devices that only further and deepen the original problem."[27]

As part of the Reagan transition team at the Equal Employment Opportunity Commission (EEOC), he at first defended numerical goals and timetables in hiring, but then reversed this position in 1984. He also rejected statistical disparities as proof of discrimination. During a commencement speech at Savannah State College in June 1985, Thomas summed up his views by saying that although racial prejudice exists, blacks should not use it as a crutch. Others, he said, jump too quickly to make excuses for black Americans, who should stand up for themselves instead. They should "overcome the lure of excuses" and the "temptation to blame others." The onus was on them. And, in a comment that may clarify Thomas's treatment of Anita Hill more than it clarifies the condition of African Americans, he charged that "we subdue, we seduce, but we don't respect ourselves, our women, our babies."[28]

In the early part of the confirmation hearings, Thomas stressed his poverty as a child and his ascent up the economic class ladder. Although he mentioned the help he received from his grandfather, from the nuns, and from affirmative action, he presented his story as one of self-help. His nomination became a public airing and national viewing of a black man rejecting affirmative action policy.[29] This was a problematic stance for one who also believed that "there is nothing you can do to get past black skin" in our society.[30] One might have expected from Thomas some recognition that you cannot substitute self-help for society's obligation to deal fairly with its members.

Thomas's black neoconservative agenda was articulated through a racialized patriarchal discourse about African American women. He used his sister's brief stint on welfare to advance the notion of the dependent black welfare woman, one of many blacks waiting for a handout. In fact his sister's story is one not only of welfare dependency but also of hard work. Emma Mae Martin's life held a series of low-paying jobs while she raised her own children and cared for other family members. Thomas simply ignored the way that his sister's options were different from his because of the way gender is encoded on her black skin.

Emma Mae Martin's story was misrepresented through the text of a dependent welfare mother. In her real story, a rich network provided support and strength in the face of racism and poverty and sexism: desertion by husbands and lack of child support even as she struggled to enable boys and men to get ahead.[31] Thomas was oblivious. His world was male. Carol Delaney, an anthropology professor at Stanford University, who also attended a Roman Catholic school in Savannah, Georgia, countered Thomas's descriptions of the nuns. They might have taught *him* how to make something of himself, but girls were taught and trained by them to "learn their place" as women and to serve others.[32]

Thomas's sexism is completely relevant here. And so is his engendered viewing of black women through a racist lens, particularly given the charges of Anita Hill that Thomas had sexually harassed her on the job.[33] Nothing in his world view would lead one to think that it was unlikely for Thomas to act in this sexist manner. The fact that Hill was a black woman, and sexualized as such, made it all the more plausible. Nevertheless, Anita Hill's charges were denied by Thomas. When all was said and done, Hill was erased as a black woman, and her charges were said to be racist.

Although Anita Hill was a black woman, Thomas treated her as though she was *not* black, but just a woman, with no claims to racist stereotyping. This is the way Thomas transformed Hill's charges of sexual harassment into his own charge of a racist "high-tech lynching." *Lynching* was used as a racial metaphor that de-raced Hill.[34] It allowed Thomas to speak of the racist stereotypes of black men's sexuality as though there are no parallel stereotypes affecting Hill as a black woman. Thomas angrily stated at the hearings: "This [charge of sexual harassment] plays into the most bigoted, racist stereotypes that any black man will face."[35] It was a "stereotype you can't wash off."[36] Thomas called upon the very racism that he argued blacks should not hide behind so that he would not have to answer individually to the charge of sexual harassment.

Thomas shifted the ground out from beneath Hill. He attempted to make the issue the racist stereotyping of African American men rather than the sexual harassment of a black woman. In this shift, he denied the existence of sexism and sexual violence against black women, which indicts black as well as white men.[37] Instead of probing the sexually discriminatory action of Thomas, the committee was served up a series of charges concerning the racist treatment of black men in order to deflect the attack. In this case, racism was used to erase gender, even though there was no racial angle between Thomas and Hill. Or, as President Bush is supposed to have said: "If they are going to use the sex thing, we can use the race thing."

The hearings bespeak the very interconnections of race and gender. In order that Thomas be confirmed, the connections between racism and sexism had to be distorted and severed. Anita Hill would be sacrificed in the process. She would be depicted as either a traitor to her own race—and therefore not black—or as a traitor to her sex—and therefore not a woman. As black feminist Barbara Smith commented, "any black woman who raises the issue of sexual oppression in the African American community is somehow a traitor to the race, which translates into being a traitor to black men."[38] Hill was also seen as a traitor to her sex in that she remained silent about sexual harassment and did not come forward because she cared too much about her professional career. She was too much like a (white) man.

The impossible situation of Anita Hill was that she was both a woman and black. Language and its politics did not afford her a way to translate this double reality during the hearings. As Nell Irvin Painter argues, Hill lacked a clear stereotype like a lynching to rally support for her as a black woman.[39] Anita Hill, a year after the hearings, indicted the Senate Judiciary Committee during an address at the conference on "Race, Gender and Power in America" at Georgetown University Law Center. She stated that she was misrepresented by Senate members because she lacked the usual institutional attachments of patronage. Moreover, her gender and race, when combined with her education and demeanor and career choice, disallowed the senators their visual stereotypes and simplistic oppositions that pigeonhole women of color. They had no way to see or hear the complexity of her charges.[40]

This ploy of separating the mesh of racialized gender worked to the extent that Thomas was confirmed.[41] But it did not succeed in silencing the issue of sexual harassment. Instead, it unleashed an outpouring of anger by women repelled by sexual harassment abuses in the workplace. After ignoring much of the feminist civil rights agenda and dealing with affirmative action as a race issue, the Bush administration and then the Senate unleashed a tidal wave of feminist consciousness among white and African American women.[42]

The Senate Judiciary Committee had not thought Hill's charges important enough to investigate at the start. Once the committee was forced to conduct an inquiry, its members appeared callous and ill informed.[43] The televised hearings presented a stark picture of white men occupying the seats of government. This visual image—of a group of white men judging a black man charged with sexual harassment by a black woman— had an impact.

The hearings underscored the racialized nature of politics. Would a white man have been interrogated publicly, the way Thomas was, with references to the size of his penis? The hearings also attested to the male privilege which pervades both white government officials and the black middle class. Clarence Thomas was able to utilize masculinist imagery even in his claims that he was being treated in racist fashion. As the testimony of John Doggett made clear, masculinist and sexist values exist within the African American community. According to Doggett, Anita Hill suffered from sexual delusions, not sexual harassment. Similarly, Orlando Patterson claimed that Anita Hill was merely overreacting to a "down-home style of courting."[44]

The Thomas confirmation hearings were not politics as usual. At the start of the hearings, it looked as though Thomas's antiabortion "right to life of the child-in-the-womb stance" would be used to mount an attack against him by feminists and other civil rights groups.[45] Although a few eloquent critical reviews of Thomas's civil rights record were heard early on, the focus soon changed. Thomas's stance on abortion became secondary as attention shifted to charges of sexual harassment on the part of Thomas. And because it was a black woman bringing the charges, the issue of sexual harassment was brought forward as an issue for both women of color and white women. Sexual harassment can happen to any woman. The connections between racism and sexism could not be effectively severed because they were too enmeshed in the person of Anita Hill.[46]

Bush had played his race card with the nomination of Thomas, but it gained him very little.[47] Barely confirmed (by a 52–48 vote), Thomas won the battle, but it is not clear who won the war. Thomas is on the Court, but as an undistinguished black man whom many people believe to be guilty of sexual harassment of one form or another. Bush was responsible for the nomination, and he discredited both the appointment process and himself by wrongly politicizing the process.

The full effects of the hearings remain unclear in terms of the repackaging of the right-wing agenda. In some ways the hearings became more subversive than constitutive of this agenda. Senator Orrin Hatch of Utah would have us believe that the whole Hill scenario was a plot by white liberals and their slick "special interest" lawyers to discredit Thomas.[48] Thomas also charged that it was "special interest" groups who were trying to ruin him. He continually spoke of "the people who concocted this" and "the people" who leaked the story to the press. The hearings were depicted by the Republicans on the Judiciary Committee as a result of the excesses of a liberal rights agenda.

But these charges were not totally successful. Instead, in some quarters there was a revitalization of the liberal feminist agenda. Many women, outraged by the hearings, recommitted their energy to the electoral arena. They were determined to transform the nearly all-male club of the Senate. In this spirit, over 119 women ran for congressional seats in 1992, up from 78 women in 1990. There are now forty-seven women in the House, up from twenty-eight. Another 2,215 women sought state legislative seats in 1992, twice as many as in 1990. Four women won Senate seats. Carol Moseley Braun, the first African American woman elected to the Senate, campaigned in protest of Clarence Thomas's confirmation.[49]

For the white public, the hearings also became an unexpected window into the internal conflicts and intraracial differences in the black middle class. The confirmation hearings exposed their audience to the diversity within the black community, to the existence within its ranks of Reagan-Bush neoconservatism as well as a new black conservatism. It clarified for whites an important reality: "the black community" is no more homogeneous than "the white community" is.

Orlando Patterson called the hearings a "ritual of inclusion" and an affirmation of the achievements made by blacks. For him, it was clear that "the culture of slavery is dead."[50] Many affluent blacks in Los Angeles, however, do not completely agree with Patterson. They still fear the possibility of finding themselves on the ground being beaten by police officers as Rodney King did.[51] In other words, slavery per se may be dead, but the racialized culture it left behind is alive and well.

During the hearings, we saw African American women who supported Clarence Thomas and disavowed any connection to Anita Hill. We also saw a group of black women who formed a network called African American Women in Defense of Ourselves—just days after the hearings—and placed ads in newspapers throughout the country decrying the attacks on Hill. Racial and sexual politics were both connected and diversified in the hearings, allowing for the emergence of new possibilities for feminist politics.

The confirmation process cannot be summed up easily. The Senate Judiciary Committee members, uncomfortable with their own racialized patriarchal views, never asked Thomas the formidable questions. He was not queried concerning his attitudes toward black women or his choice of a white wife. No one pushed him to answer questions about his alleged addiction to pornographic films. He was never really pressed on his stance on abortion. And when he disclaimed his earlier ultraconservative positions on judicial interpretation, no one on the committee decried his opportunism. The committee members' own discomfort with race and sex permeated the entire proceedings and covered over the very issues which needed to be explored. As a result, we have a justice—who happens to be black—who is one of the most conservative jurors ever to sit on the Court.

Thus far, Justice Thomas has distinguished himself as slightly to the right of Justice Scalia. In his first term, he agreed to the narrowing of the 1964 Voting Rights Act; affirmed a narrowed view of political asylum; consented to the weakening of labor unions; and further limited the rights of prisoners on death row, who are disproportionately black. In a lower court ruling, published after Thomas's confirmation, he stated that the federal government could not give preferential treatment to women in awarding broadcast licenses, even though it does so for blacks and other minority groups. His decision stated that the Federal Communications Commission's policy of giving preference to women was unconstitutional because it denied equal protection to men. He completely endorsed the rhetoric of reverse discrimination: preferential treatment of women violates equal treatment.[52] We have heard this before.

RACE, GENDER, AND THE GULF WAR

The war in the Persian Gulf formed an important backdrop for this racialized gender politics. The Gulf War included more women—especially women of color—and more female reservists—many with young infants and children—than ever before. Fighting forces were disproportionately composed of people of color: over 24 percent of the troops serving in the Gulf were African Americans. Almost 30 percent of the army's soldiers called to fight the ground war were also African Americans. Thirty-five thousand of the United States troops in the Gulf were women. Fighting forces were described for the first time in United States military history as men and women. Women flew helicopters and were medics. Melissa Rathbun Nealy was captured as a prisoner of war. Some of the imagery of the Gulf War was new: women in khaki alongside men. Some of the imagery was old: little attention was paid to race.

The Gulf War unsettled notions about gender. Both the reality and imagery were significant in challenging established ideas; the war changed perceptions of the role of women in the military and expanded their actual combat duties. After the war, Congress repealed the law barring women from flying combat planes. Women are now permitted but not required to perform combat roles as Navy or Air Force pilots.[53]

The unsettling of gender roles was in no sense linear or simple. Although women were seen on the television screen as forming an integral part of the United States fighting forces, they were also depicted by the media as being deeply troubled at the prospect of leaving their children to go to war. A few mothers of newborns even refused to go. Others, under extreme pressure, agreed to make intricate childcare arrangements for the duration of their tour of duty. These women left their children in the care of babysitters or husbands and headed for the Persian Gulf. One reservist had a twenty-one-month-old baby, and another a five-month-old baby who was still nursing. When the latter reservist tried to get an extension in order to wean her baby, she was told it was not possible.[54] Family and job appeared to be too much in conflict for many Americans as they watched the war unfold. Media messages were mixed, and the construction of family life appeared disarranged by the reality of the woman soldier. Her militaristic form of gender equality unsettled many of us.

The Gulf War brought particular attention to the large numbers of single parents in the military. There are approximately 55,000 single parents in the Armed Forces—37,000 men and 18,000 women. Of this number, there were roughly 16,000 single parents and 12,000 military couples with children who were on duty in the Gulf. Although it would have been possible to give these people exemptions, it was not done. Instead, the military said that family life would not exempt a person from military duty—whether man or woman. We saw sharply the meaning of sex equality in the military: men and women were treated as though they had the same familial responsibilities, even if the woman was still breast-feeding her infant.

In stark contrast to the United States women in khaki were the women of Kuwait and Saudi Arabia in their veils and chadors. The Saudi woman, with face and body hidden, needed protection.[55] The United States military would protect her. News of a protest by Saudi women demanding the simple right to drive their own cars underscored the problematic status of these women.[56] United States military women appeared more than equal against this backdrop of Arab women. However, United States military women remain highly ghettoized in the lowest ranks of the military. They experience sexual harassment on a daily basis. Also, a danger here, as Cynthia Enloe cautions, is that a militarized world needs for women to find rewards in a militarized femininity.[57]

Amid this gender flux, what remains constant is the privileged status of white men and of a very few black men in the military. General Norman Schwarzkopf repeatedly invoked Saddam Hussein's Arab rhetoric and spoke of the Gulf War as the "mother of all wars." Alongside this vision of a masculinized mother stood military women in uniform. And alongside them stood Schwarzkopf's outdated vision of a military filled with men. When he addressed the troops in the Gulf, he often spoke as if they were all men. In one instance he acknowledged their looking forward to seeing their wives, children, and families—but not their husbands.[58] In another instance, speaking about his upcoming retirement, he pointed proudly to the "fine young men coming up behind me whom I've trained the right way. They're going to make generals and great leaders."[59] Women remain the foot soldiers.

What of racial equality in the military? First, one should note that for many Americans it was Schwarzkopf, not Colin Powell, who became the hero of Desert Storm. Powell, as an African American, could never become the same kind of hero. Instead, he was used to deflect American racism toward the Arab world, by evoking African Americans as part of the United States concept of self.[60]

Blacks make up a higher percentage of the military population than of the general population because they have had greater opportunity for advancement in the military than in civilian life.[61] This has been especially true of black women, who now make up approximately 33 percent of the women in the military.[62] When President Bush was asked to explain the overrepresentation of blacks in the Gulf War, he said it was simple: "The military of the United States is the greatest equal opportunity employer around."[63] The truth is that there is not much competition.

WAR AND THE SILENCING OF DISSENT

The Gulf War was our first full-fledged television war. Although we had seen television reports on the Vietnam War, we could actually watch the Gulf War around the clock on CNN. However, although the constant coverage made it appear that we were getting more information about this war than about previous wars, we actually saw less and knew less about the Gulf War. News reporting was highly regulated and censored. There were strict new press restrictions for covering military operations. The information flow was managed through briefing rooms.[64]

There were Pentagon-approved correspondent pools, security reviews, and military escorts for all interviews.[65]

These new restrictions were justified by the Bush Administration largely on the basis of the Vietnam War. Too much news exposure had purportedly led to anti–Vietnam War sentiment. The Pentagon said it would not allow such an erosion of support to happen again, and it achieved its goal. In actuality, the greatest success of the Gulf War was the censoring of information and the silencing of dissent. The very idea of speaking out against the war was discredited by equating patriotism with a prowar stance, by fomenting an absolutist hatred of Saddam Hussein, and by curtailing war information.[66]

In part, Bush tried to make this war different from Vietnam (which we lost) and more like World War II (which we won). He used the imagery of World War II to call up the former associations of strength and virtue with the struggle against Nazism. Hussein was termed "a Hitler"; other countries intervening with us were called "the allies." This need to identify with our past rather than with our present or our future reflected to what degree the United States has become a country in decline. According to Doug Lummis and Mojtaba Sadria, we triumphed in the Gulf because we became what we used to be. Of course, neither Japan nor Germany identified with this World War II imagery. They did not want to be what *they* were during World War II; they preferred what they had become since 1945.[67]

Well-known *New York Times* editorialist Tom Wicker notes that the Bush administration was so successful in controlling information regarding the war that they "were able to tell the public just about what they wanted the public to know." As a result, most Americans did not know that the so-called smart bombs made up only 7 percent of all the United States explosives dropped on Iraq and Kuwait, or that 70 percent of the 88,500 tons of bombs dropped on Iraq and Kuwait in the forty-three days of the war *missed* their targets.[68] Anthony Lewis, also of the *New York Times,* describes earlier information control: "From August 2, 1991, when Iraq invaded Kuwait, to the first bombs falling on Baghdad, January 17, 1991, President Bush maneuvered the country toward war. Deception obscured the process then. Now we can see the steady, skillful march to war."[69] According to Everette Dennis, Executive Director of the Gannett Foundation Media Center in New York, this sanitized version of the war presented us with the illusion of news. The government's new censorship violated the first and fifth amendments. The yellow ribbons and American flags that decked the United

States landscape for months during the war came to represent a troubling patriotism, one which required a closing down of debate and of democratic dialogue.

In the end, over one hundred thousand Iraqi soldiers were killed in the Gulf War. Iraqi children continue to suffer terrible disease and hunger as a result of the war. The bombs and the oil spills created environmental havoc and numerous health hazards. Saddam Hussein remains in power.[70] In many ways, war continues for the Iraqis.

At first, the United States claimed victory. Bush claimed it as his finest moment. Then less was said on the war as questions persisted about Iraq and Hussein.[71] Questions have also persisted about censorship during the Gulf War. It is possible that recent attacks against "political correctness" reflect the broad impact of the Gulf War on political speech.

POLITICAL CORRECTNESS AND THE RIGHT TO SPEAK

Making full use of the postwar nationalistic fervor, President Bush, in a commencement speech at the University of Michigan, attacked what he considered to be an assault against free speech that was particularly forceful on college campuses. He said a new tyranny had replaced old prejudices with new ones and had declared "certain topics off limits." He spoke of this new censorship as responsible for crushing "diversity in the name of diversity."[72] In particular, Bush attacked the civil rights agenda as antithetical to free speech because people no longer feel free to speak out against it.

The right-wing term "political correctness"—which started out as an ironic term used by the Left to criticize its own purist strain[73]—is now being used to caricature people who support racial and sexual equality and the consequent diversity it demands, portraying them as intolerant. To connect the issue of civil rights to the issue of free speech is a smart move on the part of the right wing, because it appeals to most people's commitment to liberal individualist freedoms, especially the right to freedom of speech.

Similar charges have been made against the codes prohibiting "hate speech" which have been instituted at several universities, such as Stanford, the University of Wisconsin, and the University of Massachusetts.[74] They have been seen by critics as infringements on free speech—which, in fact, they were meant to be, in any absolutist sense of the term. Much less has been said regarding the violence that led to the adoption of these prohibitions. At the University of Wisconsin, a series of racist incidents occurred, including a fraternity-run "slave auction," before a code forbidding hate speech was put into place. At the University of Massachusetts, a white mob had chased and beaten several blacks on campus before there was discussion of such a code.

This kind of violence, which both reflects and instigates hate speech, is often not recognized for what it is.[75] And much of this violence goes unreported. The National Institute Against Prejudice and Violence reported racial incidents at 115 campuses in 1989. Clearly there is a problem here, and hate speech contributes to it.

The question of free speech is complicated because all speech is not equal in the first place, and all speech does not have the same effect. Some words have more power than others. So speech can hurt, can have real consequences, and can create complicated and dangerous terrain when it does. Because speech is dangerous, there can be no absolute freedom of speech, yet there is no sane way to limit speech arbitrarily in advance. As Stanley Fish, professor of English and law at Duke, said, "there is no safe place."[76] No code can create such a place. But it is on the basis of the political consequences of speech that one should rethink the hate speech codes, not on the basis of an abstract notion of speech, disconnected from its political effects.

These issues are opportunistically simplified in the charges against political correctness. Instead of really trying to open up discussion, the Bush administration used the issue of free speech as a smokescreen. The charge against political correctness was an attempt to close down free speech: to silence individuals who were critical of the Reagan/Bush agenda. It was an attempt to silence the discourse of racial diversity by attacking it as authoritarian in intent, as if those promoting diversity disallowed the freedom to speak or hear views against it. Such charges distort the dilemmas of a racialized and patriarchal liberal discourse which gives greater freedom to white men and to what they speak. The attack on the "politically correct"—those who support racial and sexual diversity—is really an attack on the significant changes made by the 1960s civil rights movements and the radically pluralist demands that have followed.

Members of the Bush administration—mainly white men—stated that they would "resist intimidation" from those claiming to be politically correct ("PC"). In other words, they would not allow themselves to be pushed into accepting a policy that incorporated greater racial and sexual equality. This attack on political correctness was extended beyond the challenge to affirmative action to ridicule the entire progressive agenda of the last twenty-five years.[77] It has been used to allow people their racism, sexism, and homophobia. It equates all forms of intolerance. But to speak out against intolerance is not the same as being intolerant. And speaking out is not the same as silencing others. Much is lost if one does not recognize the difference between speaking on behalf of some people and speaking against all the others. Speech that likens feminists to pit bulls, jokes about dykes on bikes, T-shirts that say "Club faggots, not seals," and signs that say "Club the niggers" are forms of speech we cannot afford to protect.[78]

Equality discourse carries little of the clout that the right wing attributes to it. Yet at the heart of the charges against political correctness is the assumption that such discourse is used to exercise authoritarian power. *Newsweek* led the attack with an article in December 1990 about the "Thought Police." These police are said to be the "tenured radicals" inhabiting campuses throughout the country. The *Atlantic Monthly* gave further voice to these charges in March 1991 with the publication of excerpts of Dinesh D'Souza's *Illiberal Education: The Politics of Race and Sex on Campus.*

A precursor to the "PC" debate was the best-seller by conservative political theorist Allan Bloom, *The Closing of the American Mind* (1987). Bloom argued that the university was failing democracy by becoming too democratic—that it was creating homogenized persons rather than truly distinct varieties. He argued that we have been left with a "drab diversity" fostered by a false egalitarianism, because we are not all created equal and the same. He argued that we need to have prejudices: they help us discriminate truth from falsity. The new relativism—challenging the classics and fostering diversity—leaves us undiscriminating and ignorant. In a phrase that is classic Bloom, "you don't replace something with nothing."[79]

D'Souza has extended these charges. He attacks the foundations of affirmative action as undermining individual achievement by exalting group membership. He calls this illiberal, because democracy is meant to nurture not equality but equal rights to opportunity, and opportunity recognizes individual merit, not subjugated groups. The underlying premise of group justice is "hostile to individual equity and excellence." Thus, affirmative action has led to a tyranny of minorities who are less qualified. D'Souza terms this a new racism: it is not that minorities *are* inferior, but that affirmative action treats them as though they were. The victim then becomes the victimizer.[80]

Part and parcel of this process, claims D'Souza, has been the dilution of intellectual expertise in the name of cultural and ethnic diversity. Core curricula have been labeled as biased and have been replaced with non-Western classics, feminist literature, and revolutionary tracts of the Third World. There are now multicultural requirements in many of the major universities, which D'Souza describes as reflecting little more than ethnic cheerleading and primitive romanticism about the Third World.[81] He contends the changes have been "revolutionary." The search for "universal standards of judgment, which transcend particularities of race, gender, and culture, has given way to a politicized Afrocentricity."[82] He claims this revolution has been institutionalized by tenuring multi-cultural radicals as faculty, as deans and college presidents, and as heads of major academic organizations.

The facts do not bear out D'Souza's charges of an institutionalized revolution. Only 7 percent of all full professors at colleges and universities are people of color. Thirteen percent are women. Although women's studies courses are offered at a majority of schools, one can major in the subject at only about fifty of them.[83] In the early 1960s, ten top history departments had a total of 160 full professors, all of whom were men, and 128 assistant professors, 4 of whom were women. Ten years later, out of 274 full professors, 2 were women. Out of 317 assistant professors, 3 were women. By the mid-1980s, 11.7 percent of all full professors in the country were women, and 2.2 percent were black.[84] There has been change. But the change has hardly been revolutionary.

It is significant that even this limited amount of change should be so threatening to the white male domination of the academy—and of the work force more generally. These men's sense of the fragility of their power may in part reflect the changing demographics of the labor force and global economy and of family structure.

Because throughout the 1980s the academy was the one place that civil rights discourse still had saliency—though lessened political clout—the attack against political correctness was launched here. After neo-conservatives had dismantled much affirmative action law and stacked the courts, college campuses remained one of the last bastions of equality discourse. The charge of political correctness was the attempt to silence such discourse. It appeared more important than ever to do so now because some one-third of professors in the country, many of whom were tenured in the conservative 1950s, are nearing retirement age.[85]

Very few people would argue that there have not been some abuses of affirmative action. Bad decisions have sometimes been made on how to create equality while recognizing racial and sexual diversity. The wrong person has sometimes been hired in the interest of multiculturalism. But these problems are not inherent to civil rights discourse. Such discourse instead is open and undetermined. Harvard professor Henry Louis Gates argues that one need not be black to write a slave narrative; that we need not overspecialize difference; that people can and must stretch themselves in order to embrace common threads. This view is not a defense of a nondiversified faculty, but it is also not a narrowly determinist or essentialist definition of a diverse one.[86] To pluralize the curriculum is not to make a new center, as the term "Afrocentric" wrongly implies.[87] It is to create many centers, between which there will often be conflict. Conflict can breed openness. This hardly describes the closed-mindedness attributed to the "PC" camp.

Pertinent to this discussion is Martin Bernal's *Black Athena: The Afroasiatic Roots of Classical Civilization,* which argues that the theories concerned with the origins of Western civilization are heavily influenced by racism and anti-Semitism. He challenges the Aryan model, arguing that Egyptian civilization came from Black Africa, that Egyptian culture was a black culture, and that Western civilization had its roots in Black Africa.[88] Bernal's analysis invites scrutiny. His argument invites discussion, as well as competing interpretation. There is no silencing intended here.

Although neoconservatives have termed political correctness the new McCarthyism of the Left, calling someone a sexist or a racist is in no way parallel to calling someone a Communist. People who were called Communists in the fifties lost their jobs. They were called before Congressional committees and queried by federal agents. They were hounded from one city to another. There is no similar punishment for homophobes or racists.[89]

The silencing of debate was initiated by the Bush administration, not faculty members on college campuses. The real "thought police" are those who oversaw the censorship of the Gulf War, insisted that racial guidelines were really quotas, and swore that Anita Hill was a pawn of liberal special-interest groups. They are also those who led the assault against reproductive rights, as we shall see in chapter 4.

THE 1992 ELECTION: MISREPRESENTATIONS OF RACIALIZED GENDER

These events—the Thomas hearings, the Civil Rights Act of 1990–91, the Gulf War and its aftermath, the candidacy of David Duke, the Los

Angeles riots—were coded into the political psyche and the language of the 1992 presidential election. This coding allowed racialized imagery to be evoked without directly calling attention to it.

Another series of events that took place before the official start of the 1992 campaign also color-coded the parameters of the election. The angry incident between Bill Clinton and Sister Soljah, a rap singer, set the racial tone for Clinton's campaign.[90] Clinton criticized the rap performer for being divisive and hate-filled in her statements about the Los Angeles riots. Clinton's remarks were made at a meeting of Jesse Jackson's Rainbow Coalition and were therefore highly divisive. Jackson saw Clinton as using this moment to distance himself from old-style democratic racial loyalties. Clinton was making clear that he was not held hostage by Jackson or the race issue as old-style liberals have been.[91]

Clinton's election rhetoric on welfare reform also distanced him from old-style democratic politics. He proposed a work force program that allows no more than a two-year stint on welfare. Many white voters read this proposal as limiting the Democratic party's tendency to give hand-outs to blacks.

Although Jackson told Clinton that he should not take "the black vote" for granted, there was little alternative for black voters. Of course Bush and Clinton differed on racial equality issues, but there was less difference than many would have liked. Clinton supported the Civil Rights Act of 1990–91 more firmly than Bush, although he, like Bush, rejects the use of quotas. During his campaign, Clinton directed very little criticism at Bush's civil rights record. Neither racial nor sexual equality issues were given a priority.

One cannot discuss the 1992 election without some mention of Ross Perot's candidacy. And although the potential electoral disorder he created was initially exciting, most of his policy initiatives were much less so. Although he espoused black equality, he had serious misgivings about affirmative action programs. Most of his employees at higher levels of management were white men. When he addressed the National Association for the Advancement of Colored People (NAACP) early on in the campaign, he called the audience "you people." He spoke in favor of the pro-choice position on abortion, but in terms of financial efficiency: abortions are cheaper than welfare payments for unwanted children. When asked about abortion rights as a guest on the Larry King show, he responded that he thought the American people needed to deal with the real issues rather than the nonessential ones that divide us. Another time, he said that the most important day in a woman's life is the day she marries. After all, the purported reason he ended the first stage of his campaign was that Bush was planning to disrupt his daughter's wedding, and this would have been too devastating for him to bear.[92]

All in all, the 1992 presidential campaign covered over racial and gender issues while misrepresenting their interconnections. There were no Willie Hortons this time around because the heightened racism of the political context did not require such an explicit foil. Instead, all three candidates used the language of family values and coded it according to their stance on abortion and on women in the work force. Issues related to race were even more silenced. Affirmative action was not even discussed. The economy was said to be "the" issue.

Given this obfuscation, it is almost impossible to sort out the real political issues of the 1992 campaign. All the candidates spoke of a "new world order," of "economic issues" as if they were separate from "family values," of domestic policy as if it were completely separate from foreign policy, and of the "forgotten middle class," as though these political phrases accurately described the issues. They did not. The effectiveness of this political rhetoric was that it partially rang true. Anyone can read whatever they like into "sound-bite" rhetoric. The new world order is both new and very old. Domestic and foreign policy are no longer separate spheres. The economy and the family are interrelated realms. The middle class *was* forgotten in the past decade, but the fact that this middle class is also a "working class" was wiped off the map.

This duplicitous cacophony set the context for the swirling, contradictory messages regarding woman and her proper identity. On the one hand, we were told that this was "the year of the woman." More women ran for Senate than ever before—and one was "even" African American. Of the final four presidential and vice-presidential candidates, two had wives who were lawyers—one of whom actually practices. On the other hand, Barbara Bush, the quintessential loyal wife, actually addressed the convention. She presented herself in a homey, self-denigrating fashion and enjoyed record popularity. She used her paper-thin persona to bring in whatever pluralist vote existed for the Republicans. She became the party's umbrella.

Hillary Clinton was the other election icon. As her husband, Bill, pointed out, one would have thought Bush was running against *her*. And in some sense he was. Ms. Clinton was dangled by the Republicans as a radical feminist, an arch-critic of marriage and family, and a defender of children's rights to sue parents.[93] Everyone, including Hillary, seemed to ignore the likelihood that if she had been a radical feminist, she would have run for the presidency herself. Instead, she had chosen to use her remarkable intelligence and skills to redefine the role of political wife. We need to remember that her early outspoken role in the campaign unfolded amid charges of her husband's infidelity. She was drawn into the Gennifer Flowers affair to speak for her husband's faithfulness. She tried to silence the rumors as only a wife can do. But one should not confuse her early active role in the campaign with a "copresidency." We will return to Barbara Bush and Hillary Clinton later.

Women's lives do not lend themselves to easy, homogeneous description, although election rhetoric attempted to do just that. The rhetoric trumpeted worn-out models that did not work for most women or their families. This did not stop the right wing of the Republican party from privileging the model of the traditional white patriarchal family, with a husband in the labor force and a wife at home.

The economy and its demand for families earning dual wages undercut the effectiveness of the racialized traditional family rhetoric. So did the vast number of poor, single-parent households, especially those headed by women. When the Republicans spoke of "family values," they dismissed the multiple realities of family life. It was a throwback to what they perceived as a better time: a stronger and more dynamic economy that allowed the traditional (middle-class and white) family structure to dominate. Even though family and a racialized economy are completely intertwined in this picture, they are treated as separate.

"Family values" became the Republicans' code words for antiabortion, antifeminist, anti–affirmative action, antihomosexual, anti–social welfare, antidrugs, and so on.[94] Those words elicited the vision of a traditional heterosexual family headed by a white male, which is supposedly orderly and free of drugs, of abuse, of AIDS, and so on.

The language of "family values" constructed the perfect postmodern moment in its elusiveness and the vagueness of its borders. As Barbara Bush purportedly said, family is whatever you say it is—although of course she thinks her kind is the best. The plural vision she alluded to is a false pluralism, because all other types of family are seen as inferior to the Bush-type family, the all-American family. Bush summed up this attitude when he said he wanted America to be like the Waltons, not the Simpsons. Interestingly, he did not choose to mention Bill Cosby's television family, the Huxtables.

The Republican theme was not families, but family "values." This sleight of hand allowed them to ignore the structural realities of families and instead focus on imagery. The discussion of values was perfect for Bush's rhetoric, which focused on individual choice and responsibility and ignored the constraints on people's choices. Of course, many people, especially women, would still not choose the patriarchal family even if they were free from economic constraints and could do so. But I do think that most men, women, and children wish to be surrounded by love, to have an interesting and well-paying job, and to be free of the degradation that nurtures addictions. Family values rhetoric sidesteps all of these clarifications.

The rhetoric of "family values" and of "women's place" allowed Republicans to stake out old territory within the so-called new world order. The new order is no longer defined by an anti-Communism located in Eastern Europe or the former Soviet Union. The new anti-Communism targets feminists, homosexuals, and people of color as egalitarians who want too much government. As Gary Wills has noted, the new enemy for born-again Republicans is inside our borders. This enemy is seen as pro-state (seeking more taxes, more civil rights legislation, more social services, etc.) and antifamily.[95]

Family values held center stage for most of the 1992 election, because this was the way the right wing of the Republican party chose to define the battle against liberal democratic politics—that is, against equality legislation for "blacks and women." This battle reflected a certain truth: family structures *are* at the core of society, and changes in these structures are changing the way we live. The traditional family is in as much trouble today as the savings and loans are—and the Republicans tried hard to bail it out.

The internationalization of the economy and the multicultural nature of the United States work force have resulted in real problems for traditional family life, which depended on good jobs for white men. There are now not enough good jobs for white men or for single parents, whatever their gender or race. Black men—except for Clarence Thomas and a few others—are largely unemployed. White families are looking more like families of color have looked for years, with married women in the labor force, single parenthood, teenage pregnancy, and so on. These family structures do not fit well with an international economy, which demands women's entry into a labor force that ghettoizes them in poor-paying jobs. And family and economy are coming more into conflict than ever before as the economy constricts. Single parents need a family wage, yet many of them cannot even find jobs.

So the discussion of family values was a cover-up of the real economic crises facing families and of the white male privilege once aligned
with an industrial (rather than the current service) economy. Bush knew
he was in trouble on the abortion issue and for pandering to the right
wing of the party. So the Republican convention was orchestrated to
show that Republicans were pro-women (whatever that means), even if
antiabortion. Former Secretary of Labor Lynn Martin gave the nomi-
nating speech. Barbara and Marilyn represented the party's commitment to "family values" by speaking on behalf of George and Dan—
although this was hardly the same as women speaking for themselves.

Barbara was spokeswoman for the old model of supportive wife,
while Marilyn represented the new breed, a professional woman who
defers to her wifely responsibilities. These women alluded to the security of the traditional model of the family: By their very presence, they
appealed to voters to stay with the familiar, because change would be
too hard. If voters were unable to trust Bush and Quayle on the economy and taxes, then perhaps we would trust them as family men (who
happen to be white). Clinton was portrayed as an untrustworthy, un-
faithful family man who was asking us to risk change. Bush and Quayle
hoped that Clinton would remind us too much of what we deem scary
in ourselves.

The family values rhetoric was also an attempt to repackage the Republican antiabortion stance in less strident terms. But this strategy does
not appear to have worked. Instead, a gender gap developed which accounted for much of Clinton's lead. Although there had been a gender
gap in 1984 and 1988, it seemed more likely that it would affect electoral results in 1992. And in fact there was a 13 percent increase in
turnout among women from 1988 to 1992. Clinton received more than
50 percent of the votes of wage-earning women; 86 percent of the votes
of black women (compared with 77 percent of the votes of black men);
and 48 percent of the votes of women aged 18–29 (compared with 38
percent for men of the same age).[96]

Barbara Bush worked hard to see that a gender gap did not materi-
alize. For more than a decade, when asked for her thoughts on abortion—and whether they differed from the president's view—she repeatedly refused to answer the question. She often commented that she was
not going to let the press make it seem like she and George were in
conflict over the issue.

Then, when her husband started to trail badly in the polls—and the
Republican party platform took a rigid antiabortion stance, which was

unpopular with a majority of Republicans and of the American public—George needed Barbara to help him out. So Barbara said publicly
that the abortion issue did not belong in the party platform. Then, the
morning after she addressed the convention, she recanted her position.
She revised her statement to read that she was neither pro-choice nor
anti-choice, and that she had gotten in over her head with her statement
regarding the platform. Barbara remained the dutiful wife.

All the political wives remained dutiful in "the year of the woman."
They were allowed to speak because they spoke for their husbands.
Barbara Bush did not have—and was not allowed—any other agenda.
Hillary Clinton had a somewhat more complicated duty to perform.
Since the election, she has expanded the constraints of her status as
political wife. As head of the task force on health care, she wields enor-
mous power. Yet her status is precarious; she has this power because
she is the president's wife.

During the election, Marilyn Quayle offered herself as the flip side of
Hillary Clinton. Educated and professional, she *chose* that her family
should come first. (Actually, she works full-time on behalf of her husband.) She offered herself as the appropriate choice for women who do
not want to be, as she put it, "liberated from their essential nature as
women." There are so many obvious incongruities in this portrait that
it is difficult to know what to say about it.[97]

Hillary Clinton and Tipper Gore did not address the Democratic
convention as Barbara and Marilyn did. In part, there was no need for
them to do so because they did not have to make up for an antiabortion
party plank. So they could just be wives. Hillary's fantastic legal record
was irrelevant to this posture. The Democrats featured women office-
holders without taking the risk of featuring any feminist wives.

Ann Richards opened the Democratic Convention with the statement
"I am pro-choice and I vote." She did so to remind voters that the next
president would choose the next Supreme Court justice, who will likely
decide the abortion issue. Women candidates running for Senate were
highlighted and did their best to remind us of the Thomas-Hill hearings.
Race and gender issues were thrown together and left oblique. Neither
party tried to clarify the meaning or significance of women's issues in
their racialized meanings; neither party brought them center-stage. There
was something very old about all this.

FOUR

Reproductive Rights and the Privatized State

The Webster *Decision, Post-*Webster *Restrictions, and the Bush Administration*

The same politics that have challenged affirmative action and rolled back civil rights law, as discussed in the previous chapter, have also restricted access to abortion and have limited reproductive rights. The Bush administration and the Supreme Court have institutionalized a restrictive and limited notion of government responsibility not only in the realm of sexual and racial equality but also in the area of privacy rights. This governmental stance underlines the politics of both abortion and civil rights throughout the 1980s. Each was used to justify the narrowed discourse of the other. The process has been incremental and insidious. It has confused and misrepresented the way people's actual privacy depends upon the protection of a state which nurtures equality.

I will argue that the connections between racial, sexual, and gender politics are threaded in and through the core of abortion politics. In order to understand abortion, one must view it in terms of the larger framework of racialized patriarchal politics. This is not to argue that the issues of civil rights, defined as the commitment to racial and sexual equality, are the same as the issues of abortion and reproductive rights, which encompass the issues of sexuality, sexual practices, and bodily privacy. But one cannot fully address the issue of reproductive rights for all women without understanding and challenging the intricate web of relationships between the conditions of equality and individual privacy. In order to do so, one must reconnect the struggle for civil rights (equality) with the struggle for reproductive freedom (individual privacy).

One must recognize the integral connections between sex, race, and gender both inside and outside the politics of abortion. And this means recognizing the connection between abortion as a fundamental right, which applies to all women, and the way this right is experienced differently according to one's race and economic class position. Welfare recipients and the poor have not had the same access to abortion that middle-class women have had since 1977. Since that time, the assault on abortion has broadened further through the dismantling of the civil rights agenda. Now the issue is not only the disparate impact of abortion law on poor white women and poor women of color, but the impact of recent restrictions on all women. The undermining of racial equality through the discourse of privatization, which has destroyed the idea of government's affirmative responsibility in creating access, has been used to undermine reproductive rights in general. The anti–civil rights agenda has been used to undermine abortion rights, and anti-abortion rhetoric has been used to undermine equality discourse. In the end, more women have been left on their own than ever before.

I examine the Court's *Webster* decision as the wholesale privatization of abortion by the state, making an abortion even more difficult to obtain. This decision opened the floodgates to further restriction on abortions, particularly for minors. This restrictive view of abortion came to full flower in the Pennsylvania *Casey* case, even though the Court reaffirmed *Roe*. I also examine *Rust v. Sullivan* as the ultimate denial of a woman's right to choose an abortion by limiting the information she is allowed to obtain. According to the *Rust* decision, a doctor or clinician working at a facility receiving Title X federal funds is no longer allowed to mention abortion as a possible alternative to a health-threatening or unwanted pregnancy. The word "abortion" is banned. One wonders who the "thought police" are in this instance.

I then focus on the Justice Department's amicus curiae brief filed in defense of Operation Rescue in Wichita, Kansas, which argued that when demonstrators try to deny women access to an abortion clinic, they are not discriminating against women per se. The government's stance was perfectly clear: the issue of abortion is not a civil rights issue. To deny a woman access to abortion is not sexually discriminatory. The Bush administration sought to sever the important connection between the issues of privacy and equality for women in their struggle over abortion.

Lastly, I examine abortion as an electoral issue. I look first at the various political positions taken by Bush on abortion. His waffling is reflective of politicians' treatment of abortion in general, particularly in the 1992 campaigns of both Bush and Clinton. Neither candidate expressed a consistent position on abortion; instead, they dealt with it opportunistically. Bush hoped to mobilize the antiabortion forces, while Clinton sought support from pro-choice quarters.

CIVIL RIGHTS AND ABORTION

The Court's preoccupation with reverse discrimination—that is, with the plight of the white male—has been intertwined with its rollback of reproductive freedom. The Reagan-Bush state affirmed childbirth over abortion and individual opportunity over affirmative action. As will be discussed here, civil rights legislation was narrowed to the privacy stance of abortion rights. The government no longer sees itself as having any responsibility for creating access to an abortion or equal opportunity for a job. The individual is on her own.

Legally, women are still free to get an abortion if they so choose, even though the responsibility of government to make it available has been completely denied by the neoconservative Court. In fact, there are grave inequalities to be reckoned with, especially for a poor African American teenager or a poor white or native American rural woman. Abortion rights—or the freedom of reproductive choice—affect women's lives differently depending on their economic abilities, race, age, geography, and so on. Any limitations on access for these women affect the cultural and political climate in which any woman, whatever the circumstance, obtains an abortion.

Approximately 1.6 million abortions are performed each year. Eighteen- and nineteen-year-olds account for one-fourth of these. Approximately one-third of abortions are elected by women of color: black and Hispanic women have more abortions than do white women. Sixty-two percent of women having abortions have incomes under $11,000; 32.5 percent have incomes between $11,000 and $25,000; and 16.5 percent have incomes over $25,000.[1]

This is the context in which recent Supreme Court cases must be viewed. The Court has further articulated a neoconservative position on reproductive rights without directly overruling *Roe v. Wade*. Although *Roe* was based not on the equality doctrine but on the right to privacy (which is much more in line with neoconservative discourse than affirmative action law has ever been), Reagan-Bush neoconservatives have seen a need to limit abortion doctrine further. Abortion impacts on the possibilities of sexual equality even though it has not been framed legally as doing so. Without being able to control and make choices surrounding one's fertility, a women is not free, nor is she treated as an equal. Instead, she is held hostage to her body.[2]

The controversy surrounding abortion is about women's lives—and the way women's potential for childbearing affects their ability to determine their own lives. All women, especially women of color, are affected by this controversy, and poor women have the most to lose. An examination of *Webster v. Reproductive Health Services* and *Planned Parenthood of Southeastern Pennsylvania v. Casey* shows just how fragile and contested the "right" to abortion has become. But it is also crucial to recognize that the battle over the right to legal abortion in the courts is only one site of the struggle.

Even before *Webster,* it was becoming more and more difficult to get abortions because there were fewer doctors willing to perform them. Doctors who do have been under increasing surveillance and harassment by antiabortion activists like the Lambs of Christ and Operation Rescue. Many of them have given in to the fear and threats and will no longer perform abortions. In a 1985 poll conducted by the American College of Obstetricians and Gynecologists of a sample of four thousand of its twenty-nine thousand members, 84 percent of the doctors thought abortion should be legal and available, but only one-third of the doctors who favored abortions performed them, and of those who did, two-thirds did very few.[3]

Eighty-two percent of U.S. counties, particularly in rural areas, were without any abortion providers by 1985. The number of abortion providers declined by 5 percent between 1982 and 1985, and only 32 thousand abortions, or 2 percent of the national total, were provided outside of metropolitan areas during 1985.[4] Meanwhile, the number of urban providers also decreased. In 1991, 31 percent of all women in the United States lived in counties without access to an abortion provider.

Janet Benshoof, director of the American Civil Liberties Union's Reproductive Freedom Project, says that about 20 percent of the women seeking abortions today cannot get them because of lack of money or geographical location. Teenagers and women in the military are some of those who are the most affected by this changing landscape.[5]

WEBSTER AND THE POLITICS OF ABORTION

In *Webster v. Reproductive Health Services,* the Court, in a 5–4 decision, basically upheld a Missouri statute's limitations on the abortion rights of women. The preamble to the statute states that human life begins at conception, that "unborn children have protectable interests in life, health, and well-being," and that these "unborn children" are entitled to the "same rights as other [constitutionally recognized] persons." The statute requires that, prior to any abortion, a test for viability must be conducted on any fetus believed to be twenty or more weeks old; it prohibits the use of public employees and facilities for performing or assisting in any abortion not necessary to saving the mother's life; and it prohibits the use of public funds, employees, or facilities for the purpose of encouraging or counseling for any abortion not necessary to saving the mother's life.[6]

Those challenging the constitutionality of the statute argued that it violated the privacy rights of a pregnant woman seeking an abortion, a woman's right to an abortion, the right to privacy between physician and patient, and a woman's right to receive adequate medical advice and treatment concerning abortion.

Although an earlier court of appeals had found that the preamble was unconstitutional in that it tried to establish a "theory of life to criminalize abortions," the Court found the preamble "precatory," meaning that it was merely a recommendation with no requirement and therefore imposed no substantive restrictions on abortions. According to the Court, the preamble is "just" a value judgment, with no real (legal) effect; it does not in and of itself regulate abortion. The focus of the Court was completely narrow here: the preamble constituted a value judgment, and was therefore disconnected from the law itself, which was supposedly not value-laden. The Court also argued that Roe "implies no limitation on the authority of a state to make a value judgment favoring childbirth over abortion."[7]

The Court further found that the preamble was simply a statement of orientation and preference, not a set of "concrete facts" that the Court could judge. The Court argued that it did not need to decide on the preamble's constitutionality, because as a set of "abstract propositions," it had not as yet been applied in unconstitutional ways. Those challenging the statute argued that the preamble was integral to all the prescribed prohibitions and not merely precatory.

GOVERNMENTAL RESPONSIBILITY:
CHILDBIRTH OR ABORTION

The heart of the Missouri statute—and the *Webster* decision—is the provision making it unlawful for a public employee to perform or assist in an abortion or for a public facility (very broadly defined) to be used to perform an abortion unless the mother's life is in danger. This limitation of abortion rights was found constitutional and consistent with former Court decisions like *Maher v. Roe*.[8] In *Maher,* the Court upheld Connecticut's welfare regulations, under which Medicaid recipients could be covered for medical services related to childbirth but not for nontherapeutic abortion. The Court found that these regulations placed "no obstacles—absolute or otherwise—in the pregnant woman's path to an abortion."[9] In a similar case entitled *Harris v. McRae,* the Court upheld the so-called Hyde Amendment, which withheld federal funds under Medicaid programs for reimbursement for abortion unless the mother's life was in danger.[10] Once again, the Court found that this statute placed no governmental obstacle in the way of a woman's obtaining an abortion. Justice O'Connor further developed this theme in *Webster* when she restated her position first formulated in *Akron Center for Reproductive Health v. City of Akron:* "A regulation imposed on a lawful abortion is not unconstitutional unless it unduly burdens the right to seek an abortion."[11] The problem here, however, is that there is a significant difference in having the right to *seek* an abortion and having the right to *obtain* one. The definition of what constitutes an "undue burden" is key to understanding what this difference really means for women.

The Court, in these decisions, upheld the notion that the state's interest is on the side of childbirth, not abortion. As it stated in *Maher,* "The state may make childbirth a more attractive alternative . . . but it has imposed no restriction on access to abortions that was not already there."[12] In *Webster,* the Court further narrowed the meaning of the right to abortion. Instead of focusing on the funding of abortion by Medicaid, the Missouri statute focused on the more indirect support of the right to an abortion: by public employees, public hospitals, or even private hospitals on public land using public water. Its restrictions affect private doctors, private hospitals, and even private clinics, which serve many more women than those who receive welfare assistance. This ruling most starkly affects poor women, who have the fewest options, but it extends to middle-class women as well.

The further significance of this ruling is its place within the 1980s discourse of equality. The neoconservative position on equality is that its true meaning is the individual's right to opportunity before the law, which in this instance would be the individual, legal right—a "privacy" right—to choose an abortion. Privacy does not extend to an individual's equal right to *get* an abortion—equal access to abortion—but only to the private opportunity to choose one. According to many neoconservatives, the wrong-headed presumption of a right to equal access to abortion reflected the excessive demands of the women's movement. Neoconservative jurisprudence has made it clear that the government should never have gotten involved in the business of "affirmative" action, either in the job market or in the area of abortion.

It should not have been surprising, therefore, when Rehnquist, writing for the Court in *Webster,* stated that the "Due Process Clauses generally confer no affirmative right to government aid . . . even . . . to secure life, liberty, or property interests."[13] Women have no affirmative right to governmental support of abortion: hence the prohibition on public employees and facilities. The core of the *Webster* decision is that the state no longer has *any* affirmative role or responsibility in abortion. The state's responsibility is to affirm childbirth and make it the more attractive alternative. One could say the Court's new preoccupation with reverse discrimination has extended into the realm of abortion: protecting the rights of the fetus against the rights of the pregnant woman.

Rehnquist argued for the Court majority that Missouri's decision to use public facilities and employees to "encourage childbirth over abortion" does not create governmental obstacles for a woman who "chooses" to end her pregnancy. "[It] leaves a pregnant woman with the same choices as if the State had chosen not to operate any public hospitals at all." He continues, "Nothing in the Constitution requires States to enter or remain in the business of performing abortions. Nor . . . do private physicians and their patients have some kind of constitutional right of access to public facilities for the performance of abortions."[14] These statements by the Court establish the state's interest in making childbirth the preferred alternative to abortion.

This neoconservative position is contradictory at best. The state is establishing an affirmative role: it is affirming a nonabortion stance. To encourage childbirth is to *dis*courage abortion. The Court views the lack of governmental support in performing abortions—in the form of the use of public hospitals or staff—as the state of Missouri's pro-childbirth stance. This *lack* of government support for abortion is both affirmative action on behalf of the fetus and prohibitive action against a majority of women seeking abortions. In some sense, my use of "affirmative action" here is a misnomer, because the Court does not give the fetus rights to anything except birth, and the fetus is even denied that in cases where women cannot afford prenatal care. Actually, the state "gives" nothing—rather, it takes away. In the end, the *Webster* decision has dismantled any "affirmative action" by government to support women's reproductive rights. It remains a woman's private right to seek an abortion, but the government does not have to say it likes it, nor does the state have any responsibility in making it available.

On the one hand, the antigovernment discourse of a privatized service state is being used to deny access to abortion. On the other hand, we are subject to a statist-moralist-antiabortion interventionism from this same government. It is the very privatized discourse of the Reagan-Bush era that undermines women's ability to act on their (private) choices. The discourse covers over statist activism that invades women's private right of choice.

Rehnquist argues that the Missouri provisions that were challenged "only restrict a woman's ability to obtain an abortion to the extent that she chooses to use a physician affiliated with a public hospital."[15] According to him, this limitation is in full keeping with *McRae* and is less burdensome than not allowing public funding. Although the limitations provided in the Missouri statute may be less burdensome, they are more far-reaching because they affect more women. Moreover, this further narrowing of the access to abortion takes place within the context of a rightist and neoconservative Court. Ronald Dworkin sees these Missouri restrictions as out of keeping with earlier decisions and restrictive in unacceptable ways. Dworkin argues that "a city cannot force newsstands in shopping centers built on public land to sell only papers it approves. It cannot force theatres it supplies with water and power and police protection to perform only plays it likes."[16] He concludes that a city should not be able to refuse abortions on these grounds, either. To do so is to distort the meaning of government support. There is also an ambiguity here between the supposed noninvolvement of the state and its imposition of far-reaching regulations. According to the neoconservative Court, regulation occurs at the level of individual states. However, the enabling of such regulation occurs at the federal level: the laissez-faire state.

VIABILITY, PRIVACY, AND THE STATE

The Missouri statute in *Webster* requires testing of all twenty-week-old fetuses to determine gestational age, weight, and lung maturity in order to establish fetal viability. The statute requires that no abortion of a "viable unborn child" be performed unless it is necessary to preserve the life or health of the woman. The Court found viability testing at twenty weeks constitutionally acceptable in that it is consistent with the state's interest in protecting potential human life, even though there is strong medical evidence that viability does not occur until twenty-four to twenty-eight weeks of gestation.[17]

In reviewing the issue of viability testing, the Court attacked the trimester framework established in *Roe* as unworkable. It extended and broadened the state's interest by allowing this intervention in the second trimester of pregnancy, whereas in *Roe* the woman's right of privacy precluded any state regulation until the third trimester. Rehnquist, writing for the Court plurality, justified this change by asserting that the state's interest in childbirth is equally compelling before and after viability, and that *Roe* had set up "unsound and unworkable" guides.

Blackmun, in his dissent, attacked this rejection of the viability standard and of the trimester framework. He argued that the viability standard effectively and sensibly operates "to safeguard the constitutional liberties of pregnant women while recognizing and accommodating the state's interest in potential human life."[18] The point of viability distinguishes between the point where the fetus has rights (like a person) which may override the woman's right to choice and the point where it has no such rights. Blackmun, concurring with Stevens, wrote that "the development of a fetus—and pregnancy itself—are not static conditions, and the assertion that the government's interest is static simply ignores this reality."[19] Viability testing at twenty weeks is in flat contradiction with *Roe* in that it assumes the state's interest in potential life is compelling before viability.[20]

Rehnquist further rejected the *Roe* trimester framework as rigid and not consistent with the Constitution, which is cast and written in general terms, articulating general interests. The trimester framework is unnecessarily specific, he argued, and is not found anywhere in the text of the Constitution; it resembles "a code of regulations rather than a body of constitutional doctrine." *Roe* had unnecessarily made the law "increasingly intricate."[21]

Rehnquist's insistence on the generality of the "body" of constitutional doctrine is more than instructive on the gender bias of *his* constitutional text. To the degree that the Constitution masquerades as gender neutral, it speaks in general terms while silently assuming the male body as the individual with protected rights. This silencing feigns neutrality through nonspecificity. Given a male individual as the starting point, it is not surprising that pregnant women are not mentioned in the Constitution. The rights of the individual have been specified for nonpregnant persons, not pregnant women.[22] The trimester framework—or some such device—is necessary to specify the rights of *the individual who is pregnant*. Specificity here is a needed corrective.

When Rehnquist insists on a close "textual" analysis, he ignores the fact that in order for the Constitution to effectively meet the needs of men and women, differences of rights must be specified when they occur. Otherwise, women's specific rights to privacy and equality within the realm of pregnancy will be denied, effectively violating her right to equal and similar (though not the same) treatment. But Rehnquist believes that women should not be granted similar rights (to those of men) in the instance of pregnancy. In earlier decisions, such as *Michael M. v. Superior Court* (1981), he argued that the "real" differences between men and women require differential treatment.[23] Rehnquist feigns the so-called neutrality and generality of the text of the Constitution. But his reading of the text is definitely not neutral. Dworkin remarks similarly that if we can look to the Constitution only for "enumerated rights explicitly mentioned in the text," then the rights of the fetus are not mentioned in the text either.[24]

On a much simpler level, Rehnquist is inconsistent. He argues that the general right to privacy was established in *Griswold v. Connecticut*,[25] but that in *Roe* it was interpreted to become overly regulatory and rigid. However, the Court has regulated and specified other constitutional rights, such as free speech—limiting speech such as pornography or screaming "Fire!" in a crowded theatre. Perhaps Rehnquist and his associates believe that the existing regulations on abortion within the trimester framework allow women too much privacy. They allow women to decide about their lives—as though they were men—to become not-pregnant.

For Rehnquist, abortion is not a fundamental right or even a "limited constitutional right," as established in *Roe*, but a "liberty interest protected by the Due Process Clause."[26] As such, the privacy of a woman in an abortion decision can be limited by governmental restrictions in order to protect "potential human life." *Webster* broadens the assumed moral authority of the state while denying its responsibility to create access. It narrows the woman's alternatives and authority over her own choices and often makes her responsible for caring for a(nother) child when she does not want to do so. In a contradictory way, the Court has expanded governmental authority and rearticulated its responsibility in defense of the fetus, while severely curtailing women's choices.

Neoconservative jurisprudence has reestablished a more authoritarian relationship between the state's authority and the individual. In this case, the individual is a pregnant woman. In rejecting the trimester framework, the Court broadened the state's authority to include the entire term of pregnancy and prioritized the rights of the fetus over the privacy rights of women. Reestablishing the authority of the state—against the excesses of individual rights (especially the right to privacy)—is a primary focus of rightist neoconservatism. It is what Bertram Gross has critically called the establishment of "friendly fascism."[27] It is what evangelical antiabortionists call the "right to life": the state's establishment of its authority over the woman via the rights of the "unborn."

Blackmun, in his dissent, stated that the plurality opinion in *Webster* "is far more remarkable for the arguments that it does not advance than for those that it does." The Court pretended to leave *Roe* standing, but refused to discuss what Blackmun considered to be the real issue underlying the case: "Whether the Constitution includes an unenumerated right to privacy that encompasses a woman's right to decide whether to terminate a pregnancy."[28] Instead, the neoconservative plurality argued specifically that the *trimester framework* does not appear in the Constitution, thereby undermining women's right to privacy without directly repudiating it.

The rightist neoconservatism of the Court set the context for its silence on this point. Privacy—and one's right to it—is an aspect of liberal individualism that has been central to public discourse. Although the neoconservatism of the Reagan-Bush era, with its critique of the "excesses of liberalism," successfully denounced liberalism as the "L" word, the right to individual privacy remains successfully embedded in public discourse and consciousness. When a woman's right to abortion is phrased in terms of her private right to choose, there is overwhelming support for it among the public. When abortion is placed within a neoconservative discourse which criticizes governmental funding, public support of the right to abortion, though still significant, lessens.

The Court's silence on certain issues that Blackmun points out takes on considerable import when one realizes the diminishment of women's actual ability to obtain an abortion even as the Court still supposedly upholds abortion as a fundamental right of privacy. Justice O'Connor does not see viability testing as being in conflict with any of the Court's earlier decisions, including *Roe*, so she argues that the Court cannot be asked "to anticipate a question of constitutional law in advance." She also states that the Court should not "formulate a rule of constitutional law broader than is required by the precise facts to which it is to be applied."[29] In her view, if and when a state's abortion statute actually tests the constitutional validity of *Roe v. Wade,* there will be ample time to address it then.

But *Roe* has been undermined in its practice and its effect. The Court's political discourse has changed significantly as well, even though the Court did not make "a single, even incremental, change in the law of abortion."[30] One must wonder where *Roe,* as law, begins and ends in relation to the political discourse within which it is interpreted and applied.

Justice Scalia and Chief Justice Rehnquist stand to the right of the neoconservatism of the Court. They call for the overruling of *Roe* as unconstitutional. Scalia's angry dissent in *Webster* was directed at O'Connor, because of her attempt to narrow the Court's protection of access to abortion while guiding the Court away from a review of *Roe.* O'Connor is somewhat more cautious in discussing Roe than the others of the plurality have been. She appears to recognize a legal right to abortion as long as the state is completely absent in endorsing it, either indirectly or directly. Scalia rejects O'Connor's view of judicial restraint, arguing for an aggressive court that will speak broadly on the issue of *Roe.* He argues that O'Connor protects *Roe* in contradictory fashion because Roe established a "broader-than-was-required-by-the-precise-facts structure."[31] O'Connor obviously does not agree.

This redefinition recognizes women's opportunity for privacy in the realm of abortion. But that opportunity remains within the purview of individual freedom of choice, not governmentally provided access. Within this context, the "undue burden" standard has extremely limited effect, because almost no burden seems too great. It is not until the Court's decision in *Hodgson v. Minnesota* that the troubling contours of "undue burden" begin to be clarified.[32]

RESTRICTING ABORTIONS FOR MINORS

In *Hodgson v. Minnesota,* decided in the spring of 1990, the Court upheld a Minnesota law requiring parental consent and a forty-eight hour delay for adolescents seeking abortions, so long as judicial bypass procedures were in place. Justice Stevens, writing for the Court, stated that the immaturity, inexperience, and lack of judgment of minors justified a "state-imposed requirement that the minor notify and consult with a parent." He noted that the family has a "privacy interest in its children's upbringing." In an instance where a minor woman felt unable to discuss abortion with her parents, she would be free to seek permission from a judge. The judicial bypass allows a young woman who is unable to speak freely with her parents to obtain an abortion. The burden of consent was not found by the Court to be unjust.[33]

Justice O'Connor attempted to clarify her understanding of "undue burden" by stating that requiring notification of parents *without* a judicial bypass option would constitute an "undue burden." As long as another option exists, no matter how narrowly procedural it is, the woman's freedom of choice is intact. The fact that many teenagers are unable either to tell their parent(s) or to negotiate a judicial bypass is irrelevant; O'Connor says the choice remains theirs.[34]

One might term this a neoconservative feminist position. A woman's right to abortion is recognized as a narrowly legalistic individual right to private choice, which can be restricted by the state as long as abortion is not legally impossible. O'Connor recognizes the female body and the problem it poses for privacy, but denies the relationship between equal rights, equal access, and real choice. Her reading is different from Rehnquist's. O'Connor's starting point in deciding both *Webster* and *Hodgson* is *Roe*, which recognizes the pregnant woman and protects her right to abortion. Rehnquist's starting point is the text of the Constitution, which mentions neither pregnancy nor abortion.

Justice Marshall's dissent in *Hodgson* states that "neither the scope of a woman's privacy right nor the magnitude of a law's burden is diminished because a woman is a minor."[35] But this remains a minority view on the Court. The decision in *Ohio v. Akron Center for Reproductive Health* reaffirmed *Hodgson:* a requirement of parental notification, as long as a judicial bypass is in place, does not present the minor with an undue burden.[36] But of course it does. These decisions stymie teenagers seeking abortions. In the United States, 11.15 percent of all abortions, or about 182,000 abortions a year, are obtained by women under eighteen. On any given day, approximately 2,825 teenagers get pregnant. Parental consent requirements would have a serious impact on these young women's lives. In Minnesota, after the law requiring parental consent for adolescents seeking abortions went into effect, the percentage of minors who had second-trimester abortions— which are more dangerous than first-trimester abortions—increased by 26.5 percent.

It is also the case that the judicial bypass procedure operates differently around the country. In some cities, judges grant waivers easily, whereas in other cities, judges will not even hear these cases. While it is relatively routine to get a judge's approval in Massachusetts, this is not the case in Indiana. Jane Stout, director of the Indianapolis Clinic for Women, says that in the six years she has been working at the clinic, she does not know of a single case in which a judge approved an abortion. "With the judges here, it's just not going to happen."[37]

Given the already extremely high rate of teenage pregnancies and the growing number of poor teenage mothers, these limitations seem troublesome at best. As the National Abortion Rights Action League (NARAL) has admonished, we need to make abortions less necessary, not more difficult to get. Two-thirds of all the teenagers who had babies in 1990 were unmarried; of black teenagers having babies, only 10 percent were married.[38] Poverty is a real issue in these young women's lives, and it is a major problem facing their newborns as well. Requiring these teenagers to get permission from their parents for an abortion adds to an already burdened situation.

THE *CASEY* DECISION

The burdens on women seeking abortions were substantially increased by the Court's summer 1992 decision in *Planned Parenthood of Southeastern Pennsylvania v. Casey*. This decision further clarified the meaning of "undue burden," while authorizing an increasingly restrictive view of abortion. The decision legitimated more intervention by the state on behalf of the "unborn," while espousing a narrowed defense of *Roe*. Its outcome is devastating for women who cannot negotiate the newly articulated regulations. The devastation for these women is masked by a confusing court rhetoric that reaffirmed *Roe* in principle.

In the *Casey* decision, the Supreme Court upheld a Pennsylvania law that required parental permission or court approval before a teenager could obtain an abortion; imposed a twenty-four-hour waiting period on women after deciding on abortion; and required "informed consent" from the pregnant woman after being given information as to why she should continue the pregnancy. The Court did not uphold the law's requirement that married women must have spousal consent before having an abortion.

The opinion for the Court was unusual in that it was written jointly by Justices Sandra Day O'Connor, Anthony Kennedy, and David Souter. Justices Harry Blackmun and John Paul Stevens joined the opinion, in part, to affirm *Roe v. Wade.* The anti-*Roe* stance of Justice Scalia was supported by Justices Rehnquist, Thomas, and White.[39]

The Court, by a narrow margin, retained and reaffirmed *Roe*'s essential holding: that abortion is a liberty interest, although it is not spelled out as such in the fourteenth amendment. Instead, the full scope of liberty must be read as "a rational continuum" which has "no formula or code spelling it out." The liberty of women is unique to women and must be construed by the law as such.[40] But woman's liberty, the majority found, is not so unlimited that the state cannot show its concern for fetal life—even at the *outset.* This principle allows the state to take steps to "ensure that this choice [abortion] is thoughtful and informed." As in *Webster,* the Court affirmed that "the state has an interest in protecting the life of the unborn." Going beyond any other decision to date, *Casey* dismantles the trimester framework completely and allows state intervention (as opposed to obstruction) *at the start* of pregnancy. The trimester framework is said to "undervalue the State's interest in the potential life within the woman."[41]

The Court carved out a more restrictive interpretation of *Roe.* "What is at stake is the woman's right to make the ultimate decision, not a right to be insulated from all others in doing so." The state will ensure that women have carefully appraised their decision, and we are to assume that any new regulation toward this end will be acceptable as long as it does not create a "substantial obstacle to the woman's exercise of the right to choose."[42] Obviously the Court does not recognize the fact that most women already deliberate intensively and carefully before deciding to end a pregnancy. Nor does the Court recognize that the restrictions it has already endorsed are "unduly burdensome" for most women.

This view of such restrictions as not "unduly burdensome" reflects a shift in O'Connor's stance, for instance, on an enforced waiting period before having an abortion. In the earlier *Akron* decision, she found a waiting period to be an undue burden.[43] In *Casey,* however, she wrote: "The idea that important decisions will be more informed and deliberate if they follow some period of reflection does not strike us as unreasonable."[44] The Court takes this stance even while recognizing that a waiting period will require two visits to the doctor, necessitating more time and money. Even though the justices recognize that many women must travel long distances to obtain abortions and may have increased trouble explaining their whereabouts to husbands, employers, and others, they do not find these burdens to be "substantial" obstacles: "A particular burden is not of necessity a substantial obstacle." According to the *Casey* decision, *Roe* does not guarantee a constitutional right to abortion on demand. Rather, it only protects women's right to decide to terminate a pregnancy free of undue interference.[45] *Roe* has not been overturned, but it has been rewritten.

One part of the Pennsylvania law which was not endorsed by the Court was the requirement of spousal permission. Interestingly, the Court found that requiring permission of one's husband would create a substantial obstacle and would be likely to prevent a significant number of women from obtaining an abortion. Why? Because millions of women are victims of physical abuse, and if they had to inform their husbands of their decision to have an abortion, these women might face further violence.[46] Whereas the Court seemed to suggest that minors might benefit from consultation with their parents, a parallel assumption could not be made about adult women and their husbands. The Court seems to have listened carefully to much of the feminist literature concerning family violence. Yet this understanding did not carry over into the Court's view of restrictions on minors (who also suffer family violence) or the twenty-four hour waiting period (which increases the possibility that an angry husband or boyfriend might find out about an intended abortion).

So what has happened to *Roe* in this decision? A woman's right to choose to have an abortion without undue interference from the state is still guaranteed. But "undue interference" has been redefined to mean outright obstruction. Otherwise, a woman's right to abortion can be restricted, meaning that the state can try to deter the process—even in the first trimester. The only thing the state cannot do is prevent the woman from exercising her choice. But with the limits on access, especially for poor women, a woman may not be able to carry out her choice.

One loses some important political insights, however, if one leaves the discussion of *Casey* at this point. Although the decision attacks women's access to abortion in fundamentally damaging ways, it also evinces—in a limited way—the impact of feminist concerns and the effects of the abortion rights movement. In *Casey,* the Court notes that the 1973 *Roe* decision has had "a rare precedential force." *Roe* has affected the lives of women profoundly, and to overrule it would damage the Court's credibility, as well as curtail women's ability to control their reproductive lives. This deference to *Roe* is a political, not a constitutional, one. It is significant that even such a conservative Court did not reject abortion as a right. Instead, it denied abortion as a right with unencumbered access. This position bespeaks the power of abortion rights discourse today, as well as its significant liabilities. The Court affirmed the holdings of *Roe* against the backdrop of the *Webster* decision in order to define its newly restricted meaning.

RUST V. SULLIVAN

As if poor women were not already hard pressed to negotiate and attain abortions, the Court in *Rust v. Sullivan* upheld legislation limiting their access to information about abortion. Here we enter the uncomfortable terrain of the limiting of freedom of speech and informed choice. The decision in *Rust v. Sullivan* upheld federal regulations that barred employees of federally financed family planning clinics from all discussion of abortion with their patients.[47] This decision affected 4,500 clinics and approximately 4 million women each year. Women of color make up over 30 percent of Title X clients, who were most directly affected by this ruling. Poor women make up a majority of the Title X clients using federally financed clinics, public hospitals, and public health department facilities. Planned Parenthood predicted that the number of unintended pregnancies would increase by 1.2 million annually, and approximately 400,000 of these women would be teenagers.

The 1970 law establishing family planning had been interpreted as allowing the discussion of abortion as an integral part of family planning. The 1988 Reagan regulation barring all discussion of abortion represented a sharp departure from this earlier interpretation of policy. Although federal funding and availability of abortions for poor women had been curtailed since the early 1980s, this newer federal stance was predicated on the belief that abortion was not an appropriate method of family planning. Title X projects were therefore prohibited from engaging in abortion counseling or referral or any activities advocating abortion.[48]

The Court ruled in *Rust v. Sullivan* that the regulations did not violate the First Amendment free speech rights of the counselors or doctors. Nor did the regulations violate a woman's Fifth Amendment liberty right, the right to choose whether to terminate a pregnancy. The Court stated that, "of course, it would be easier for a woman seeking an abortion to be able to get the information . . . but the Constitution does not require that the government do so." The Title X grantee was not denied the right to engage in abortion-related activities, but Congress had refused to fund such activities publicly.[49]

The regulations were recognized by the Court as being "viewpoint discriminatory," but were not considered to be in violation of the Constitution. The Court ruled that the government could "make a value judgment favoring childbirth over abortion." In doing so, the Court found, "the government has not discriminated on the basis of viewpoint; it has merely chosen to fund one activity to the exclusion of the other." As for its particular effect on poor women, the Court's finding was similar to the decision in *MacRae:* poor women had the same choices as if the government had never chosen to subsidize health care in the first place.[50] This finding continued the line of argument found in *Webster:* the refusal to fund abortion counseling and advocacy left a pregnant woman with the same choices as if the government had chosen not to fund family planning services at all. The Court found that the due process clauses do not confer affirmative rights to government assistance even when such aid is necessary to secure life, liberty, and property. The government has no duty to "subsidize an activity just because it is constitutionally protected."[51]

The decision in *Rust* continued to elaborate a state discourse of privatization which had become increasingly restrictive. This time, the state not only had no obligation to fund abortion services, but also had no obligation to provide information about such services. The Court moved one step further in defending an activist, antiabortion stance: the government could actively deter women seeking abortions because it was an unacceptable method of family planning. As a worker, one was not allowed to speak of abortion if one was receiving federal funds. As a poor woman, one was not allowed access to full information. As Justice Blackmun stated in his dissent, "For these women the government will have obliterated the freedom to choose as surely as if it had banned abortions outright."[52]

Whittling away at the right to abortion targeted poor women and teenagers most particularly. The politics of such a policy are self-defeating. Few people believe that teenagers are ready to be parents. Few believe that a poor woman who has decided that she cannot provide adequately for another child should have to birth it anyway. What child—if he or she could choose—would want to be the child of such a parent? Of course, such arguments carry little weight with right-wing antiabortion activists who say that sex education promotes incest; that "it's healthy for a young girl to be deterred from promiscuity by fear of contracting a painful, incurable disease"; or that it is unfair to punish a rapist by killing his unborn child.[53]

Such politics are mean and punitive. The welfare system of New Jersey in January 1992 promoted a plan to deny additional payments to welfare mothers who have more children while on welfare.[54] This policy ignores the limited options of many who are affected by it. If a poor woman is on welfare and her program will not cover new children, yet she cannot afford an abortion, then what exactly is she—not to mention her newborn child—to do? The state does not have the responsibility to make access to abortion available. Nor does it have any responsibility to the new child. How can the "pro-life" movement make sense out of this contradiction?

The New Jersey welfare revisions, known as the "Family Development Initiative Act," are supposed to take away the financial incentive for having too many children. According to columnist Anna Quindlen, the existing financial incentive worked out to only about 50 cents a day per child.[55] The act also requires that mothers will have to attend school or job training to qualify for their subsidies. This seems fine, but the program offers no assistance in finding jobs once these training programs are completed. In his 1992 State of the Union Message, Bush endorsed the principles behind New Jersey's welfare revisions as encouraging self-help and individual responsibility. Such callousness is the flip side of the privatized service state.

Restrictions on abortion create mixed responses. Whereas the majority of the public supports parental notification, there was much less support for the *Rust* decision. Both the House and the Senate voted to overturn the Bush administration's ban on abortion talk, but failed to override a presidential veto. Bush, in an attempt to assuage some of the bitter feelings over the ruling, said he would allow doctors, but not counselors or nurses, to give limited advice about abortion at federal clinics. Instead of silencing abortion rights forces, he further enraged them, because it is counselors and nurses who primarily see the women at the clinics. Meanwhile, antiabortion forces were furious with what they viewed as a cop-out. Then a federal district judge, Charles Richey, declared that Bush's newest restrictions violated the initial law, "that the exception for doctors was not just an interpretive change, but a legislative change requiring public notice and comment."[56] This ruling was upheld unanimously by a federal appeals court. President Clinton, in his first days in office, reaffirmed the ruling and also signed an executive order repealing the ban on abortion counseling in federally financed clinics.

WICHITA, KANSAS, AND THE KU KLUX
KLAN ACT OF 1871

Although there has been a change in administration, the Court's decisions in *Webster, Hodgson,* and *Casey* still hold. And this neoconservative treatment of abortion appears again in *Women's Health Care Services v. Operation Rescue.* In this case, the Justice Department attacked the use of civil rights law to defend women's access to abortion. According to the government brief, abortion rights are unrelated to civil rights. Denying a woman an abortion does not discriminate against her as a woman.

Operation Rescue, a militant antiabortion group that demonstrates at abortion clinics to prevent women from obtaining abortions, had targeted the clinics in Wichita, Kansas, in the hopes of closing them down. Women's Health Services, an abortion clinic in Wichita, argued that on the basis of Section 2 of the Ku Klux Klan (KKK) Act of 1871 (also known as the Civil Rights Act of 1871), women's rights were being violated.

This act had initially been applied to prevent persecution of newly freed slaves. It was an attempt to end the intimidation, violence, and terror tactics used against blacks and against those whites who supported the attempts of blacks to vote. In the Wichita case, U.S. District Judge Patrick Kelly found in favor of the clinic. He stated that the Civil Rights Act of 1871 "makes it illegal for two or more people to conspire 'for the purposes of depriving any person or class of persons' from exercising their constitutional rights."[57]

The Justice Department challenged this view, arguing that women seeking abortions were not protected under the law aimed at the KKK. The Justice Department asked for a stay of the preliminary injunction ordered 5 August 1991 against Operation Rescue.[58] The department's brief argued that several acts of Congress which have excluded abortions from federal funding have not been found to be gender discriminatory. The respondents would have to show a "racial, or perhaps otherwise class-based, invidiously discriminatory animus behind the conspirator's action" in order for the 1871 act to apply. According to this argument, there is no intentional discrimination toward women; Operation Rescue targets anyone who is involved in the abortion process, whether man or woman. The class of people defined as pro–abortion rights is not exclusively female.[59]

The Justice Department did not view abortion as a "class" need of all women in order that they might enjoy their full constitutional rights.[60] A woman's right to abortion is allegedly separate from her civil (equality) rights as a woman. Demonstrators who block access to abortion clinics are not singling out women for discriminatory treatment, but seeking to prohibit the practice of abortion. Their actions are not against women, but against abortions.[61] We are asked to distinguish people seeking abortions from women, as if it were not women who seek abortions.

Operation Rescue chooses to intimidate and harass women and make them fearful. Action against abortion is action against women, against women as a class with a particular need.[62] Yet the government argued that nothing in Operation Rescue's actions "indicates an affirmative intention to reach conspiracies based on gender." It also argued that it would be "fanciful" to say that the 1871 law was intended to extend to gender intimidation; rather, it was designed to "combat the prevalent animus against Negroes and their supporters."[63] Once again we have a narrowed reading of the intent of discrimination law. This time the narrowing negates the connections between antiabortion activism and its sexually discriminatory content. According to the Bush administration, Operation Rescue may intimidate women seeking abortions, but it does not "discriminate" against them as such. And in any case gender intimidation would be allowed under the Constitution, even though gender discrimination is not. In January 1993 the Supreme Court finally found in favor of Operation Rescue.[64] They ruled that the civil rights law enacted to protect blacks from the Ku Klux Klan does not provide federal judges with jurisdiction to bar antiabortion protesters from blockading abortion clinics.

When one views the neoconservative jurisprudence of the Supreme Court alongside the antiabortion politics of the Bush administration, the attack on reproductive rights appears devastating.

BUSH ON ABORTION

The Bush administration's antiabortion policies were antidemocratic. Yet the connection between reproductive rights and democracy is seldom made when assessing Bush's record. The United States press has no trouble making this connection when it comments on the outrageous and undemocratic rule of Ceausescu in Romania. The major examples used to capture the totalitarian aspects of his regime were his antiabortion and pro-natalist policies and the state's surveillance of women's bodies.[65] True, Ceausescu made birth control as well as abortion illegal. He instituted laws requiring that women of childbearing age had to have monthly examinations; otherwise, they would no longer be eligible for free medical care or be able to apply for or renew drivers' licenses.[66] Although the Reagan-Bush policies never reached such a point, the comparison should not be lost. Many poor women who currently have no access to abortion might not view the comparison as so far-fetched.

Bush's record on abortion was never consistent. Although most of his domestic and international policies can be described as neoconservative, his antiabortion stance became increasingly rightist. The rightist position on abortion is that it should be illegal: it is murder, and therefore it is almost never justifiable. Neoconservatives, in the main, say little regarding the legal status of abortion, but instead support restrictions on access to it.

Bush's rightist abortion stance was a minority position; most political observers agree that it was endorsed by only about 12 percent of the American public. When he attempted to make it government policy, he misrepresented a majority of the American public, as well as the approximately 1.6 million women who choose abortion each year. Instead of representing a diversity of views within his administration, he used policy position "litmus tests" for all appointees and administrative vetoes to authorize his minority position.

One wonders why Bush adopted the rightist antiabortion stance relatively late in his career. In 1970, Bush coauthored with Senator Edward Kennedy the original Title X National Family Planning Program, although he later became largely responsible for its demise.[67] The program subsidized contraceptives and counseling for low-income women and teenagers. Bush thus was an early advocate of the use of family planning to address issues of civil rights, without calling attention to the highly charged issue of race. He was influential in establishing family planning and population control to replace open housing legislation as a way to address civil rights issues.[68] At this stage in his career, Bush also applauded family planning as an answer to the problems of hunger and poverty. As chair of the House Republican Task Force on Earth Resources and Population Planning, he advocated the liberalization of abortion laws "to eradicate the increasing number of unlicensed and unqualified practitioners who jeopardize the health and safety" of American women.[69]

Bush continued to support legal abortion until he was chosen as the vice-presidential running mate by Ronald Reagan in the summer of 1980. He then adopted the position that abortion was permissible only to protect the life of the mother; otherwise, it was murder. In the 1988 presidential debates, candidate Bush implied that if abortions were made illegal, he would probably have to treat women who obtained abortions as criminals. Then he shifted his position again, saying he did not mean that women should be treated as criminals, but rather as victims: doctors should be treated as criminals.[70] Perhaps Bush thought that because most doctors are men, they are therefore more rational and accountable, whereas women are merely victims.

As President, Bush then vetoed the proposed extension of federal funding for abortions for poor women in cases of rape or incest. The bill he vetoed, H.R. 1990, had been passed by a House of Representatives which included the highest number of women ever: women voted 18–8 in favor of the bill.[71] Defending his veto at a press conference, Bush stated, "I'm not looking for any conflict on this. I'm not going to change my position any. But let's see how those negotiations come out . . . but I have not changed my position." When asked if he might accept a compromise, he stated flatly that a compromise was out of the question. Then he said that there might be some room for flexibility. He explained: "The conference language may be able to avoid a veto on my part" if the criterion for abortion funding were changed from rapes "promptly" reported to rapes reported in forty-eight hours. This severe time restriction, he reasoned, would prevent women from using false claims of rape to finance their abortions.[72]

Bush *then* said that his only concern was to protect the taxpayer. It was an issue of overseeing the "management and implementation of federal taxpayer dollars, and whether you can control them." He wanted to stop the potential abuse of federal financing of abortions by "women who falsely asserted they have been raped in order to get the government to pay for their abortions."[73] In other words, Bush vetoed publicly financed abortions for rape and incest victims because he assumed that women would lie about rape and cheat the government. Forgotten in all this is his position that abortion is murder. Also forgotten is his "gentler and kinder nation."

One wonders exactly what his purpose *was* in this veto. The impact of this revised legislation would have been negligible at best. In 1979, the last year in which data were available, the federal government paid for only seventy-two abortions which were the result of rape or incest, of a total of more than 1.6 million abortions performed that year.[74] Bush's antiabortion stance was more symbolic than realistic. It is symbolic of the antidemocratic demagoguery of the right-wing evangelicals.

Shortly after Bush's veto of federal funding, he sent a letter to the Senate Appropriations Committee vowing to veto the $156.7 billion bill providing fiscal 1990 funding for the Departments of Labor, Health and Human Services, and Education because of the bill's abortion language. He also ordered the Justice Department to file a brief urging the Supreme Court to use one of the three abortion cases coming before it in 1990 to overturn *Roe v. Wade*. He continued a nineteen-month-old ban on federally funded research involving fetal tissue. He vetoed a funding bill (H.R. 3026) for the District of Columbia because it did not include a ban on the city's use of its own tax money to pay for abortions. He also vetoed a foreign aid appropriations bill because he thought some of the funding would go to countries that support abortion as a method of population control.[75]

Bush named Dr. Antonia Novello, who was opposed to abortion, as Deputy Director of the National Institute of Child Health and Human Development. Many other candidates withdrew from the competition for this office because they did not share Bush's antiabortion position and they refused to accept an ideological litmus test. The litmus test had replaced more rigorous requirements of competency and excellence. Spokespersons for the president denied that there was a litmus test for working in the administration, but said that it was important that such people be willing to support the president's position.

In February 1988, the Department of Health and Human Services had finalized the regulations that were then under review in *Rust*. Family planning clinics that violated the ban on discussion of abortion would lose all federal funding. Along with this set of directives came a Food and Drug Administration (FDA) revision of the information that was to be included in oral contraceptive packets. Formerly, these inserts had mentioned all types of birth control, including abortion. After the FDA revision, these inserts no longer mentioned abortion; instead, they proposed "periodic abstinence."[76] All of these restrictions greatly limited the information available to women about abortion as an option.

Such an authoritarian limiting of information did not speak well for the democratic process. Nor did it bode well for issues and concerns other than abortion, as seen in Bush's veto of the $14 billion foreign aid bill. He vetoed the bill for its alleged support of abortion. But the bill he vetoed did not contain one dollar for abortion. Fifteen million dollars would have gone to the United Nations Population Fund, which devotes itself to family planning excluding abortion. It was explicitly stated that none of this money would be allowed to support abortion services, even indirectly.[77] To make certain, the Senate stipulated that no United States money could be used to aid China—because China authorizes abortion and sterilization—and that the $15 million be kept in a separate account that Washington could audit. Bush still vetoed the bill, thereby depleting United Nations funds for a variety of purposes.

United States policy disallowing federal funding to any international program supporting abortion was counterproductive. According to the World Health Organization, approximately 200,000 women were dying each year from illegal abortions. These numbers were expected to rise after the U.S. government successfully curtailed the activities of the international arm of Planned Parenthood—which was then responsible for providing contraceptive services to some 1.4 million people. A 1987 study at the University of Michigan School of Public Health predicted that a cutoff of United States funding for family planning international assistance would result in 69,000 more abortions, 1,200 additional pregnancy-related maternal deaths, and 311,000 more births in three years.[78] Fortunately, Clinton has already reversed these policies of right-wing zealotry.

As a result of considerable public criticism of his antiabortion policies, Bush shifted his posture *slightly* in November 1989 in anticipation of the 1990 congressional elections. In the post-*Webster* fallout, abortion rights forces had claimed new electoral status that worried the Bush administration. Bush even held a meeting with four Republican pro-choice women and campaigned for two of them, Claudine Schneider of Rhode Island and Lynn Martin of Illinois. He was trying to show that the party could be an umbrella for diverse views on the issue, even as Bush maintained his "personal" stance against abortion.[79]

Shortly before his death, Republican strategist Lee Atwater said that Bush wanted "to make sure that everybody feels comfortable as Republicans, regardless of what their position on abortion is."[80] Vice-President Dan Quayle picked up this line and argued that the Republican Party was a big tent, with room enough for differing views on abortion. Yet Quayle supported the 1992 party platform that endorsed the notion that the "unborn child has a fundamental individual right to life which cannot be infringed" and advocated a constitutional amendment to overturn *Roe v. Wade*. He said it was not necessary to change the platform so long as "we are a party that is diversified."[81]

Contradictions remained unresolved. If Bush *really* believed that abortion was murder, did he mean to say that the party had room for murderers or advocates of murder? And what did he mean when he said that it does not matter what your stance is on abortion, so long as you are consistent and strong about it?[82] Barbara Boxer, Democratic senator from California, reasoned that Bush realized that he had to give members of his party the right to choose their own position on abortion. Yet he did not extend this same indulgence to the rest of the American public. Instead, he continued to veto abortion legislation.

The hollowness of Bush's rhetoric on abortion is unsettling. While arguing against abortion, Bush vetoed the Family Leave Bill, which was designed to assist wage-earning parents with newborn infants by ensuring that employers would grant them unpaid leave. Bush said that although he supported the idea, he did not see it as the role of government to enforce such policy.[83] In other words, it was the government's responsibility to enforce childbirth over abortion, but it was not the responsibility of government to assist parents in caring for infants once they were born. The government was acting as an interventionist yet privatized state.

In contrast to Bush administration policies, the public's view of the right to abortion, however loose and fragmented it may be, is that abortion is one of our democratic rights. This is as true for Republicans as it is for Democrats. In reaction to the anti-choice Republican Party platform, and in the hope of changing it for the 1992 presidential election, a group formed calling itself "Republicans for Choice."[84] As Republicans, its members opposed government interference in people's private lives; they believed that the decision to choose an abortion must be made by the individual, not the state; and they argued that theirs was the majority position of the American public as well as the Republican Party.[85]

The "Republicans for Choice" had no impact on the outcome of either the 1992 platform or the Republican convention. The platform remained antiabortion, even in cases of rape and incest. And the convention was dominated by the "family values" theme, with its antiabortion subtext.

There was, however, some post-convention shifting on abortion. Marilyn and Dan Quayle, by late September, were softening the "pro-life" agenda, saying that they could understand the need for abortion in cases of incest. Both Bush and Quayle also went on record as supporting the decision of a pregnant granddaughter or daughter, whatever it might be.

The Democratic candidates in the 1992 election espoused the "right of choice" as distinct from pro-abortion rhetoric. Clinton stated in his acceptance speech at the Democratic National Convention that "abortion should be safe, legal, and rare." Neither Clinton nor Gore has been consistently pro-choice. In the fall of 1986, Clinton wrote a constituent in Arkansas that "I am opposed to abortion and to government funding of abortions." In March 1989, he signed a bill requiring notification of the parents of teenage girls seeking an abortion. But by the fall of 1991, Clinton held that the government has no right to interfere with decisions that must be made by the women of America. And since his election he has supported government funding of abortions.

Al Gore repeatedly voted to ban federal financing of abortions from 1977 through 1979. In 1983 he likened abortion to the taking of human life. However, in 1988 he voted to loosen restrictions on Medicaid funding of abortions. And in 1992 he stated that "the decision to have an abortion is an intensely personal one, and I do not believe that the federal government should participate in the decision."[86] The Clinton-Gore platform evolved to support a woman's right to choose: "Personal privacy is a fundamental liberty guaranteed and protected by the United States Constitution." More specifically, Clinton and Gore endorsed the Freedom of Choice Act, the repeal of the Hyde amendment preventing federally funded abortions, and the repeal of Bush's "gag rule." They opposed any federal limitations on access to abortion such as waiting periods or parental consent.[87]

Although the platforms of the two parties differed significantly on abortion, neither one reflected a coherent long-term stance. Both bespoke the controversial and contested nature of abortion and the opportunistic politics that surround it. In the 1992 election neither party got out in front of the issue; both parties were more comfortable saying as little as possible.

Post-election politics have been somewhat different. In addition to overturning the gag rule, Clinton lifted the restrictions on federal financing of research using fetal tissue; eased the policy on abortions in military hospitals; reversed the policy prohibiting aid to international family planning programs which provide abortion-related services; and, at the time of this writing, had initiated plans to ask Congress to end the nearly total ban on federal financing of abortion for poor women.

Nevertheless, much remains to be played out in the abortion arena. The hesitant posture toward the Freedom of Choice Act introduced in Congress in 1992 reflects the continued dissension over abortion policy. The act would have established in statutory law the same reproductive freedom that women were initially guaranteed in constitutional law in *Roe v. Wade*. When the time came to push for the act, however, its Democratic supporters feared that it would not be passed without severe restrictions. Instead of risking outspoken and forceful debate on both sides of the issue, they withdrew the act from consideration.[88]

ABORTION, ELECTORAL POLITICS, AND LIBERAL DEMOCRACY

It is important to recognize that there is a considerable disjuncture between the American public and rightist politicians on abortion. This public, of mixed political persuasion, is more supportive of guaranteed health care, support for the poor, abortion rights, and reproductive choice than were the Reagan-Bush politicians. The disjuncture reflects a real tension between administration policy of the 1980s and the rest of us.

In a *Los Angeles Times* poll conducted in July 1989, after the *Webster* decision, 63 percent of U.S. women said that the Court's decision hurt women's rights in general. In another poll, when asked whether restricting access to abortion interfered with a woman's right to make a personal moral decision, 67 percent of the American public said that it did.[89] The ability to obtain an abortion is thus viewed as integral to one's freedom of choice. Access to one's rights matters. This is exactly the point with which the neoconservative Bush administration disagreed.

For the first time in the November 1989 state and local elections, the American public used its votes to express disapproval of the *Webster* decision and of the Bush administration directives on abortion. Although abortion had been a contested issue in the 1980 and 1984 presidential elections, it did not manifest itself in terms of a vote against the antiabortion stance of either Reagan or Bush.

November 1989 appeared different, and antiabortion politicians were particularly uneasy with this new terrain. Because abortion is a "nontraditional" political issue, people cross party lines to vote on it.

In polls taken before the *Webster* decision, a majority of Americans had responded that they would not vote for a candidate on the basis of his or her abortion stance alone. When asked whether, if the Court overturned *Roe v. Wade,* they would be more likely to support Democrats in the next election, a majority of the respondents said such an outcome would have no effect. Abortion was still not identified as an electoral issue. However, in a July 1989 Gallup poll taken after *Web-*

ster, 61 percent of those polled said they were more likely to take a candidate's position on abortion into account in deciding their votes.[90] And, according to *The Polling Report,* 36 percent of Republicans and 35 percent of Democrats said they would cross over to vote for a pro-choice candidate of the opposite party.[91]

It was in the period between October and November 1989 that the climate surrounding abortion shifted. Abortion rights forces seemed to be getting the upper hand. Special antiabortion legislation sessions were canceled in Illinois, Texas, and Minnesota. Then-Governor Bob Martinez of Florida was rebuffed by the state legislature in his antiabortion initiative. The Florida Supreme Court, in a 6–1 decision, overturned a law requiring parental consent for teenage girls. The court argued that the law violated a clause of the Florida constitution that guarantees citizens the right to be left alone, free of government intrusion into their private lives. In April 1990, the Connecticut senate overwhelmingly approved a bill that would ensure a woman's right to abortion in that state, in case the Supreme Court overruled *Roe v. Wade.*[92] In February 1991, Maryland passed a similar provision.[93] Senator Alan Cranston and Representative Don Edwards, both of California, introduced the Freedom of Choice Act into Congress. Cranston also initiated a companion bill, the Reproductive Health Equity Act, to begin to redress the 1977 Hyde amendment, which had banned abortion coverage for women on Medicaid, Native American women living on reservations, and women in the military and the Peace Corps.

At the same time, antiabortion forces were also making gains and inroads. Governor Mike Hayden in Kansas successfully called for curbs on late-term abortions and for required parental notification for girls under sixteen years of age. A similar battle was fought long and hard in Louisiana, where the legislature finally overrode Governor Buddy Roemer's veto of a new, highly restrictive abortion law.[94] Similar legislation was passed in Nebraska. The Idaho legislature approved an abortion bill specifically intended to overturn *Roe.* Utah passed legislation permitting abortion only in cases of rape or incest or to protect the life of the mother. Similar legislation is pending in Wyoming, Ohio, and Missouri. Guam passed legislation allowing abortion only when the pregnant woman's life is in danger.[95]

While a majority of the American public supports a woman's right to abortion, the polling data reflect significant differences in the way people think about this right. These partial and conflicting views are grist for the political mill. Seventy-three percent of Americans polled in

1990 were in favor of guaranteed abortion rights, yet 77 percent of those polled also regarded abortion as a kind of killing.[96] When people were asked in 1989 whether abortion should exist as it did then, only 48 to 59 percent of the respondents answered yes. When asked whether abortion should be legal with the advice of a doctor, the support ranged from 63 to 74 percent. On the whole, respondents did not like government interference in private decisions. But there was also wide-ranging support for restricting abortion: parental notification was favored by 71 percent of the respondents, and fetal viability testing by 60 percent. However, 54 percent opposed spousal consent, 57 to 65 percent opposed prohibiting public employees and public hospitals from performing abortion procedures, and 63 percent wanted abortion to remain legal in their state.[97]

Given this mixed consciousness, restricting abortion is acceptable to and even preferred by many. Parental notification requirements tap parents' fears about their daughters and their own parental rights. It also evokes the sometimes conflicting identities of mothers as parents and as women themselves. For these reasons, revisionist positions on abortion have become a part of the political landscape.

RADICALIZING DEMOCRACY VIA ABORTION RIGHTS

A real issue facing the reproductive rights movement is whether abortion can be successfully maintained in the public consciousness as a "rights" issue—and radicalized as such. The American public does seem to be viewing abortion in this light: 62 percent of respondents to a CBS News poll in September 1989 agreed that they favor abortion because "every woman has the right to control her own body," and 61 percent of respondents said they do not believe that life begins at conception. According to a *Los Angeles Times* poll conducted in March 1989, 39 percent believe that abortion is a human right. This belief lays the groundwork for radicalizing a democratic rights discourse on abortion. So does the belief of 63 percent of respondents that the *Webster* decision hurt "women's rights."

But there are problems with the "rights" discourse related to differences between women on abortion. In some polls, only 32 percent of respondents with incomes under $12,500 a year think abortion should remain legal and unrestricted, as it was before *Webster;* in contrast, 56 percent of those with incomes of $50,000 or more favor the law as it now stands. Only one-third of respondents with the lowest income think poverty and inability to support a child are sufficient reasons for abortion.[98] These responses can be read many ways. But one is left with the question of how to discuss abortion and reproductive rights while being sensitive to the differences of racialized economic class.

One of the difficulties is that differences of economic class create different choices. To be poor and to choose an abortion because one is unable to care for a(nother) child financially is different from choosing an abortion when finances are not the issue: because one has had all the children one wants to have, or one simply does not want a child at that time. If one is poor and wants a child, one might not readily agree that being poor is sufficient reason for an abortion. It is important that the feminist discourse surrounding abortion take these differences into account. Abortion, though a fundamental right, is only one choice within a matrix of choices.

Differences of race and ethnicity also raise important issues for the reproductive rights movement. The unemployment rate for black high school girls with babies is nearly twice that for white girls in the same situation.[99] Forty-nine percent of white women respondents to a CBS News poll thought abortion should be legal as it was before *Webster*; 45 percent of black women concurred.[100] Yet the April 1989 pro-choice march held in Washington, D.C., was 95 percent white. This is not to deny the presence of African American women in the abortion rights movement. The National Black Women's Health Project in Atlanta sent thirteen busloads to the April march. The weekend of the march, a conference called "In Defense of *Roe v. Wade*" was also held in Washington; three-fourths of the women on the core organizing committee were women of color.[101] The Coalition of Women of Color for Reproductive Health has called for increasing political activity by women of color on the abortion issue.[102] However, an effective coalition between women of color and white women remains to be built.

African American women have made clear that they see much of the feminist agenda as wrongly focused for them. Given differences of family structure, different placement in the labor force, greater levels of poverty, and the problems of racism, their attitudes toward abortion, sterilization abuse, and infertility differ from a feminism defined largely by white women. But their different positions should not be understood as either antiabortion or antifeminist. African American women remain overwhelmingly supportive of feminism.[103]

Feminists have often had to define their politics within a political discourse that they have not chosen for themselves. This is true today in the battle over abortion. In part, the "issue of abortion" reflects the framing of feminist politics by rightists and neoconservatives, who have disembodied abortion from the concerns of sexual and racial equality and sexual freedom. Although many feminists argue that reproductive freedom is vital to the struggle for women's equality and sexual freedom, we do not equate the larger concern of reproductive rights with the legal right to abortion, nor do we believe that guaranteeing the right to abortion is sufficient to create sexual and racial equality. The feminist agenda also includes economic equality, rights to sexual freedom and choice, comprehensive day-care policy, available prenatal care and affordable health care, equality on the job, and much more. This larger reproductive rights agenda cross-cuts racialized economic class lines.

The narrow focus on abortion is thus problematic. The 1990s started with an already narrowed feminist agenda. Positioned defensively for over a decade, it has become more and more limited. This said, it is also the case that feminists have had little choice in the matter, although some. Feminists need to remap the abortion issue to address these larger concerns, while holding firmly to the idea that reproductive rights and the right to abortion (and bodily control) are fundamental democratic rights. The interplay between sex, race, sexual preference, age, and economic class must set the feminist discourse on reproductive rights.

It is difficult to address the Court's position on abortion as feminists, because women's rights—the rights to equality and sexual freedom— are not part of the Court's discourse on abortion. The *Webster* decision is about fetuses, not women. It redefines privacy for the state, not for women. Such privatization encodes the right to abortion as a right for women who can afford it—if they can find someone to perform it.

White women and women of color of all economic classes are affected by the *Webster* decision, but differently, according to whether they live in rural communities, whether clinics exist in their area, and whether new restrictions on leasing of public land affect the hospitals and doctors in their community. One local doctor, who implants seaweed in the cervix of pregnant women to cause bleeding so that they will be admitted to the local hospital for an abortion which otherwise would be denied them, says of *Webster,* "People say that the Supreme Court will make it like the old days. Out here sometimes it feels like the old days."[104]

The assault against women's right to abortion was a major part of the Reagan-Bush rightist and neoconservative attack on earlier gains made toward racial and sexual equality and sexual freedom. It has become almost impossible to get an abortion if you are without financial means in much the same way as it has become almost impossible to prove discrimination. As long as no legal barrier exists for a black woman seeking a promotion, discrimination does not exist, even if she can prove harassment and bigotry. As long as it is legal for a woman to seek an abortion, no undue burden exists, even if economic constraints or the lack of a doctor or unavailability of a clinic in fact prevent her from obtaining one. In actuality, both the promotion and the abortion may be impossible to get. I do not mean to overstate the parallel between abortion rights and the job market. After all, there is a difference in not getting a job—or a promotion—and having to birth a child against one's will.

If democracy is based on individual freedom of choice to determine the decisions that affect one's life, then abortion, along with other reproductive rights, is crucial to the practice of democracy. Women's bodies and their capacity for pregnancy require this specification of rights for democracy to exist in general. Such specificity is not necessary for Chief Justice Rehnquist or for former President Bush. A man's body structures rights discourse for them, and a man's body poses no problems of reproductive rights.

Because democratic rights were established for nonpregnant individuals, it is up to feminists to claim them for women's bodies, which can be pregnant. And if they are pregnant and do not want to be, all women must have the right to abortion in order to protect bodily privacy.

Instead, we are left to read about newborns being thrown down garbage chutes and into trash compactors by young, distraught teenage girls.[105] Women have been left to deal with the painful consequences of restrictive abortion policy. What of the women who are HIV-positive and pregnant? What if they are unable to find clinics willing to perform abortions for them?[106] What of the teenage girl who desperately does not want a child, but cannot negotiate an abortion—with either her parents or the court? What of the woman with a severely deformed fetus in the later stages of pregnancy, who has decided on abortion but is unable to find a doctor willing to perform one in late term?[107]

The politics of abortion are complicated. By the 1992 presidential election, abortion policy had become more punitive and restrictive toward women and their choices than at any other time since *Roe*. Abortion clearly played a role in the Clinton victory, which explains many of the policy shifts on abortion already under way in the new administration. Exactly how effective these changes will be remains open to question. After all, we have been left with a neoconservative Court, the leftovers of the interventionist moralism and selfish privatization of the Reagan-Bush years, and their antidemocratic legacy.

FIVE

The Contradictory Politics of AIDS

Public Moralism versus the Privatized State

Much of the "pro-family" antiabortion rhetoric has carried over into talk about Acquired Immune Deficiency Syndrome (AIDS).[1] The Reagan and Bush administrations believed they should be able to tell people what they were allowed to do in the intimate sexual realm of their lives: with whom they should sleep, what they should watch on TV, what kind of art was moral, and so on. These same government officials believed they had no responsibility for the public health.

The privatized state formed the backdrop for dealing with AIDS. Its establishment meant that there never was any coherent federal policy to deal with AIDS during the Reagan and Bush years. The AIDS virus was allowed to run rampant. By the end of the Reagan decade, AIDS had a complex political history. This history embodies the relations of heterosexism as they are interwoven into a racialized, patriarchal system of discrimination.

As Dennis Altman has pointed out, "we are not used to thinking of illness as political,"[2] but AIDS is politically constructed. It reflects and nurtures a system of inequality and discrimination that is already in place. AIDS is a disease of the "other": the general population is defined as white and heterosexual, and anything else is specified as deviant. So although AIDS is caused by a virus which can affect anyone who takes part in particular practices or is exposed to blood containing the virus, it is also a socially constructed disease, which reflects the lives of marginalized groups while creating a new marginality.[3] It was treated as a "special interest" disease by the Reagan and Bush administrations.

The politics that have surrounded AIDS from its outset in the United States have been characterized by a rightist moral absolutism along with a neoconservative revisionism of liberal equality discourse. It is a contradictory political view, which advanced a public moralism and denied the right to choice in the private realm while advocating a privatized service state that redefined public responsibilities as private. The Reagan-Bush state disclaimed public responsibility for AIDS while challenging the private rights of individuals living with AIDS through an interventionist public moralism. We were left with the disjuncture of a state that required the *de*privatization of sexuality, a state in which social services were displaced by moral crusades.

Initially, moralist rightists and neoconservatives argued that AIDS was caused by gay men's lifestyle: by "perverted" and "unnatural" sexual practices. Neoconservatives such as Norman Podhoretz viewed AIDS as the punishment for men who "buggered" other men. More than a decade later, this kind of "moral" stance still held despite its spread to the nongay population, especially heterosexual intravenous (IV) drug users and their sexual partners. The construction of the "other" had been refocused to include the "difference" of poverty, ghetto life, and drugs. IV drug users are disproportionately black, Latino, and poor. AIDS has institutionalized *new* discriminatory discourses from these categories. The Reagan-Bush state's orientation toward AIDS was similar to its attitude toward drugs and the so-called "drug war." The criminal status of IV drug users weaves through the status of all persons with AIDS. Sex, drugs, and their racialized meanings became indistinguishable in the representation of the crack-addicted, pregnant, HIV-positive woman of color.

THE "OTHER," DISCRIMINATION, AND THE CONSTRUCTION OF AIDS

The construction of the meaning of AIDS simultaneously assumes a biotechnical reality and a political discourse. As Simon Watney argues, "ideology seeps in exactly where language is medical or scientific."[4] AIDS is something more than a virus. It reflects meanings given to it from a political culture.[5] This is problematic because, as Paula Treichler notes, "language is not a substitute for reality; it is how we know it."[6] As a result, the construction of AIDS is only "true" or "real" in particular and partial ways.[7]

AIDS has been defined in and through the hierarchical differentiations of hetero-homosexual, white/person of color, middle-class/poor, safer sex/deviant sex practices, drug-free/drug abuser—that is, in terms of divisions between "self" and "other." AIDS activated this prior agenda of oppositional differences. As Dr. Jonathan Mann, former head of the World Health Organization's Global AIDS Program, put it, "The AIDS virus entered an imperfect world, a world of prejudice and fear, ignorance and want, and the plague has thrived in part because of these imperfections." [8]

The discriminatory construction of AIDS distinguishes between innocent victims—such as infants born with the HIV virus and individuals who were infected through blood transfusions—and victims who are in some sense held responsible for their illness, because of their sexual activity or drug use. Differentiating and blaming are key to the discourse surrounding AIDS. If Ryan White, the young boy who fought to remain in school after becoming HIV-infected from a blood transfusion, is portrayed as an especially *innocent* victim of the disease, then others with AIDS, by implication, must be guilty. Similarly, if Kimberly Bergalis, the young woman infected with AIDS by her dentist, is seen as innocent, then others with AIDS are not. The same is true for Arthur Ashe, the tennis pro, who was unknowingly infected by a transfusion during heart surgery: emphasizing the innocence of the few presumes the guilt of the many. As Susan Sontag has stated, "societies need to have one illness which becomes identified with evil, and attaches blame to its victims." [9] And if AIDS is the responsibility or the fault of the sick—because they liked sex or drugs too much—then it is no longer the responsibility of the state to provide funding for care, treatment, or research. In a CBS / *New York Times* poll in September 1988, nearly one-half of those interviewed expressed sympathy for people with AIDS, but less than one in five shared that sympathy with homosexuals and IV drug users who had AIDS.

The notion of the "other" and the problem of difference is positioned against the image of the "general" population as heterosexual. [10] Dr. Otis Bowen stated in February 1988, while Secretary of Health and Human Services, that "we do not expect any explosion into the heterosexual population. . . . The much feared explosive invasion of the general population is not occurring and never will." [11] Meanwhile, *Newsweek* in March 1988 ran a cover story on "Sex in the Age of AIDS," featuring a new book by Masters and Johnson which argues that the number of heterosexuals infected with the HIV virus has been seriously underestimated. The authors argue that the AIDS virus is "running rampant" in the heterosexual community, and that it will continue to spread at a frightening pace.[12] Note that the heterosexual community is the major concern.

Others in the medical community have also argued that the epidemic is spreading rapidly among some groups of sexually active heterosexual teens, with equal numbers of males and females infected. "We think it's a crisis emergency situation."[13] In October 1989, the Centers for Disease Control (CDC) reported 415 known cases of persons thirteen to nineteen years old who were HIV-positive. This number is similar to the number of homosexual men initially affected by AIDS, in 1981. By March 1990, there were 1,429 young people aged thirteen to twenty-one who were infected with HIV.[14] Researchers assume that about one-fifth of infected people who are now in their twenties were exposed in their adolescent years. By 1991, AIDS was the sixth leading cause of death among fifteen- to twenty-four-year-olds.[15] Nevertheless, heterosexual AIDS goes unrecognized because AIDS still activates a discourse of "otherness": it will happen to someone else, who uses drugs, likes anal sex, is a prostitute, is black, and so on.

The identity of AIDS has always been tied to specified groups. First, the disease was defined through white gay men. Now it is often identified with poor African Americans and Hispanics and with drug addicts and their partners. When we hear about the epidemic in Africa, where AIDS is transmitted heterosexually, with as many women affected as men, it is said that African sexual practices account for its spread.[16]

A series of articles in the *New York Times* in September 1990 depicted African AIDS as a "raging epidemic," out of control due to high rates of sexually transmitted diseases, cultural customs, anal sex, poverty, and so on. African AIDS is presented as different from United States AIDS. According to journalist Jane Perlez, women are more vulnerable to AIDS in Africa than in the U.S. because of African women's economic impoverishment and the demands made on them sexually.[17] AIDS supposedly affects African women to a higher degree because they are already overburdened by work, bearing and caring for children, and low pay. Some women in the United States might argue that this description reflects similarities rather than differences between women in the United States and women in Africa.

Such depictions attempt to keep AIDS separate and different from the "general"—white, heterosexual—population in the United States.[18] In this process, Africa, as a false unity, stands in for U.S. blacks and people of color. Cindy Patton notes that United States cities with high numbers of people of color with AIDS are often described as being like Africa.[19] Simon Watney argues that talk of African AIDS deflects attention away from white heterosexuals. "African blackness is reconceptualized as an analogue of the sexually perverse."[20] Groups of people who are "different" get AIDS, whereas a nondiscriminatory view would recognize that, "until there is a cure, we are all living with it."[21]

According to Paula Treichler, the facts about AIDS changed very little in the period between 1981 and 1986, while its presentation changed greatly.[22] She argues that the perceived gay nature of AIDS was in part an artifact of the way in which data were collected and reported.[23] The CDC categorized people with AIDS who were gay *and* IV drug users as gay. The common perception that all gays were white and all drug users were black existed until around 1985, when the gay press called attention to the numbers of black and Latino men who were overrepresented in the homosexual category. As of December 1986, when the United States news media first reported that heterosexuals were at risk for AIDS, there had been no new scientific discoveries. What had shifted was the way in which data were being construed within the AIDS text.[24]

Since mid-decade, AIDS has concentrated in new communities. But its depiction and representation remains confused and often misleading. For example, in a *New York Times* article entitled "AIDS among Prostitutes Not As Prevalent As Believed," William Darrow, an AIDS epidemiologist at the CDC in Atlanta, is quoted as saying, "I don't know of any proven cases of female prostitutes infecting clients."[25] Other times lack of representation, rather than misrepresentation, characterizes the depiction of AIDS. It was not until March 1987 that the *Village Voice* discussed the relationship between AIDS and minorities, in an article entitled "The Hidden Epidemic: AIDS and Race."[26] Silence about Native Americans continues to construct the AIDS discourse. Between 1989 and 1990, the number of Native Americans with AIDS increased by 23 percent, but little attention has been focused on it.[27]

The AIDS discourse covers and uncovers the shifting nature of politics. Throughout the 1980s and early 1990s, the political struggle has continued between the rights of individual privacy and the authoritarian moralism of the state, along with the state's attempt at privatizing the service sector. Let us look more carefully at the constructions of the "other" in AIDS—the images of homosexuals, the black poor, and women of color—and the way this construction led to new restrictions on individual privacy and access to government services.

THE SHIFTING DISCOURSE OF AIDS

AIDS allows for a "counterrevolution against tolerance for minority rights"[28] because it reminds us of human variety and diversity within an already discriminatory context.[29] AIDS not only affects multiple marginalized groups but also affects people who are members of those groups. As a virus, it does not recognize the socially constructed risk groups as categories unto themselves. It travels across and through them.

Most often, the representation of AIDS has severed the connections between risk groups and risky activities. In 1990, homosexual contact was the predominant AIDS risk category among black and Latino males, and although some women are infected by the HIV virus through their own IV drug use, more are infected by sexual partners who are either IV drug users or bisexual. Although it is much more likely that some individuals will contact the AIDS virus than others, the risks are as dispersed as the virus.

Because AIDS reveals the plurality of sexual choices and preferences, it "exposes the artificiality of the categories and divisions" prevalent in the moral stance of rightist neoconservatism.[30] But because AIDS is a disease of the disenfranchised, AIDS discourse has not dislodged the powerful "pro-family" stance. As Jeffrey Weeks argues, sexuality is never fixed and is always open to change,[31] so the process of defining risk groups becomes part of the process of controlling sexuality while constructing AIDS. A racializing of gender has become a part of this mapping as well.

HOMOSEXUALITY AND AIDS

The first reporting of AIDS was on 2 July 1981; it was identified as a rare cancer found in homosexuals. The initial identification of AIDS as a gay man's disease (Gay-related Immune Disease) institutionalized AIDS as a disease of the "other." It also established the sexual nature of the transmission of the disease. The state responded with authoritarian moralism instead of with a federal policy that was open and truly pluralist about sexual practices and sexual orientations.[32]

Ethicist Dan Beauchamp has called for policies that would combine "the right to be different with the view that in matters of the common health and safety we are 'one body' with a common good."[33] Initiatives such as his would necessitate the repeal of state laws that proscribe homosexuality and sodomy as unlawful. Homosexuality would need to be fully decriminalized.[34] While there had been some movement through the sixties and seventies in the direction of recognizing the rights of sexual minorities, this impetus all but ended with the onset of AIDS.[35]

Some sodomy statutes had been liberalized through the 1950s, but these changes were seriously set back by the *Bowers v. Hardwick* decision in 1986. In this case, the Supreme Court reaffirmed sodomy as criminal and as not protected under the due process clause.[36] Despite this hostile stance of the Court, along with the obstacles it created for outreach and education about the disease, gay men launched an astounding safer-sex campaign to stem the spread of AIDS within the homosexual community. One wonders what might have been possible in the earlier stages of the epidemic if the campaign against AIDS had been given the assistance of an affirmative state.

The government, except for former Surgeon General C. Everett Koop, took no part in the safer-sex campaign. Presidents Reagan and Bush absented themselves from discussing sex and the transmission of AIDS. Their choice was abstinence. The choice of the gay community was more creative. As Douglas Crimp writes, "our promiscuity taught us many things, not only about the pleasures of sex, but about the great multiplicity of those pleasures."[37] It pushed gays to discuss exactly how they could have sex safely.

Safe sex is a complicated issue, particularly as one moves into the reality of poverty that defines much of the disease at present. As Michael Jones, an inhabitant of a federal housing project in Chicago, aptly put it, "there is no safe sex in Cabrini Projects. Cabrini Projects is not a safe place."[38] Nor does the safer-sex campaign adequately address some of the regional aspects of the disease. One can engage in high-risk behavior in the Dakotas with much less risk of acquiring AIDS than if one engaged in those practices in the Bronx.[39]

WOMEN OF COLOR AND AIDS

Nationally, women account for approximately 10 percent (up from an earlier 8 percent) of all AIDS cases since 1981.[40] It is projected to become one of the top five causes of death for young women, especially for poor women of color. In December 1990, the *New York Times* announced: "AIDS in Women Rising But Many Ignore the Threat."[41] Many women have become infected through their sexual partners who are IV drug users. Some women are IV drug users themselves. Some are heavily dependent on crack (cocaine) and sell sex for the drug. Some are infected by sexual partners who are bisexual.

There has been little recognition that the spread of AIDS to poor women of color should define women as a risk group. Race denies gender here. To connect women of color to the larger category of women opens up the risk group to include white women. Instead, women of color are classified as black or Latino—as a woman *who is black*, for example, rather than as a black woman. She is named by the specifics of her race, not by her racialized gender. Recognizing that the category of women cuts through racialized divisions tears down the wall between white women and women of color—a wall that is necessary to the construction of women of color as "other," as determined by their race and poverty or their sexual preference.[42]

Women of color are also viewed as vectors for the transmission of AIDS: as drug-addicted or HIV-infected mothers (infecting their babies) or as prostitutes (infecting men).[43] This view again differentiates women of color from the "general" population of (white) women. If women—read white women, rather than the specified category women of color—are at risk, so are men—read white men, which in turn means the general public. Women are defined as poor, as persons of color, or as poor persons of color. As such, they are seen as poor and drug dependent, not as women. Their color and poverty and drug status define them as lawless and immoral—like the others affected by AIDS.

The denial that women are a risk group is clearly seen in the official definition of AIDS by the Centers for Disease Control. Until 1 April 1992, to receive a diagnosis of AIDS an individual had to have HIV antibodies in the blood plus at least one opportunistic infection or cancer that was listed by the CDC. However, this list, which was derived from initial studies of gay men, did not include any of the opportunistic infections particular to women, such as vaginal thrush, pelvic inflammatory disease, or cervical cancer. Not one female gynecological complication was included in the original federal guidelines.

This narrow definition meant frequent incorrect diagnosis of women with AIDS and subsequent delayed and inadequate treatment. It has limited women's access to experimental drug trials, and it has wrongly denied poor women federal health benefits, because the social security administration, using the CDC definition, denied their claims of disability. According to writer Sarah Schulman, one study conducted at the CDC found that of 1,100 women aged 15–44 with AIDS listed on their death certificates as the underlying cause of death, only half met the initial CDC definition.[44] As Sonia Singleton put it, "Read my lipstick—Women do not have the same symptoms as men."[45] This situation may soon change with the implementing of a broader, more inclusive definition of AIDS. The new definition has added pulmonary tuberculosis, invasive cancer of the cervix, and recurrent bacterial pneumonia to the list of opportunistic diseases. The post–April 1992 definition of an AIDS sufferer is: "Any infected person with T-cell levels below 200." This broadened definition, though an improvement, still overlooks ailments common in women which occur at higher T-cell levels.[46]

The category of women cuts through racial and economic differences. And these differences cut through gender; therefore, race and economic class must also be specified so that gender does not stand in as a cover-up for other marginalized realities.

The number of reported AIDS cases nationwide is growing faster among women than men. From 1989 to 1990, cases among women increased by 33 percent; cases among men increased by 22 percent. The transmission of the virus is significantly different for women than for men; 33 percent of all women with AIDS, as opposed to 2 percent of all men with AIDS, report exposure through heterosexual conduct.[47] Up to eighty thousand women of childbearing age carry the AIDS virus, and approximately two thousand babies each year will develop the disease, according to 1991 data. It is thought that as many as three million females and one million children worldwide are presently infected with the virus. The World Health Organization estimates that by the year 2000, 15 to 20 million women will be infected, representing approximately half of the projected number of HIV infections worldwide.

AIDS is already becoming a leading cause of death for women who live in cities and are between twenty and forty years old. In New York City, 1,364 women were reported to have AIDS as of December 1987, along with 231 children. As many as fifty thousand women in the city are thought to be HIV-positive. Eighty percent are African American or Hispanic. AIDS is already the leading killer of black women aged 15–44; it is the third-ranking cause of death in New York and New Jersey among all women in this age group, and the leading cause of death for New York City women 25–34 years old. Among black women, the AIDS death rate rose from 4.4 per 100,000 in 1986 to 10.3 in 1988. For white women, the AIDS death rate increased from 0.6 in 1986 to 1.2 per 100,000 in 1988.[48]

In the United States, 51 percent of the women with AIDS are black, and 21 percent are Latina, whereas they make up only 18 and 11 percent of the population, respectively. Twenty-six percent of women with AIDS are white. Of men with AIDS, 61 percent are white, and 23 percent are black.[49] Over 90 percent of affected children under five are children of color.[50] Most of these women and children have no private health insurance and rely on Medicaid for treatment.[51]

This picture of "the" woman of color with AIDS lays the basis for discrimination against her; it initiates and reproduces her suspect identity. The stigmata of race, gender, poverty, and drug addiction are added onto the affliction of AIDS, which is already threaded through these realities. The drug-addicted mother is presented as an unfeeling criminal who requires state policing rather than as a person who needs drug treatment and a way to earn a living.[52] Any discriminatory practices based on such a representation, such as mandatory HIV testing of pregnant women, might easily be extended to apply to all women.

AIDS and drug use are represented in rightist neoconservative discourse as willful and criminal. Only drug users and sexual outlaws get AIDS. Women who get AIDS are drug users or sexual outlaws and are not part of the general population of women. They are guilty; their infant children are innocent.[53] AIDS reconstructs this hierarchy of difference as one of discrimination.

RACISM AND AIDS

Racism lays the basis for the neglect of blacks with AIDS and simultaneously constructs the "otherness" of AIDS and of the people living with it. Despite the Bush administration's official rhetoric, Kimberle Williams Crenshaw argues, blacks have remained a subordinated "other," while formal reform has merely repackaged racism.[54] One out of every three blacks still lives below the poverty line, and health care for blacks is well below the care for whites.[55] Substandard care complicates AIDS, allowing it to establish a firm foothold within African American communities.[56]

As discussed above, AIDS is disproportionately found among African American and Latina women and, to a lesser degree, among black IV drug-using, homosexual, and bisexual men. In 1991, 38 percent of all those with AIDS in the United States were people of color; 87 percent of the women with AIDS were women of color; and 91 percent of the children with AIDS were children of color. This means that four out of every five women and nine out of every ten children who have AIDS are either African American or Hispanic. Sixty percent of people with AIDS living in Newark, New Jersey, and 50 percent of those in Washington, D.C., are African American heterosexuals. In Belle Glade, Florida, 97 percent of the people with AIDS are black and about one-third are thought to be infected from heterosexual intercourse.[57]

Not until the fall of 1987 did the Department of Health and Human Services, through the Office of Minority Health, give recognition to AIDS as a serious minority health issue. The CDC was equally negligent. Its first report on AIDS and minorities was in the fall of 1986; its first conference to address the issue was in 1987. Not until July 1989 did black doctors begin to urge the study of the risk factors of AIDS for blacks.[58] In May 1990, Representative John Lewis, a Georgia Democrat and member of the Congressional Black Caucus, finally acknowledged that "AIDS is having a tremendous effect on the black community."[59]

The early neglect of African American communities which allowed the spread of AIDS is even more troubling given the fact that blacks in the United States were at special risk for AIDS because sickle-cell disease is treated through transfusions. But, as Sander Gilman points out, blacks were not considered in the same risk category as hemophiliacs because they were "deemed to be at risk because of their perceived sexual difference, their sexual practices, their hypersexuality."[60] Denying the prevalence of AIDS among blacks was (and is) part of this sexual stereotyping.

Homophobia within the black community has also played a part.[61] *Ebony* and *Essence* carried no articles on AIDS until Spring 1987. Official magazines of the NAACP and the National Urban League were also silent until 1987.[62] Blacks, like whites, did not want to be identified with a disease that was associated with homosexuality and its "otherness."

The announcement by Earvin "Magic" Johnson in the fall of 1991 that he had tested positive for the HIV virus and would be retiring from professional basketball further forced open the discussion of AIDS within African American communities.[63] Johnson, a black basketball superstar, told the public that he was infected during unprotected heterosexual sex. He then became a spokesperson for safer (hetero)sexual practices.

Because Magic Johnson speaks as a heterosexual, the specificity of his race almost seems neutralized. He speaks about AIDS across the color line. His hero status as a super-sportsman allows him this versatility. He also speaks as a man who says he was infected by a woman. The death of Rock Hudson from AIDS, even though he was white, had less impact nationwide than Magic Johnson's announcement because Hudson had contracted AIDS through homosexual activity. The public's (and Hudson's own) understanding of AIDS remained ghettoized by his homosexuality. Magic Johnson challenged this view of AIDS. Johnson's challenge meant that anyone—meaning any heterosexual man—can get the virus from a woman.

There was, however, some shifting of this emphasis after the initial shock. More and more was made of Johnson's sexual promiscuity. This issue narrowed the inclusiveness of heterosexuality and repositioned the AIDS discourse to include only particularly promiscuous heterosexual men. Emphasis was also shifted to the idea that men could catch AIDS from women. Little was made of the fact that only 2 percent of AIDS cases in the U.S. are men who have been infected by women. Since the only way HIV is transmitted is semen-to-blood or blood-to-blood, open sores and skin breaks have to be present for female to male transmission.

Sarah Schulman points out that this emphasis on female transmission may save women's lives, in that it gets men to wear condoms when they otherwise might not. But it also focuses on women as transmitters of the disease (to men and to their children), rather than as people who are living with AIDS. Schulman urges that it is a real tragedy that Magic Johnson's claim reignited this view of women as carriers when women remain the most underserved AIDS population in America.[64] And women of color make up a majority of that population.

The CDC reported in 1987 that blacks represented 25 percent of the reported cases of AIDS, and 51 percent of the cases among women. As much as 1.4 percent of the African American population may be infected with the AIDS virus. Whereas in 1981, New York City's AIDS cases were mainly homosexual men who were predominantly white, in 1987 nearly half of the AIDS cases were in the heterosexual community; 54 percent were minorities, and four out of five women were either African American or Hispanic.[65] In 1989, 36 percent of newly diagnosed persons with AIDS were black; among women, 84 percent were black or Latina.[66] By 1993, it was expected that 73 percent of new AIDS cases in New York City would be minority men and women.[67]

We turn now to an examination of the federal neglect and incoherent policy on AIDS that has allowed this situation to occur. This process reflects the kind of outcome an anti–affirmative public health state can lead to.

PRIVATIZATION, THE UNITED STATES GOVERNMENT, AND AIDS

The number of full-blown AIDS cases reported by the CDC in 1988 was 64,506. In 1990, more than 3,000 new cases of AIDS were reported every month in the United States; in 1991, the number of new cases per year had increased to 115,000. In 1992, the epidemic reached 200,000 new cases, "with the second 100,000 coming four times as quickly as the first." The cumulative total bespeaks the terrible rapidity with which AIDS is growing.[68] Dr. Jonathan Mann of the Harvard School of Public Health says that the rate of growth is more alarming than anyone had previously thought. He estimates that in the next three years alone, the number of infected people who develop AIDS will exceed the total who developed the disease during the entire history of the epidemic. Mann also stresses the particular plight of women, who accounted for 40 percent of HIV infections worldwide in 1992, up from 25 percent in 1990.[69]

In 1981, 244 people had died of AIDS; by the end of 1990, approximately 100,000 had died. The CDC estimate that by the end of 1993, between 285,000 and 340,000 will have died from AIDS. Some 20,000 children have already lost one or both parents to AIDS. If this trend is allowed to continue, by the year 2000 there will be 100,000 orphans.[70] The CDC believes that approximately 1.5 million people are presently infected with the HIV virus. Others estimate that 5 million people in the United States will be carrying the virus in the very near future. The World Health Organization estimated in June 1991 that ten million adults and children worldwide have been infected with the HIV virus and that the number will reach 40 million in the year 2000.[71]

Obviously, the need for federal policies for prevention and treatment is extraordinary. Prevention can make a significant difference, and treatments like the drug Azidothymidine (AZT) can be effective for varying amounts of time for people infected with the HIV virus who suffer no symptoms. Studies show that those taking AZT have been half as likely to develop symptoms as those taking placebos.[72] AZT, however, is not available to many who need it, nor is it clear that it is as beneficial for African Americans and Hispanics as it is for whites.[73]

Pneumocystic infections remain the leading killer of AIDS patients, largely because many are not receiving prophylactic treatment.[74]

An aggressive, preventive governmental outreach program is needed, along with the dismantling of discriminatory legislation—regarding hiring, testing, confidentiality, and sexual practices—that affects the prevention and treatment of AIDS. This need stands in stark contrast to the fact of governmental retrenchment throughout the 1980s.

The Reagan years, from 1980 to 1988, were years of neglect. AIDS first appeared in 1981.[75] In 1983, the HIV virus was isolated. By 14 June 1983, AIDS was defined as the number one health priority by Margaret Heckler, then-Secretary of the Department of Health and Human Services. But in that same year, the Committee on Government Operations, in its report "The Federal Response to AIDS," revealed that the administration "has not exercised sufficient leadership to ensure that adequate resources have been available for its number one health priority."[76] The committee specifically criticized the executive branch for inadequate funding levels for research and surveillance and for delays in requested funding. Although Congress had moved to authorize emergency funds, these still had not been appropriated at the time of the 1983 report. The Food and Drug Administration, the National Institutes of Health, pharmaceutical companies, and governmental regulations have all been cited as contributing to the ineffectiveness of AIDS policy. Funding delays, bureaucratic tangles, and insufficient funds have plagued the research and treatment of AIDS from its outset.

In June 1983, a $12 million supplemental AIDS appropriations bill was finally passed and signed. At that time, public health officials were requesting $52.3 million. Dr. Marcus Conant of the University of California at San Francisco Medical Center declared that "the failure to respond to this epidemic now borders on a national scandal."[77] There was still no federally funded AIDS prevention campaign or even a plan of attack through 1983. Indeed, the administration remained deficient in this area throughout the Reagan and Bush years. Federal inattention was so egregious from the start that California allocated state monies for AIDS research to the University of California in 1983. Since then, states have responded to the lack of comprehensive AIDS legislation by enacting their own laws related to the disease.

Secretary Heckler addressed the International AIDS Conference in 1985 and stated that "we must conquer AIDS before it affects the heterosexual population and the general population. . . . We have a very strong public interest in stopping AIDS before it spreads outside the risk groups, before it becomes an overwhelming problem."[78] Her position was clear: AIDS affected specific risk groups and was not a real threat for white heterosexuals. It would become a real threat if it attacked the "general" public. Heckler had no plan as to how to protect the public, in general, or how to deal with the risk groups already being affected.

Because there was no definable, coherent federal policy, the number of AIDS cases increased significantly after 1981. The number of deaths increased twentyfold. By 1987, six years after the first diagnosis of AIDS and two years after the death of Rock Hudson, Reagan first asked the Department of Health and Human Services to "determine to what extent AIDS poses a problem."[79]

As late as July 1985, Reagan still had not said one word publicly about AIDS. In 1986, he finally mentioned it as a major health priority. In 1987, he made his first speech on AIDS. In this same year, Reagan set up a thirteen-member presidential commission to study the situation, but the commission did not include a single physician who treated AIDS patients, major AIDS researcher, or person living with AIDS.[80] The silence and inaction of the Reagan administration were deafening.

During the Reagan administration, the civil rights of people living with AIDS were not protected, even though federal health officials made clear early on that AIDS could not be spread through casual contact in the workplace. The Justice Department decided that federal civil rights law did not extend to persons with AIDS who were dismissed from their jobs because their employers feared the spread of the disease. In 1987, however, in *School Board of Nassau County v. Arline,* the Supreme Court held that a person with a contagious disease could be protected by section 504, the "handicapped individual" standard of the Federal Rehabilitation Act of 1973. In 1988 a federal court in California made the definitive ruling to date concerning discrimination and AIDS on the basis of the *Arline* decision. The court found that the Federal Rehabilitation Act applies to HIV-infected individuals, and that institutions receiving federal funds cannot discriminate against the handicapped.[81] AIDS is defined as a handicap and it is therefore illegal to discriminate on the basis of AIDS if the person is otherwise qualified. Nevertheless, the federal government has continued to discriminate against persons with HIV infection: one is ineligible for military service, the Peace and Job Corps, foreign service, and other positions.

The report of the Presidential Commission on the HIV Epidemic in 1988 called for an end to discrimination against people with AIDS. The commission argued for strong new federal legislation and directives to prevent discrimination against those carrying the HIV virus.[82] The report condemned the absence of strong federal leadership in the fight against AIDS.[83] The commission recommended increased education about AIDS and its prevention; quality-assured, voluntary testing; more reporting of HIV infection with confidentiality; a program to institute confidential partner notification; greater prevention and treatment of intravenous drug use; and more research and study of the spread of AIDS in the heterosexual population.[84] The report also stated that the "context in which the epidemic is occurring must be addressed." AIDS increases "the urgent need to address problems of poverty, unemployment, teenage pregnancy, drug abuse and homelessness."[85]

Reagan did not respond to the report. Instead, his aides downplayed its findings. The day after the report was released, a senior White House aide spoke for Reagan: "He feels deeply about it personally and Mrs. Reagan feels deeply about it. I think the President will want to move rather rapidly on this."[86] Neither Reagan nor his aides ever clarified what he felt deeply about. And he did not move rapidly—even then, in 1988.

By 1989, although there was still no implemented federal plan to deal with AIDS, Congress had increased federal spending for AIDS research, prevention, and education. The allotment of approximately $2.2 billion was comparable with expenditures for other life-threatening illnesses. Congress funded $4.3 billion for 1992.[87] In contrast, it is estimated that the federal government will spend as much as $500 billion, or about $5,000 for every U.S. household, to bail out the failed savings and loan industry.[88]

While Bush was Reagan's vice-president, he endorsed legislation and other federal measures that would discourage discrimination against persons with AIDS, but only on a voluntary basis. Yet he held that AIDS was a "federal responsibility." As president, he did almost nothing to counter the disease. He continued federal discriminatory practices in the hiring of new military recruits.[89] And he rarely broke Reagan's legacy of silence about AIDS. On one occasion, he stated that it makes no sense to blame those who are suffering from the disease, and that instead we must "try to love them and care for them and comfort them. . . . We do not fire them, or evict them, or cancel their insurance."[90] He nevertheless did not subscribe to mandatory federal legislation to protect the rights of those with AIDS. At another point, he stated, "I'd hate it if a kid of mine got a blood transfusion and my grandson had AIDS and the community discriminated against that child, that innocent child."[91] His statement of compassion distinguished the "innocent" person from the others, who by implication have brought AIDS upon themselves. Moreover, when speaking of AIDS, he spoke personally, rather than as an official of federal policy.

In the fall of 1991, Bush spoke about the weekend demonstrations by AIDS activists near his home in Kennebunkport, Maine, demanding more federal attention to the disease. He was upset that the marchers would disrupt local businesses. As for the issue of greater federal funding for AIDS research, prevention, and treatment, Bush said that he thought "behavioral change" was the best way to halt the disease's spread: "Here's a disease where you can control its spread by your own personal behavior."[92] His focus was once again on what the individual could do for him/herself, not what the government can do for the person. He ignored the fact that many individuals are homeless, poor, or already IV drug users. His lack of government support was at least consistent. He continued to deny support for federally funded needle exchange programs for IV drug users throughout his administration, even though they have proven effective in limiting the spread of infection from shared needles.[93]

Bush defended his administration's efforts on AIDS. In response to the heightened awareness of HIV infection in heterosexuals—due to Magic Johnson's announcement—he said he would renew efforts to educate the public. He stated further: "If I need to do more—and Barbara does—to express the concern we feel, we'll do it."[94] He never did.

Federal funding, such as the $2.9 billion approved by the Senate in May 1990 for emergency relief to the cities and states hit hardest by the AIDS epidemic, reflected the disarray of Bush's AIDS nonpolicy. There was no real plan of action; instead, there were piecemeal proposals. Even senators openly hostile to AIDS and the issues surrounding it voted for this piecemeal funding. As Orrin Hatch, right-wing Republican senator from Utah, pointed out, federal funding for AIDS does not end the debate over the "causes of this disease or the methods of its prevention."[95] The Bush administration continued to have "no comment" on the various proposals pending in the Senate and House. After a decade of the disease, the country witnessed decision-making through *nonde-cision-making and decisionless decisions*.[96] This lack of a coherent policy initiative has left a ten-year-old nonpolicy of discriminatory practice in place. The neglect was *not* benign.

The National Commission on AIDS, in its interim 1990 report, criticized the Bush administration much as it had the Reagan administration. It claimed that the federal government had not taken the necessary steps to get health care to people with AIDS; that the epidemic was growing in crisis proportions; that the government had to be willing to make the necessary expenditures, which could reach $15 billion but would still be less than one-third of a percent of the total health care costs of the nation; and that drug treatment must be available for all those who request it. The commission criticized the growing complacency surrounding the epidemic and the "anti-drug" policy of the Bush administration. And it predicted that many more people will be afflicted with AIDS in the 1990s than had the disease in the 1980s. The report calls for the state to take a much more active role in creating access to health care for people living with AIDS.

President Bush had no direct response to the interim report. Rather, a spokesperson from the Department of Health and Human Services claimed "this department, under the previous secretary and the present secretary, has taken strong leadership against the epidemic."[97] The final report by the commission, released in the fall of 1991, stated that a key obstacle in dealing with AIDS has been the lack of leadership by President Bush. It reiterated the importance of a "consistent national policy concerning AIDS."[98] The report indicted the problems of racism, homophobia, poverty, unemployment, homelessness, and the crisis surrounding health care as endemic to AIDS. More specifically, the commission called for universal health care for all persons to ensure access to quality care, a national HIV prevention initiative, access to a government system of health care for all people with HIV disease, Medicaid coverage for all low-income people with HIV disease, and inclusion of more people of color and women in clinical testing of drugs and treatments.

The report also looked forward into the second decade of AIDS and argued for a more aggressive education and prevention program as the only hope for altering the further spread of AIDS. Members of the commission further argued that AIDS education must be increased and broadened to address the people needing it most, especially heterosexual women. Following suit, research should be devoted to exploring a wider array of chemical and physical barriers to block vaginal HIV transmission.[99]

Members of the commission saw no resolution to the AIDS epidemic without a significant shift in the government's focus. The government must recognize AIDS as part of a wide and complex network of social and economic inequality. The problem of drugs must be seen as integral within this structuring. The commission once again called for a federal government initiative to provide drug treatment for all who apply for it.

Bush once more had no comment on the report when it was released. Once again, he invoked his moralist rhetoric and sidestepped the underlying realities conducive to the spread of AIDS. Magic Johnson, appointed by President Bush to the commission after his announcement that he was infected with HIV, resigned in protest (less than a year later) over Bush's lack of action. In his letter of resignation to President Bush, he contended that the administration had "utterly ignored" the commission's recommendations: that Bush had "dropped the ball" on AIDS.[100] President Bush made no public comment on Johnson's resignation, except that he was sorry to hear of it.

Bush's election rhetoric of 1992 was no better than his record. AIDS policy had no priority in the Republican platform. Instead, Mary Fisher, a woman who has AIDS, addressed the Republican convention. She said the administration must do more to combat the disease. She also characterized the Bush administration as open and caring: "I've always found the doors open to me on AIDS." She wore the only red ribbon among those addressing the convention the night she spoke. The next day, Barbara Bush wore one also. President Bush did not.

During the campaign, the Bush administration supported a federal court ruling that employers can limit the health insurance coverage of workers who develop costly illnesses like AIDS. In a campaign speech Bush delivered to Kentucky Fried Chicken franchise owners, he stated, "Yes, AIDS is a national tragedy. But we don't need a bureaucratic czar in our nation's capitol. . . . We need more caring."[101]

The Democratic Convention and platform paid considerably more attention to AIDS than did the Republicans. The Democrats were openly critical of the lack of a coherent AIDS policy. Red ribbons were worn by most who addressed the convention. Elisabeth Glaser, who is infected with the AIDS virus, as is her son, spoke to the convention about her life and her daughter's death due to AIDS. A member of Clinton's campaign, Tom Hattoy, addressed the convention as a gay man with AIDS. No woman of color or poor person addicted to drugs spoke, however.

The Clinton-Gore ticket promised to make fighting the AIDS epidemic a top priority. Clinton stated in *Putting People First* that there must be increased funding for AIDS research, prevention, and treatment and that he would set up an AIDS policy director to coordinate federal policies to implement the recommendations of the commission on AIDS. He also said the government must provide quality health coverage to all with HIV as part of a broader national health-care program, and that we must encourage compassion, promote education, and end AIDS-related discrimination.[102]

We are left, nevertheless, with the legacy of a passive, *non*affirmative state in the realms of health care and drug prevention, and of an interventionist state that required the *de*privatization of sex, sexuality, and family life.[103] Both legacies have left an indelible mark on AIDS. And one wonders if these legacies are in part responsible for the lack of a clear initiative on AIDS by the Clinton administration. Christine M. Gebbie was not appointed White House AIDS coordinator until June 1993. One wonders why action in the AIDS arena has been so slow, whereas actions were taken quickly to reverse abortion restrictions.

STATE PRIVATIZATION VERSUS STATE MORALISM

The lack of government leadership in formulating AIDS policy reflects the privatized stance of the service side of the state. The Bush administration claimed it did not have enough budgetary allocations to spend more on AIDS-related research or other programs. In contrast, the administration was willing to expend $2.2 billion a month for the Gulf War.

Bush's privatized stance on AIDS was seriously flawed. He preferred to depend on private sources to sustain AIDS research and treatment programs. He did not support a tax shelter for drug companies to create an incentive for developing new medicines. He was unwilling to recognize that private health insurance is not adequate to cope with HIV infection because of the limited range of services covered. The National Academy of Sciences argued that more research was needed on antiviral agents and secondary infections, as well as on gender and racial differences related to early drug treatment, but monetary support was not forthcoming.

The dependence on private sources for research became more problematic as time went on. Whereas a few years ago AIDS was in the limelight for private funding, by 1992 it had been shoved into the wings. Many of the major AIDS service organizations which had been disproportionately funded by individual donors and private sources have now lost their funding. Many of the large corporate funders decided to invest their money elsewhere. In Dallas, Texas, the three large private foundations that supported AIDS services no longer do so. Many of the grants which were initially funded privately have ended, and the federal government has not stepped in to fill the void. Nor have state or local governments. To the dismay of John Mortimer, director of advocacy services for the AIDS project in Los Angeles, the California government announced in January 1990 that it was cutting funds for AIDS by 12 percent. And there was no source to replace these funds, even as the crisis grew.[104]

The privatized stance of the state in dealing with AIDS was further complicated by the relationship between the medical establishment, big business, and government. In these arenas, it is difficult to see government interests as separate from those of business. In the case of AIDS research, the National Institute of Health (NIH) allied with Burroughs Wellcome Drug Company, with the assistance of the Food and Drug Administration (FDA), to steamroll AZT as the only approved treatment for AIDS. And, according to author Bruce Nussbaum, Dr. Tony Fauci squandered one billion dollars on research without developing a single new drug.[105] The problem is not only that the government did not commit enough money to researching AIDS, but that the money was misused by private concerns with the encouragement of the NIH and FDA. The government operated as part of this privatized network, not as a separate entity. The discourse of the Reagan-Bush state justified this privatization alongside a health care system already dominated by private interests.

The regulatory or interventionist role of the FDA in restricting innovative drugs and therapies has been actively challenged by activists in the AIDS Coalition To Unleash Power (ACT UP). By 1988, the FDA had begun to change some of its policies in order to facilitate more experimental development of AIDS drugs.[106] The process of deregulation by the FDA points to the need for careful scrutiny of state regulatory action. In this case, FDA policies should be held accountable to those people living with AIDS rather than the needs of those within the AIDS bureaucracy. The state must operate as a public concern, not as a facilitator of private interests. Its regulatory policy must hold drugs accountable to safe standards while allowing those living with AIDS to have some say in what those standards should be. And the standards must not be determined by the private interests of drug companies or by a particular political/moral stance of the state. If we extend this standard of review to other realms of public health, then the FDA ban on the abortion pill RU486 is also highly suspect.

Because of the rightist, neoconservative moralism that defined the state's inadequate and ineffective education campaign on AIDS and the ban on RU486 the government failed in its moral duty to create public health policy and access to medical services. According to Allan Brandt, professor of the history of medicine and science at the University of North Carolina at Chapel Hill, because AIDS violates a moral code, moral rectitude was used to guide the campaign against it.[107] The 1988 Department of Health and Human Services appropriations bill required that all AIDS educational and informational materials and activities for school-aged children and young adults emphasize (a) abstinence from sexual activity outside monogamous marriage, and (b) abstinence from the use of illegal intravenous drugs.[108]

C. Everett Koop's policy initiative as Surgeon General differed from the administration's official policy in that it discussed the importance of condom use and assumed that suggestions of abstinence and monogamy were in and of themselves insufficient. In his message to the nation, which was distributed countrywide to every household, he stated, "Condoms are the best preventive measure against AIDS besides not having sex and practicing safe behavior."[109]

William Bennett, the architect of the "war on drugs," thought the mention of condoms endorsed immoral sexual activity. He insisted that the government's message must advocate self-restraint until a person is ready to begin a "mutually faithful monogamous relationship. . . . The federal government has an obligation, a duty, to provide . . . information . . . which encourages sexual abstinence and sexual fidelity."[110] He argued further that the government must point out the dangers of sexual promiscuity and the need for self-control. Jesse Helms, a Republican senator from North Carolina, campaigned to outlaw AIDS education that directly or indirectly encouraged homosexuality. Edwin Meese also endorsed this position. Cardinal John O'Connor of New York voiced his concerns when he criticized the Catholic bishops' draft of "The Many Faces of AIDS: A Gospel Response" for implicitly condoning "immoral" practices.[111] The archdiocese of Boston argued similarly that a focus on condom use encourages promiscuity and hedonism.

The condom campaign was endorsed in states like Oregon, Michigan, and New York in spite of the active lobbying against it. In New York City, debate raged over the distribution of condoms in the schools, as well as the content of AIDS education information. The New York City Board of Education approved rules requiring that AIDS education in the public schools stress abstinence and downplay the discussion of condoms. Critics of this policy, who included Mayor David Dinkins, said these guidelines greatly hamper education on safer sex and endorse a problematic censorship within the schools.[112]

"Pro-family" moralism can do little to stem the spread of AIDS for those who are sexually active and/or addicted to drugs. The United States has the highest teenage pregnancy rate in the Western world, as well as high levels of sexually transmitted diseases. Telling people not to have sex simply does not work.[113] Curtailing information and access to contraceptives does not work either.

The controversy over the public funding of the National Endowment for the Arts (NEA), particularly in relation to the work "The Perfect Moment" by Robert Mapplethorpe in June 1989 and the show (and catalog) "Witnesses: Against Our Vanishing" curated by Nan Goldin in November 1989, reflects this same authoritarian moralism about sexuality. People like Jesse Helms said that "Witnesses" depicted and represented AIDS and homosexuality in a way that made it morally unacceptable for federal funding. According to Helms, Mapplethorpe's art violated all sense of moral standards;[114] it depicted unnatural acts and homoeroticism and exploited children.[115] Although President Bush supported continued funding of the NEA in the short term, he endorsed the idea of immoral art and felt that federal funding should not support it.[116] His firing of NEA director John Frohnmayer in February 1992 reflected this interventionist moralism.

The debate over NEA funding and what constitutes acceptable art—or acceptable sex—is part of the same moralist text in which AIDS has been addressed. The moralism of Bush, Bennett, and Helms did not allow public funding to endorse private choices with which they did not agree. An antiabortion stance became as much a prerequisite for governmental appointment as a public stance supporting monogamy. A government defined by a monolithic morality makes your private sexual choices for you. Constructions of sex, sexual practices, and fantasy become the domain of public policy.

The Bush administration, by dealing with AIDS as a disease representing immoral lifestyles, also justified its "drug war." Both AIDS and the drug war necessitated a police mentality. The state policed more than it supported research, prevention, and treatment.

AIDS AND THE DRUG WAR

Drugs, sex, poverty, and AIDS are part of a complex web. The Bush administration's drug war falsely isolated the problem of drugs and used it as a stand-in for the other issues. President Bush named drugs as our gravest domestic problem, as though it stood alone.[117] The drug war falsely focused rage on one symptom of a complex and seemingly unmanageable problem. It was a wrongful quick fix that justified a police state. Columnist Ellen Willis argues that drugs bespeak the intolerable frustrations people seek escape from. Drug addiction represents one outcome of the unbearable poverty of the Reagan-Bush decade. The drug war is a political surrogate for the problems of the urban poor, racial ghettoes, and unemployment, which have been ignored.[118]

The Bush administration used the drug war as a substitute for an active, affirmative state in the realm of education, anti-discrimination, the struggle against poverty, AIDS prevention, and so on. It refused to acknowledge the need to make high-quality treatment services available as part of its drug program. Bush opposed Senator Daniel Patrick Moynihan's attempts to amend the administration's package to include "treatment on request" for drug-addicted individuals, especially pregnant women.[119]

Benjamin Playthell, writing in the *Village Voice*, described his drug-ridden neighborhood and declared that he wanted a "real" war on crack dealers, not President Bush's phony war.[120] Official policy was directed to a militarist interventionist politics in Latin America rather than to domestic policy dealing with the poverty of the ghetto.[121] The international militarist model constructed the focus of domestic drug policy on the police state. Bush's drug plan called for an increase in federal funding for "more prisons, more jails, more courts, more prosecutors."[122] He argued that we need to enlarge the criminal justice system to allow for easier and more effective punishment.

The drug war set out and justified what Michel Foucault has named the process of disciplining and punishing.[123] Drug abuse is seen as criminal rather than as part of a larger societal and economic network of problems, or as an addictive disease needing treatment and prevention. Bush continued to call for more of the same militaristic action in order to intensify efforts at curtailing the flow of drugs in the United States, even though years of such action had met with limited success. By 1992, the drug war seemed like a failure. Billions of dollars had been spent on criminal prosecution and incarceration, while less than 20 percent of the funds had been spent on drug abuse treatment, prevention, or research. Because of its failure the war on drugs was omitted from Bush's campaign in 1992.[124]

Nevertheless, the drug war was successful in consolidating a neomoralist state: one that further limits access to groups already subject to discrimination, while cloaking this process in a discourse of moralism. The White House Report on Drugs called for intolerance toward the problem: "That intolerance must be embodied in law, and expressed in action."[125] To speak of "drugs"—a vague and homogeneous term, which includes too much and too little at the same time—is to treat drugs such as marijuana and crack cocaine as though they were equally harmful. Drug kingpins, drug addicts, small-time users, and small-time drug sellers are also treated alike.

This moral stance of right and wrong simplifies the issue of drugs much as it simplifies the difference between acceptable sexual practices and "deviant" ones, and the difference between innocent victims of AIDS and those who supposedly brought it on themselves. The White House Report on Drugs recognized the need for prevention, but defined prevention as including only antidrug education that instills in children the values that contribute to a drug-free life.[126] This strategy was consistent with the earlier Nancy Reagan solution: "Just Say No." Individuals were supposed to be able to take care of the problem by themselves, with a bit of self-restraint.

William Bennett represented the most aggressive formulation of the absolutist moral "pro-family" stance. He argued that the prevalent use of drugs in the United States reflected a crisis of authority. It therefore became the renewed responsibility of the state to authorize the values conducive to strengthening family life. In a letter in the *Wall Street Journal* to Milton Friedman, the well-known free-market economist, Bennett criticized Friedman's support for legalizing drugs. Bennett argued that the government needed to reestablish a sense of moral order. "A true friend of freedom understands that government has a responsibility to craft and uphold laws that help educate citizens about right and wrong."[127]

Friedman rejected Bennett's proposals for more police, more jails, the use of the military in foreign countries, and so on as adding repressive sanctions to an *already* bad situation. "The drug war cannot be won by those tactics without undermining the human liberty and individual freedom that you and I cherish."[128] Friedman has it partly right:

Bennett's armed camp mentality sets a troublesome context for individual rights of privacy. Whether Bennett in fact cherishes these freedoms is less clear. He needs an outlaw culture to justify a police state.[129]

Drugs and the moral order were made into national security issues. The drug war required surveillance and other invasive strategies. A billion dollars was slated for prison construction in 1990. The antidrug campaign was targeted at $10.6 billion for 1991. The state enlarged its responsibility for law enforcement while reducing its responsibility to assist the poor and the sick. The drug war was not a real attempt at dismantling the infrastructure of drug culture. Rather, it reoriented and redirected the purpose of the state toward policing.

Worse still, the drug war included no policy for dealing with AIDS. The 1989 National Research Council report on AIDS and IV drug use argued that a policy on AIDS was desperately needed, that the media presentation of drug users as self-destructive and uninterested in their own health is largely untrue, and that changes in risk-associated behavior have already been reported among IV drug users, even given the limited number of education programs available to them. The council report also documented that well-designed, staged trials of sterile needle programs have been successful wherever they have been implemented. Lastly, the report noted that many opportunities exist to halt the spread of AIDS among drug users, and that more preventive action was badly needed.[130]

When the exchange of sex for drugs is added to the practice of sharing needles it becomes clearer than ever that the criminal framework of the drug war cannot deal with the problem of AIDS. Heterosexual transmission of AIDS is occurring particularly where illegal drug use and prostitution are prevalent. IV drug users constitute 25 percent of AIDS cases, and 70 percent of all heterosexually transmitted cases in native-born citizens come from contact with this group. Seventy percent of children with perinatally transmitted AIDS are born to IV drug users or their sex partners. And the number of these cases continues to rise.[131] The general increase in sex-related diseases is linked to the increase in sex-for-drugs activity.[132]

The increase in the use of crack, a cheaper form of cocaine used primarily by the urban poor, has created a particular medium for the spread of AIDS. Crack appears to stimulate "pathological levels of sexual activity" because one does not achieve orgasm while on the drug. The crack user supposedly craves more and more sex, and with it, more drugs. This craving increases the likelihood that sex will be exchanged for the drug. Also, syphilis, which is often contracted from sex in crack houses, can increase the spread of HIV: the genital ulcers and lesions are a receptive channel for transmission. As a result, AIDS is increasingly spreading in the nation's poorest neighborhoods through heterosexual contact.[133] "Thus AIDS may be piggybacking on the hypersexual crack culture."[134]

The issue of sex and drugs becomes most problematic when it is combined with pregnancy. The drug war appears most inadequate in this realm, whether one is thinking in terms of the fetus or of the pregnant woman. The White House Report on Drugs in 1990 cited an estimate that some 100,000 babies are born to cocaine-addicted mothers each year. Some of these infants are affected by the mother's drug use and/or infected with the HIV virus. Jails, punishment, and charges of neglect have little to offer either the fetus or the mother in such cases.[135]

Yet criminal prosecution, particularly of black women, appears to have been the principal response to this situation, rather than prevention or treatment.[136] Most drug treatment programs are not even open to pregnant women. Fifteen percent of all pregnant women, rich or poor, white or black, may be currently using drugs while pregnant. White women more often use marijuana, whereas black women use crack or another form of cocaine. Both are potentially damaging to a fetus, yet black women are more likely to get reported to the authorities than white women. In a Florida study, black women were 9.58 times more likely to be reported for substance abuse, even though white women were 1.09 times more likely to have abused a substance prior to their first prenatal care visit.[137] The racialized system of justice is obviously in play.

Criminal prosecution pretends to protect the fetus from the derelict mother on drugs. But it does no such thing. Rather, it punishes the woman by challenging her right to custody of her children. It does not provide her with prenatal care, drug treatment, job training, or a job. As Alan Dershowitz, professor at Harvard Law School, argues, "you can't apply a law written for drug dealers to pregnant women." George Annas, professor of health law at Boston University School of Medicine, submits that these women have real problems besides drugs, such as "poverty, discrimination, living where services aren't available."[138] Such arguments have not kept several states from prosecuting women for cocaine, heroin, and alcohol abuse. In 1992, the drug-addicted mother often also has AIDS, bringing us full circle in the chain of related problems.

An aggressive outreach policy, along with a series of policies that end discrimination by race or sexual orientation, will have to be initiated by the public health system if drug-addicted women are to be reached for treatment. Because these women are highly vulnerable due to their dispossession, policies must focus on getting them the care they need, not merely identification or discipline.[139]

The CDC first reported an AIDS-like syndrome in infants in December 1982, but did not have the needed funding to conduct follow-up research on this group.[140] In June 1990, scientists were hopeful that they had found a connection between a specific string of molecules in the mother's antibody system and the protection of her infant.[141] Such findings should instigate new research and support for related treatments for the fetus and mother. But such research can take place only if we take a nonpunitive orientation to drugs and AIDS, and provide outreach programs for women's prenatal care without the fear of punishment. Such an approach requires affirmative public health programs that are free of neoconservative moralism and criminalization. The Reagan and Bush years provided us with a privatized, discriminatory state: one which defined its fiscal responsibilities more and more narrowly and its moralist prerogatives and functions more and more broadly. Because AIDS is utterly democratic—anyone can get it who partakes in certain practices—it cannot be addressed sufficiently by a discriminatory discourse.

PRIVACY, THE PRIVATIZED STATE, AND THE POLITICS OF TESTING

Because AIDS is "an epidemic with roots in private acts,"[142] it has allowed the state easy access into the private realm.[143] As Simon Watney has argued, AIDS is increasingly being used to underwrite a widespread ambition to erase the distinction between the public and the private, and to establish in its place a monolithic and legally binding category: the family.[144] This conflation of the private and public realms defines the moralist interventionist state. However, the Reagan and Bush administrations maintained the distinction between public and private when useful for their own purposes of privatization.

The issue of AIDS and its impact on individual privacy is complicated because homosexuals have no constitutionally guaranteed right to privacy in the first place. Homosexuals have no right to choose their sexual practices. Most people living with AIDS have discriminatory status. They have no privacy from the state, and AIDS publicly represents their private "violations." This lack of privacy impacts the issues of mandatory testing and confidentiality.[145] There are no easy answers here.

Instead, one finds a painfully complex set of issues. Homophobia, racialized patriarchy, and poverty already pose spectacular problems for individual privacy, and AIDS poses even more problems as a transmittable disease. Whose privacy counts more when a person infected with the HIV virus does not choose to disclose this information to his or her sexual partner? Whose privacy takes precedence in a rape case when the assailant is thought to have AIDS?

The American Civil Liberties Union (ACLU) is against all mandatory testing; all reporting of AIDS cases by doctors or laboratories; and against all tracing of or to partners.[146] In New York State, no one can be tested for HIV without the person's informed consent. Such requirements may be appropriate most of the time. But not always. "It's hard to tell a rape victim that testing her rapist is a terrible invasion of his privacy."[147] Unlike New York, at least eighteen states, as of September 1989, had adopted legislation that mandates testing of sex offenders.[148]

There is a political agenda inherent in the focus on testing—especially mandatory testing—given the lack of treatment programs. It prioritizes identifying and isolating those with the virus over preventing or treating those with the virus. Before the development of AZT and other drugs which can deter the onset of infection, the focus on testing appeared highly suspect to those thought to be infected. Why mandate testing when there was no treatment available, and no commitment to making treatment accessible and affordable?

Testing is justified in order that individuals who have been exposed to the virus know that they carry it, so that they can seek treatment and take precautions not to infect others. Thus, education and treatment programs are as important as the testing. Yet one does not hear of mandatory treatment, but only of mandatory testing. Testing as an isolated activity singles out people as infected. It is wholly inadequate as an effective public health initiative.

To begin with, there is still controversy about the conclusiveness of the testing process. Cindy Patton argues that testing is not as definitive as it is deemed to be, and very often continual testing over a period of time is necessary to detect the infection because of its period of latency.[149] But these charges remain inconclusive; the researchers who initially made this claim have been unable to reproduce the data confirming this latency period.

In 1991, the major AIDS story was the question of enforced testing of health care workers and doctors. If one read the *New York Times* for the year, one might conclude that the spread of AIDS could be curtailed through testing of doctors. Yet, at the time of this writing, only one doctor—a dentist, Dr. David Acer of Florida—has transmitted the AIDS virus to his patients. One of the five patients infected by Dr. Acer, Kimberly Bergalis, with the help of much publicity, became a vocal advocate for mandatory testing of medical workers. Whereas there are a number of cases where health workers have been infected by patients, Dr. Acer remains the single case of transmission from a doctor to a patient. The scarcity of cases did not, however, limit the speculation and discussion. Even though there are no known cases in which AIDS has been transmitted in any operation, the CDC says it estimates that from 13 to 128 patients may have acquired AIDS from health care workers doing invasive procedures in the last decade. Even though no such patient has yet to be identified, the CDC recommended that doctors infected with the virus inform their patients and refrain from performing invasive procedures.[150]

In September 1991, Senator Jesse Helms authored a bill requiring prison terms of at least ten years and fines up to $10,000 for doctors infected with the HIV virus who do not inform their patients. Congressman William Dannemeyer, a Republican from California, called for mandatory testing of all health workers. He thinks that "too many people are treating AIDS as a civil rights issue."[151] Senate majority leader George Mitchell and Senate minority leader Bob Dole sponsored another proposal requiring testing of doctors who perform invasive procedures. In the end, Congress approved a bill suggesting, but not requiring, that health care workers and doctors be tested for the HIV virus.[152]

Everett Koop spoke out against the trend toward testing doctors as costly, ineffective, and providing no additional protection from infection. He argued that the risk of being infected by a doctor "is so remote that it may never be measured."[153] Many in the medical community maintained that the government guidelines were scientifically unwarranted, because the danger of transmission is infinitesimal. According to a report in the *New England Journal of Medicine,* the risk of getting AIDS from a doctor during surgery is one in twenty-one million for each hour of the operation.[154] Most medical organizations refused to draw up lists of high-risk surgery, and New York State took the lead in rejecting the federal guidelines, declaring that health care workers infected with the AIDS virus should be able to perform surgery and other invasive procedures without informing their patients.[155] Overwhelmed by opposition from the medical profession, the CDC decided to drop its plan to list procedures that should not be performed by doctors and health workers who had been exposed to the HIV virus.[156] In July 1992, the National Commission on AIDS recommended against the mandatory testing of doctors and other health workers. Instead, it called for policies that would eliminate real, rather than theoretical, risks.[157]

A woman who has received much less news coverage than Kimberly Bergalis is Belinda Mason, a woman with two young children who contracted AIDS from a contaminated transfusion received during a cesarean section. Shortly before her death, she argued in a letter to President Bush that the "blanket screening of health care workers will create the false illusion that people with AIDS are a threat to others," and that universal precautions and sterile instruments would protect patients from infection more than testing their doctors would.[158] Testing, however, remained a focus for the restrictive framework which defined Bush's nonpolicy on AIDS. The United States is the only industrial nation in the world that restricts temporary entry and bars permanent entry to people infected with HIV.[159] As a result of this policy, the 1992 International Conference on AIDS, the most important scientific forum on research and treatment developments, was moved to a location outside the United States.

In conclusion, as late as 1992 the United States government was still devoid of any coherent policy on AIDS. Instead, governmental policy presented testing as its mode of protection and abstinence as its mode of prevention. Policy depends on private initiatives in the scientific arena, despite the fact that the private corporate sector has been slow to fund research or to underwrite drug development research where liability is high.[160] The 1988 Presidential Commission on AIDS called for appropriate protection from excessive legal liability for vaccine manufacturers of AIDS drugs, and sufficient funding for "rational drug development."[161] But such proposals have largely been ignored. On the contrary, the Office of Management and Budget went so far as to suggest that the research arm of the National Institutes of Health be privatized.[162] Interestingly enough, similar moves toward privatization were suggested for the National Endowment for the Arts.[163]

The lack of a federal initiative to deal with health policy for people living with AIDS highlights the desperate situation of medical care in the United States. Private industry cannot effectively address the medical and scientific issues surrounding AIDS or health care in general.[164] The pricing of the drug AZT is a case in point. The drug is priced out of the realm of accessibility for most people with HIV infection. The manufacturer of AZT, Burroughs Wellcome, defends its pricing as reflecting the "cost of research, development, production, and the need to generate revenue to support continuing research."[165] Bush administration rhetoric attributed the lack of governmental subsidies to its own lack of funds.[166]

The situation is likely to change under the Clinton administration. The negative consequences of the Reagan-Bush years for the American people are becoming clearer: the very, very rich got richer, while everyone else paid the bill. In several CBS News polls, respondents showed resistance to budget cuts in social security, environmental expenditures, and education and have begun to accept the necessity of tax increases. Seventy-eight percent of the respondents expressed approval for increasing taxes on incomes over $200,000, and 86 percent expressed disapproval for reductions in spending on education.[167] Such data in part explain the election of Clinton.

The question remains whether the prevailing anti-tax discourse, which is part of the anti–social service state, can be exposed and its hold weakened. It remains to be seen whether the idea that government has a responsibility for guaranteeing health care, a full-growth economy, and a civil rights agenda, especially for those who have been marginalized, can be recaptured from the neoconservative Right. Such a policy would need to be situated between the privacy rights of all individuals and an affirmative service state. It would require replacing neoconservative moralism with a radical pluralism. This is the major challenge for today: to retrieve the discourse of equality *and* privacy for a radicalized democracy which can move beyond liberalism, neoconservativism, and totalitarian statism. To achieve this goal we must reimagine civil and reproductive rights.

ACT UP AND A DEMOCRATIC POLITICS FOR THE 1990S

The AIDS Coalition To Unleash Power (ACT UP) has been important in demanding and drawing attention to the problems of people living with AIDS. By the mid-1980s, ACT UP had alerted the U.S. public to many of the unrecognized needs of the AIDS community, including increased funding for scientific research, alternate therapies, and drug trials.

ACT UP remains the most vocal and organized group criticizing government's lack of action on AIDS. Their political tactics and strategies disrupt the silence and complacency surrounding the disease.

ACT UP's early start was within the gay community. One should not use the construct of gay, however, to cover over the fact that there have always been people of color within the gay community. At first, the politics of AIDS articulated by ACT UP—much like the early history of the virus in the United States—was defined as white, male, and gay. The politics surrounding AIDS in the early years focused on the needs of this community. This focus allowed ACT UP to develop a radical critique of the homophobia that underpinned government policy and highlighted the need for a safer sex campaign that would be effective for the gay community. This specific focus allowed for a deep-cutting radical politics.

As AIDS has become a more diverse disease, affecting more communities, the politics of ACT UP have also become more diverse. The identity politics of some within the gay community and of ACT UP have given way to a broader focus that attempts to connect the issues of homophobia to racism, sexism, poverty, and drug use. However, some in ACT UP fear that as its base is broadened, becoming more inclusive, AIDS will be "de-gayed." [168] There is concern that the issues of homophobia will be silenced in the interest of creating a more inclusive politics. [169] Some members of ACT UP fear that their gay and lesbian identities will be subordinated in order to attract newer communities. However, as stated by Stephen Manning, executive director of the AIDS Commission of Toronto, "An authentic ally never demands that you cease to be yourself in order to include them." [170]

Today the statement that "AIDS is not a gay disease" is both accurate and troublesome. It speaks to the diversity of the disease: it is not limited to gays. The problem occurs when one uses this diversity to erase the fact that gay men still account for half of the AIDS cases, or when one disassociates AIDS from needs in the homosexual community. The question for many in ACT UP is whether it can "stay gay" and also become more diverse. [171] Can it build coalitions that cut through the homophobia and racism that exist within different communities affected by AIDS? Can it build an effective umbrella politics that incorporates the various radical agendas of these specific interests? Will ACT UP be allowed to speak for other communities, or will homophobia silence it? [172]

The Bush administration said that it supported equal rights, not special rights. We need a politics that does not allow this kind of caveat. However fragile, coalitions between groups are acutely needed. Between people with AIDS, cancer, heart disease, and multiple sclerosis. Between these people and groups formed out of their other identities: their race, gender, sexuality, and economic class. Although the differences are endless, politics can emerge out of what connects them.

Donna Haraway notes that because differences are "power-charged," we cannot treat our differences as though they do not create conflict. Instead, acknowledging our differences may allow us the construction of "just-barely-possible affinities" which will allow us "just-barely-possible" connection.[173] The AIDS conundrum is that we must move out from the ghetto and become deghettoized, while not forgetting any of the ghettoes.

I return here to the initial concerns of a radicalized democracy: one that recognizes universal human rights, but specifies these rights across the "power differences" that stunt their actual meaning. Identity politics can never be enough because we are ghettoized by our differences. We need to build connections, no matter how fragile, to move outside partialness.

We therefore need a revisioned and radicalized democratic politics to address AIDS. Why? Because the virus is universal and specific at the same time. It can attack anyone at the same time as it defines specific communities.

PART 3

Read Our Lipstick

Further Imaginings

SIX

Revisioning Privacy for Democracy

One can choose to rethink and reimagine democracy in any number of ways. I do this while imaging female bodies, which always have a color. Doing so locates me in the right to privacy—in the right to my body. So I feel the need to revise democracy to privilege bodily integrity and access to contraception, abortion, and health care. By starting out in the body, I mean to reconstruct the abstract individualism of rights discourse.[1]

My starting with female bodies is not exactly the same as Adrienne Rich's concern with rethinking the female body as a resource rather than a destiny, although it is close.[2] I start with bodies because political states always have an interest in them; because politics usually derive from such interests; and because, as we move increasingly toward new technologies that redefine female bodies, we must recognize these interests as utterly political. Feminists can insist on using our bodies to push out the boundaries of democratic theory.

My reenvisioning of privacy, then, starts with a recognition of female bodily integrity—in terms of health, control, and self-determination—as fundamental. Reproductive rights must be constructed as part of the matrix of hu(wo)man rights. They are absolute, much like the claim to food, shelter, and clothing. The control over one's body is not up for negotiation. I cannot imagine a time in which I would choose to give over the control of my body to someone else. This was true when I was pregnant with my daughter, and it was true when I was deciding about the appropriate treatment for my breast cancer.

In this reenvisioning of privacy, one other realm where the individual must not have to negotiate with the state is about one's sexual identity. One must always have the right to determine one's sexual orientation— free of the state. This is no one's business but the individual's.

My concern to write female bodies into democratic theory has been initiated in part by the exclusion of women's bodies from epistemology and theory and in part by the political struggle to deny women our reproductive rights. It is the political attacks against privacy rights that have led me to focus on those rights. My female body and the never-ending importance of personal and bodily boundaries have led me here as well. The changing contours of bodily space and integrity, given new reproductive technologies, underscore these issues. Because the meanings of privacy are multiple and politically constructed, feminists must struggle against attempts to restrict their meaning.

We have seen how the Rehnquist Court has attempted to conservatize democracy. The legal discourse of equality, which is necessary to actualizing one's freedom of choice, has been delegitimized. And privacy has been reprivatized. This particular kind of antidemocratic democracy has utilized an antigovernment discourse. The state has no responsibility for creating racial or sexual equality through governmental programs. Nor does it have an affirmative obligation to protect one's privacy. The Reagan and Bush administrations privatized the public sphere and publicized the private.

My radical reenvisioning of privacy rights requires that equality of access must become part of the discourse of freedom of choice specified for female bodies. The right to privacy and the right to equality are not one and the same, although each greatly affects the meaning of the other. The privatization of state services attacks the essence of one's privacy if it affects one's ability to actually obtain one's choice. After all, the right to use contraceptives has little effect if they are not available, or one cannot afford to buy condoms or a diaphragm. The rightist attack on privacy has been twofold: the legal status of privacy has been narrowed, especially in the reproductive realm of women's lives, and civil rights law has been decimated. Without a commitment to racial, sexual, and economic equality, privacy rights for women are reduced to a sham. They remain abstract rights for white, heterosexual men.

My vision of a radicalized right to privacy requires an affirmative and activist, yet noninterventionist, state. The state has to be willing to provide equal access to enable women's bodily integrity. Ensuring this integrity entails a notion of privacy that is underwritten by sexual and racial equality. Such equality is not part of the history of the constitutional right to privacy, which never included black slaves, and has never been extended to homosexuals. (It is not part of the history of the statist / totalitarian bureaucracies of Eastern Europe, either.) Constitutional protection of the right to privacy has been granted to white women and women of color in the U.S. with significant restrictions; it is the exclusive right of those with the ability to utilize it.

Neoconservatives within the Bush administration embraced privacy in its negative sense: one must be protected from government; one is not entitled to anything from the government, such as a Medicaid-funded abortion. Although privacy doctrine holds out the promise of a severe critique of governmental invasion of individual rights, it has instead been used as a justification for government privatization. As the state has become more privatized, society has become less equal, and privacy rights have become encoded racially and sexually along economic lines. It is from this complex of multiple meanings that I want to retrieve the idea of privacy for democratic theory.

RADICALIZING PRIVACY AND THE DISCOURSE OF RIGHTS

For me, democracy means individual freedom, which requires privacy of and for bodies as well as social, economic, political, sexual, racial, and gender equality. It does not mean rugged individualism as envisioned by Hobbes or Locke, or by John Stuart Mill, for that matter. It is a commitment to the individual, nevertheless—to an individual who has social connections and commitments but also autonomy. This conception of equality does not mean that everyone must be treated the same, but that everyone must be treated fairly, while recognizing individual diversity. This construction of individuality and equality necessitates a recognition of individual differences.

Key to this vision of democracy are freedom for our uniqueness and equality for our similarity. We need freedom for individuals, and we need the various kinds of access that allow us to enjoy our freedom. For lack of a better or more precise language, we need a little bit of liberalism (the unrelenting focus on the individual) and a little bit of socialism (a commitment to equality between people).

Individual freedom and a right to privacy go hand in hand. Privacy as a concept connotes a preoccupation with the individual's right to be free: to be free from others' invasions, to be free from an interventionist

state. It connotes the tremendously subversive and radical notion of the
sovereignty of the individual and one's right to be left alone. Supposedly, we must be free to be different; be free to speak our minds; be free
from bodily harm. This radical vision of privacy has never been actual-
ized in liberal democratic society, or even fully theorized. It is because
of its radical dimensions that privacy has always been restricted and
qualified by the interests of the state.

The radical side of privacy is not without its problems. Liberal theorists have always recognized this fact. Individuals cannot be completely free to do what they want, with no regard for the impact of their
actions on others. Privacy, by definition, recognizes the tension between
individual and collective needs. The boundaries between individuals and
states are fragile, resulting in the troublesome tension between state
neglect and state interventionism.

Because the concept of privacy focuses unabashedly on the individual, it makes both Marxists and neoconservatives uncomfortable, albeit
for different reasons. Traditional Marxists reject the very idea of autonomous individuals. Rightists do, too, but from an utterly different viewpoint: that of religion. Neoconservatives attempt to restrict the construction of privacy as a constitutional right because there are no inherent
restrictions to privacy. The very existence of restrictions on privacy speaks
to the subversive aspects of a nonrestricted understanding of it.

Many feminists and other progressives have argued that the right to
privacy is an insufficient basis on which to establish the rights of women
to control their own bodies or the rights of homosexuals to choose their
sexual expression. Some argue that privacy doctrine is misguided and
flawed by definition, that its meaning and its continual restructuring
will always rest with the state.

In contrast to this position, Elizabeth Fox-Genovese, a self-pro-
claimed Marxist and feminist, criticizes what she terms the absolutist
individualism of feminism. She argues that feminists fail "to develop a
notion of individual right as a product of collective life"; that feminism
reflects the "excesses of individualism" that deny the needs of society.
The "right to choice," in her view, reflects a misguided notion of "wom-
en's absolute right to their own bodies."[3] One wonders what social
needs would make her willing to give up her rights to her own body.

Rosalind Petchesky has a much different approach. For her, the
problem is not that feminist politics embraces privacy and the right to
choice, but that feminists must insist on enlarging the right to privacy
to include the social changes and public efforts that will make choice

real for all women. Rather than rejecting "rights" theory, Petchesky asks that we extend its individualist moorings to a recognition of "social rights."[4] Such recognition will require a rethreading of privacy through an affirmative discourse that deprivatizes the state and assigns it responsibility for creating access to medical care, prenatal care, drug treatment programs, abortion, and other necessities.

An absent, privatized, yet interventionist moralist state will not do. A radicalized notion of privacy requires a noninterventionist state in the realm of private choice, and an activist one in creating and enabling the host of options from which one makes a choice. In more traditional language, we need freedom from the state in order to be free to choose, and we need equality that is open even to the most vulnerable in order to protect privacy.

I argue, cautiously, for a state that is affirmatively friendly to women and families.[5] I do not mean to glorify or misrepresent the troublesome history of state invasion into the lives of women, especially poor women. But it is also necessary to recognize the firm hold of the current discourse of state privatization. It forms the backdrop for my discussion of public responsibility and state activism on behalf of women.[6]

My radical vision of privacy, defined as the individual's freedom to choose and the ability to get what one chooses, lands me squarely in the uncomfortable terrain of defending liberal rights discourse while critiquing it. Individuals need privacy from unwanted interference from the state, yet sometimes individuals need assistance from the state in order to get what they need, and in such cases a noninterventionist state is insufficient. Privacy is *always* needed but is never enough.[7]

I inscribe the liberal notion of privacy with an egalitarian text that does not assume sameness as a standard, but rather recognizes a radically pluralist individuality. Radical pluralism means that differences are not ordered hierarchically; they are not set up as oppositions; they are not tied up with, or reflective of, power relations.[8] They merely reflect diversity.

The radical premise of privacy rights derives from their universal meaning in a society where discrimination exists. Because not all individuals are treated equally in the first place, privacy allows for a radical critique of its own violations. Liberal democratic discourse promises, rather than actually extends, the right of privacy to all. This is where the critique of liberalism begins. The promise of universality must be made real by extending privacy equally to all persons. Liberal discourse as promissory will not do. The most frightening thing about a neoconservative moralism is that it rejects the promise of universality from the start. Once one enters this discourse, there is no space for radical critique.

Defining the relationship between privacy and publicness frames conflicts between liberals and neoconservatives. How much freedom does the individual have from the state? How much responsibility does the state have to the individual? How much does the state need to limit an individual's right to privacy for the sake of the community? Liberal Democrats focus on the rights of individuals to privacy from the state, while radical rightists and neoconservatives focus on the responsibilities of individuals for themselves. Neither view highlights the importance of inscribing privacy with sexual and racial equality. Nor does either specify privacy for female bodies. Both actually specify the opposite.

Conflict over the parameters of privatization also exists within neoconservatism. Whereas neoconservatives in the Republican Party were pushed to yield on these issues to the radical rightists, neoconservatives within the Democratic Party have had to contend with "old-style" liberals like Jesse Jackson. The outcome of these struggles will define the next decade. Bill Clinton alluded to this process in the 1992 campaign: "Our policies are neither liberal nor conservative, neither Democratic nor Republican. They are new."[9]

However new these ideas might seem, they are highly interlaced with the old. White, able-bodied, youthful heterosexual males have more rights to privacy than do most others. They need less assistance in the creation of choices and possibilities. Women need a special type of privacy because they have the potential to have an unwanted pregnancy. As Rosalind Petchesky argues, the notion of "my body belonging to me" descends from the radical strains of Western democratic theory of self-ownership. Such self-ownership is necessary in order to participate fully as a member of society.[10]

REVIEWING PRIVACY AND PUBLICNESS

The notion of privacy develops, shifts, and changes in relationship to the way the world changes,[11] particularly in terms of how the understanding between private and public space is negotiated.[12] Each realm is defined in and against the other. The difference between them creates an uneasy tension. Today, in the United States, privacy rights concentrate in the realms of sexuality, family, and procreation. In the Roman Empire, when abortion and infanticide of slaves' children were common and perfectly legal practices,[13] public and private domains were delineated differently. Current shifts in the interpretation of privacy are evident in the abortion controversy. In this context, definitions of body, person, human being, and fetus construct and limit notions of women's privacy.

The meaning of privacy changes according to the meaning of publicness. There are multiple private spheres—such as family, church, and home—and multiple public spheres—such as the official economy, the state apparatus, and arenas of public discourse.[14] All of these spheres overlap. Increasingly, the mass media define a dominant arena of public life; television presents a vision of publicness through talk-show audiences that speak of "private" matters.[15] Issues once thought of as private are open to public discussion, which begins to transform the meaning of privacy for both realms.

Alida Brill argues that the common-sense notion of privacy has turned into everybody's business, in order, perhaps, to make it nobody's business.[16] The meanings of privacy in terms of abortion and the right to die, for example, are now open to public debate. In complicated ways, privacy is being reformulated as a public issue.

Although the very definition of privacy has always implicated its relation to publicness, and the personal realm has always been defined in and through political realms, these relations became more public as the Reagan-Bush state increasingly declared its moral authority to intervene in questions once perceived as private. The state became more active in declaring its pro-childbirth, antiabortion stance as the preferred morality.

New technologies shift our understanding and perceptions, particularly when they are placed within the framework of neoconservative moralism. Petchesky has argued that fetal imagery has redefined the notion of privacy for women: women's bodily integrity is misrepresented through images of fetuses that portray the fetus as independent and a person unto itself, rather than a part of a woman's body.[17] Donna Haraway argues that as boundaries become newly permeable to both "visualization" and "intervention," rights to privacy become dependent upon those who are in a position "to control the interpretation of bodily boundaries."[18]

I have argued throughout that neoconservatives narrow the radical implications of the discourse of individualism. From a much different direction, feminists and gay rights activists have politicized privacy in order to depoliticize it in the end. Abortion, up until the mid-nineteenth

century, was for the most part an uncontested issue. But throughout the
Reagan and Bush years, it was a main site for declaring the moral stance
of the state. These shifts and boundary moves weave confusion, particularly between the discourse of individual privacy and the discourse of
the privatized role of the state.

Public consciousness reveals this confusion. The United States public
is inconsistent and variable in its understanding of the relationship between individual privacy and sexual and racial equality. A majority of
the people think that a woman has the private right to decide whether
or not to have an abortion. A majority also think that public funding
and public hospitals should be available for abortion services. However, the connection between access and privacy is less clear in the realm
of civil rights and job opportunities, where the prevailing concept of the
privatized state appears to have gained acceptance through the discourse of reverse discrimination.

PRIVATIZATION OF THE U.S. STATE: A POLITICS OF DISINVESTMENT

I turn now to the politics of disinvestment in the United States economy,
government deregulation, and the rhetoric of "choice" as integral to
this process of privatization. Although the politics of racialized patriarchy and disinvestment in the economy have different specific priorities,
they are of a piece. They articulate the same antigovernment, anti-tax
stance.

Neoconservative politics have redefined the relationship between the
individual and the state so that the responsibility of the state to the
individual is lessened while the "moral" prerogative and authority of
the state are enlarged. State functions that were previously delegated as
public duties have shifted to private organizations, where the market
defines the level of response.[19] Government has become less responsible
for people's well-being: for public transportation, public health, and
much more.

The 1992 presidential campaign was fought on this complicated terrain. Whereas the Bush campaign defended the Reagan-Bush decade of
privatization, Clinton and Gore spoke of a "new covenant," in which
government would help rebuild the country. Clinton spoke of the need
for a national strategy of public investment in the economy's infrastructure. He spoke of the need to encourage private investment; rebuild
schools; create affordable, quality health care; make taxes fair to the

middle class; and protect the environment. At the same time, he also spoke of the need for "more empowerment and less entitlement."[20] Both political parties, to differing degrees, remained locked in an anti-government, anti-tax rhetoric.

The politics of government privatization are firmly in place. They have both accompanied and exacerbated a troubled national and international economy. Economist Arthur MacEwan has traced the downward spiraling of the United States economy since the loss of the Vietnam War in the 1970s. Up until that period, more than 26 percent of the Gross National Product (GNP) was spent on domestic programs. Public spending on roads, schools, and other aspects of the infrastructure of society remained at these levels until the U.S. economy began to decline and the trade deficit grew. As the economy declined, the demands upon government by business increased considerably.[21]

According to economist Robert Heilbroner, the gravest problem facing the United States today is the inadequacy of public capital. Due to a lack of such capital, the infrastructure of streets, highways, bridges, tunnels, airports, and water and sewage systems has been steadily deteriorating for the past twenty years. What is needed is an "extensive program of public capital construction." Heilbroner argues that such public spending can be achieved through diverting money from the military, through borrowing, and through taxation.[22] David Alan Aschauer argues that such public expenditures would not only provide needed infrastructure repair but would also increase productivity within the private sector. Public investment in roads, bridges, mass transit, and the like is essential to private-sector productivity. The two spheres need each other to be healthy.[23]

No such public investment was ever endorsed by Bush. Instead, taxes were used to bail out the savings and loan associations, which had misused their funds for private speculation. Moreover, these taxes were levied on the United States public in unfair ways. Between 1966 and 1985, the effective tax rate for the richest 1 percent of taxpayers fell by at least 27 percent. Recent data show that the richest 1 percent of American families enjoyed most of the gains from the past decade. The 1980s were "a very good time for the very rich."[24] By the end of the decade, the top 1 percent of American households together had more wealth than the bottom 90 percent of Americans combined.[25]

The anti-tax talk of the Reagan and Bush administrations may have sounded good to a great many people trying to keep taxes down in order to increase their limited incomes. Yet the group who benefited the most were the wealthy, who needed it the least. Meanwhile, the poverty rate in the United States rose sharply: 2.1 million more people were living in poverty in 1990 than the previous year.[26] The increase in poverty further problematized the process of state privatization.

Benjamin Friedman argues that the economic deficit spending during the Reagan years, as well as the lowering of taxes for the rich, may have been part of a larger program to force the "permanent reduction" of governmental responsibility in the service sector. These actions may reflect "the deliberate curtailment of the nation's economic growth in order to preclude the next generation of Americans from using government for social purposes."[27] In this scenario, government debt was the linchpin in a wider neoconservative program. In this reading, the lack of a coherent federal policy for crucial problems such as AIDS, drug treatment, and the homeless can be viewed as a part of the process of disinvestment in the economy: in industry, education, roads, bridges, scientific research, and other kinds of government-based infrastructures.[28]

Robert Reich, now the main strategist for Clinton's economic policy, has argued more aggressively that disinvestment in the United States economy was deliberate and had devastating effects. According to Reich, federal funds for training and retraining workers dropped by more than 50 percent during the 1980s. He argues that Americans, especially wealthy Americans, are not overtaxed; that in 1989 they paid less in taxes (about 30 percent of the GNP) than do the other citizens of any other industrialized country. Nor does the United States government overspend, according to Reich. If one excludes defense, the combined spending of state, local, and federal governments as a percentage of the country's GNP is lower than the government spending of any other industrialized country. By the late 1980s, the United States government spent less than Sweden, Norway, Japan, Denmark, Austria, and Canada on non-defense items.[29]

Whereas former President Bush said we have the will, but not the wallet, Reich contends that we must find the wallet. He argues that we must develop an educated work force and first-class transportation and communication systems. Instead, since the early 1980s, little spending has been directed in these areas. The United States has not maintained or created new infrastructure; the United States has not built a new airport since 1974. Reich argues that debt created by investing in our future wealth is necessary at this point, which is quite different than creating debt for greater consumption, as was done throughout the 1980s.[30]

Presidents Reagan and Bush oversaw and orchestrated the idea that the welfare state is the enemy, because it has wasted our money. They demanded that we look instead to private individuals and institutions, which can do better. "By and large, government should be limited to policing the streets and protecting the national security."[31] The process of privatization they put in place not only reduced public spending in the public realm and shrank public services but also redistributed scarce public resources into private hands. The public sphere, except for defense, received fewer public funds, and the private sphere, more.

Some analysts, such as David Osborne and Ted Baebler, argue that government must become more entrepreneurial, by which they mean that it needs to become decentralized and competitive, and create more choice in the process. Osborne and Baebler argue that we need our own American *perestroika*.[32] Yet they seem to ignore politics in this process. Although they say they do not mean simply to privatize government functions, they leave the way open to do just that.

Bush's rhetoric on public education also reflected the politics of privatization. He postured: "Throwing money at the schools will help nothing." The imagery is telling. One wonders who has ever thrown money at the schools? He applauded a partial privatization of the school system through a strategy he called "choice": individuals and families should be able to choose their schools, creating an element of competition between schools as incentive to improve themselves. Tax dollars might even be used for private schools in this scheme. Former Education Secretary Lamar Alexander endorsed this model, telling Americans that they were the only ones who could fix their schools. In the end, "you've got to save yourself."[33]

Robert Crain of Columbia University Teacher's College viewed this plan critically. "In any choice plan, the families who have the least resources in terms of information, energy and money will be left behind."[34] The educational system already suffers from the process of governmental privatization; inequities have grown and deepened.

The process of school privatization was well under way by the end of the Bush administration. Christopher Whittle's plan to develop an innovative private school system to create "choice" for parents who are unhappy with the public schools was a major step toward the destruction of public education as we have known it in the United States. Whittle, along with Benno C. Schmidt, a former president of Yale University who now heads the Edison Project, argue that competition from private schools is the only way to force change in the public schools.[35]

Millions of children go to school suffering from the "insidious effects of poverty and lack of access to regular health care."[36] As a result, 12 percent of the children in the United States are said to be learning-disabled before they even start school. A system of "choice" amidst this inequity would merely reproduce the inequalities surrounding choices. These parents can barely afford to supply nutritious food for their children, let alone tackle the additional burdensome price tag of private school. Bush's late-term decision to sign the bill increasing federal spending for preschool children in the Head Start program—while applauding privatization throughout public education—made clear that there was a crisis at hand.[37]

No part of everyday life has been untouched by the insidious process of privatizing the state. A highly privatized health care system and its spiraling costs created a crisis for millions of Americans as the government dismantled programs for the poor. Millions of Americans are without health insurance. During the Bush administration, measles once again became a problem among poor children for lack of a universal immunization program. Preschool children—particularly the poor in the New York City region—came to have a worse immunization record against measles and other diseases than children in countries like Uganda and Mexico.[38] A tuberculosis epidemic took hold as a result of searing budget cuts in public health programs. The lack of public housing created a record number of homeless people throughout the country.

By the end of the Reagan-Bush years, efforts were underfoot to privatize an even wider range of former government services. President Bush issued an executive order making it easier for state and local officials to sell public properties like airports, bridges, and roads to private businesses.[39] The city of Chicago began contracting for vehicle towing and parking ticket collection. Phoenix fostered competition between government and private services for street sweeping, garbage collection, and ambulance service.[40] In New York State parks, visitors now have to carry out their own garbage: because there is no trash collection, there are no longer public garbage receptacles.

Part and parcel of this process of government privatization has been the limiting of access, which has even extended to the gathering and dissemination of information. James Ridgeway noted that governmental cutbacks necessitated first a moratorium on new federal publications, then a reduction of their number, and finally a shifting of control of government publications to the private sector. The government became heavily dependent on private sources for even the knowledge it needs to govern. Information was privatized.[41]

Deregulation by government of industries such as the airlines and the limiting of its role as watchdog of industry was also a part of the process of privatization. The deregulation was partial and capricious. The arenas of military, defense, and law enforcement remained largely untouched. The savings and loan industry was bailed out at a minimum estimated cost of $500 billion.[42] The banks were said to be also in need of government assistance.

Meanwhile, the economy continued to stagnate. There were mergers, acquisitions, and junk bonds at the same time as there were continuous "upper bracket tax reductions."[43] The very rich got richer, while the government *claimed* it got poorer. More to the point, income distribution became more unequal: white households today are typically ten times more wealthy than black households.[44]

The inconsistent privatization affected people differently according to their relationship to specific spheres of the state. The dismantling of the social welfare state affected the poor most directly. It had particular impact on women in that they, along with their children, are disproportionately poor; they are the key recipients of the social service state, and they have been heavily employed in the state's service sector.[45]

Given the large increase in the number of single-parent black families headed by a woman,[46] the percentage of women of color who are on welfare or receiving assistance is higher than that of white women. Variations in the poverty rate and in family structures account for these differences. Privatization has hit women of color more acutely, both in terms of losing benefits and in terms of state intervention. If one is dependent on state programs, one is more easily kept under surveillance. It is also a terrible reality that a growing number of children are finding themselves parentless as inner-city families collapse under the added pressures of drugs, jail terms, and deaths related to AIDS.[47]

Although the privatization of the state has affected poor people more than others, very few have been able to escape its effect completely. Anyone who travels in a car can find oneself stranded in traffic while being routed away from roads in disrepair. Anyone who travels on commercial airlines can find oneself unable to find a flight that goes directly to one's destination. Anyone who sends one's children to public schools can be dissatisfied to find out that there are not enough teachers, textbooks, or computers. Anyone who needs a drug prevention program for oneself, a child, or a loved one can feel the sting of unavailability of social services. People suffer differently from privatization according to their economic class, sexual preference, race, and gender. But to the extent that almost everyone—except the incredibly rich— must frequently enter public places and spaces in their everyday lives, the effects of the diminishing responsibility of the state to provide services or access to them will have a significant impact.

Let me return to the specific case of how the politics of privatization affect abortion. Privatization and moral absolutism have been in effect in this arena since the rulings in *Maher v. Roe* in 1977 and *Harris v. McRae* in 1980 declared state funding for abortion unconstitutional.[48] These rulings directly affected poor women in need of public assistance. The *Webster* decision further privatized the state's role in abortion, affecting a much broader base of women. The restrictiveness of abortion law impacts any woman living in an anti-choice state. It affects any woman needing a late-term abortion. It affects teenagers needing parental consent.

PRIVACY AS A CONTINGENT RIGHT GRANTED BY THE STATE

The restrictions on privacy related to the procreative rights of women reflect a series of negotiations between state interests and individual women's rights. *Roe v. Wade* in 1973 made quite clear the political construction of the right to privacy: the right is not absolute. A woman is not free "to terminate her pregnancy at whatever time, in whatever way, and for whatever reason she alone chooses." The Court found that "this right of privacy . . . is broad enough to encompass a woman's decision whether or not to terminate her pregnancy," but that it does not constitute an unqualified right.[49]

State interests define the contours of privacy. There is no "unlimited right to do with one's body as one pleases."[50] The zone of privacy extends to women's reproductive choices, but remains restricted. The restrictions on women's reproductive choices are defined by a liberal democratic and patriarchal state. The "liberal" dimension of the state extends the rights of privacy to women as individuals. The "patriarchal" aspect of the state extends these rights to women as though they were men. Women's privacy is restrictive; it is not defined as a right to reproductive freedom.

The right to privacy, interpreted as a right to be left alone, first gained currency in 1890 with an article authored by Samuel Warren and Louis Brandeis (later to be appointed to the Supreme Court), entitled "The Right to Privacy."[51] Nevertheless, critics such as the unconfirmed Supreme Court nominee Robert Bork have argued that the right to privacy has been plucked out of thin air—that it is a new, undefined, unconstitutional right.[52] Law professor Jed Rubenfeld responds that the right to privacy is a constitutional right because the Constitution is the document that establishes democracy. It is inherent in the document because the state is implicated in private life, and we need privacy from the state. The right to privacy "is not the freedom to do certain particular acts determined to be fundamental. . . . It is the fundamental freedom to not have one's life too totally determined by a progressively more normalizing state."[53] He argues that other, specified constitutional rights establish the general status of privacy.

Privacy rights are often set within the legal context of the due process clause of the Fourteenth Amendment, which says that no state shall "deprive any person of life, liberty, or property, without due process of law; nor deny to any person within its jurisdiction the equal protection of the laws." The Fourth and Fifth Amendments are also used to justify the construction of privacy. Privacy was extended to childrearing in *Pierce v. Society of Sisters* (1925); to procreation in *Skinner v. Oklahoma* (1942); to the use of contraceptives in marital sexual intercourse in *Griswold v. Connecticut* (1965); to the use of contraceptives in nonmarital sexual intercourse in *Eisenstadt v. Baird* (1972); and to abortion in the first trimester in *Roe v. Wade* (1973).[54]

Griswold established the notion that privacy was to be construed as a "peripheral right"; it made other, more specifically noted rights more secure. Using the Fifth Amendment's self-incrimination clause, the Court stated that a citizen could create "a zone of privacy which the government may not force him to surrender." In other words, although privacy may not be expressly stated, it is understood as "necessary in making the express guarantees fully meaningful." *Griswold* established, through the use of *Boyd v. United States* (1886), that the individual is protected against "all governmental invasions 'of the sanctity of a man's home and the privacies of life.' " The use of contraceptives in marital relations lies within the "zone of privacy created by several fundamental constitutional guarantees," and any government regulation "invades the area of protected freedoms."[55]

Justice Goldberg, in a concurring opinion, stated that although the constitution does not name the right of privacy in marriage, "I cannot believe that it offers these fundamental rights no protection." He argued that marital privacy was on a par with other fundamental rights already specifically protected. He distinguishes marital privacy from adultery or homosexuality, which are "sexual intimacies which the state forbids." The intimacy of husband and wife is not to be regulated.[56]

Justice Hugo Black, in his dissent, argued that there is no right to privacy per se; that instead there are "specific constitutional provisions which are designed in part to protect privacy at certain times and places with respect to certain activities."[57] He rejects the comprehensive and broad right of privacy, which he argues can be too easily misconstrued. But the notion of marital privacy was upheld by the Court again in *Eisenstadt v. Baird* (1972). Privacy was declared to be a "right of the individual, married or single, to be free from unwarranted governmental intrusion into matters so fundamentally affecting a person as the decision whether to rear or beget a child."[58]

If *Griswold* established a right to privacy, *Bowers v. Hardwick* (1986) clarified its limitations: privacy is restricted to heterosexual sex inside marriage. *Bowers* makes clear that privacy is not a generalized construct without limits: that privacy is "given" by the state and can be either granted or not. In a 5–4 decision, the Court held that the Georgia statute criminalizing homosexual sodomy, even if consensual, was constitutional.[59] The *Bowers* decision makes clear that there is no constitutional right of privacy for homosexuals. Privacy-based arguments do not support those who have no recognized right to privacy.

Justice White, writing for the court in Bowers, stated that privacy applies to the realms of marriage, procreation, and (heterosexual) family relationships. Homosexual activity remains outside these spheres and therefore exists outside the scope of privacy doctrine.[60] Justice Warren Burger, concurring in the decision, states that "there is no such thing as a fundamental right to commit homosexual sodomy."[61] Justice Harry Blackmun, in his dissent, stated that the question was not whether the federal Constitution conferred "a fundamental right to engage in homosexual sodomy," but rather whether it conferred the "most comprehensive of rights . . . namely, 'the right to be left alone.'" Blackmun criticizes the court for refusing to recognize "the fundamental interest all individuals have in controlling the nature of their intimate associations with others."[62]

Privacy as a construct of the state has clear limits that can be added or taken away. The dilemma of privacy is that the state should not have the last word on who gets to have privacy, and yet the state must play a role in affirming its actual availability. In constitutional doctrine, the right to privacy is recognized in the realms of the bodily integrity and personal autonomy of heterosexuals.[63] Privacy also locates us with the "network of decisions relating to the conditions under which sex is permissible . . . the social institutions surrounding sexual relations, and the procreative consequences of sex."[64] Reproductive issues are at the heart of the right to privacy, because they involve issues of bodily integrity which are deeply connected to our individual autonomy.[65] Privacy demands that a woman have the right to choose the circumstances of her reproductive life. Jed Rubenfeld argues that the denial of privacy in this realm is a "totalitarian intervention into a woman's life."[66]

The everyday discourse of privacy has come to have much more radical meaning than its constitutional rendering ever intended. Rather than being envisioned as a partial and restricted right *granted* by the state, privacy is more often understood as an individual right that supersedes the interests of the state. This view underlies much of the popular support for abortion rights, however variable and confused this support may sometimes be. A majority of the American public are more ready to restrict state interference than to limit individual privacy. I do not mean to overstate the radicalism of popular notions of privacy, which can have a conservative side, as manifested in taxpayers' revolts and anti-welfare sentiments. Such notions can coexist with very contradictory discourses, such as the opinion that women who get abortions or delay pregnancy are selfish.

To the extent that the right to abortion has been constructed as a right to privacy, it operates in popular discourse as though it is fundamental to women's freedom of choice. So even though the right to abortion was initially constructed in and through a restrictive posture, the restrictions on it often appear as assaults on freedom of choice. This complex posture may in the end save *Roe*. But I do not want to make too much of the power of public discourse, particularly since the present Court seems so at ease with ignoring it. So let us stay for the moment with the restrictive side of abortion doctrine.

Although *Roe v. Wade* protects a woman from undue interference with her freedom to choose an abortion, it does not prevent a state from encouraging childbirth over abortion. Nor does one's right to choose an abortion translate into a constitutional obligation for the state to subsidize abortion.[67] After all, Congress has no constitutional responsibility to subsidize health care.[68] These limitations on the access to abortion greatly clarify the economic bias of privacy rights: women who can afford to pay for their own abortions have a right to their privacy; other women do not. As we saw reiterated in *Webster,* the due process clause does not establish "entitlement."

But these restrictions are not inherent to privacy in a conceptual sense. Rather, they are part of the political negotiations that have established the control of the state over women's bodies. There is no inherent reason why privacy cannot be an unlimited right in the realm of procreative choice; there are only political reasons. And these reasons—which are based in the privatization of public responsibilities by the state—extend beyond the abortion debate.

The Rehnquist Court has little interest in expanding the right of individual privacy any further than it has already been expanded. Some on the Court, like Justices Rehnquist and Scalia, seek to narrow and curtail its meaning further. And they have successfully done so in the post-*Webster* period. Decisions of the Court involving issues of prisoner rights and the rights of defendants also reflect a narrowed vision of privacy. At the same time, a moralistic, interventionist stance has dominated the Court's expansive reading of the state's power over the individual, whether it be controlling the freedom of speech of a nude dancer or limiting the right of the individual to view child pornography.[69]

The issue of privacy has come before the Court in many guises. Chief Justice Rehnquist, in *Deshaney v. Winnebago County Department of Social Services* (1989), argued that the "due process clauses generally confer no affirmative right to governmental aid." The purpose of the clause is "to protect the people from the State, not to ensure that the State protects them from each other."[70] There is no guarantee of any minimal level of safety or security.

In this case, Joshua Deshaney, who lived with his father and was repeatedly beaten by him, was not removed from the home by the local social service agency even though the agency was monitoring the situation. As a result of the beatings, the child now suffers from permanent brain damage and is profoundly retarded. Joshua's mother sued. Rehnquist, writing for the Court, stated that there is no government responsibility to provide members of the general public with adequate protective services. To find otherwise would require an "expansive reading of the constitutional text."[71] Privacy defines the rights of the individual to be free from the interference of the state. It does not define any responsibility of the state to the individual.

There have been other variations on this theme. In *Cruzan v. Director, Missouri Department of Health* (1990), Nancy Cruzan's parents asked for the right to allow their daughter, who existed in a vegetative state connected to life support systems, the right to die. The Cruzans tried to establish that disconnecting the support systems would be Nancy's wish if she were able to communicate it. The issue of bodily integrity was essential to this case: whether Nancy Cruzan had the right to control her own body, free from restraint or interference. The Court found that although "every . . . adult . . . has a right to determine what shall be done with his own body," and although the state's interest weakens and the individual's right to privacy grows as the degree of bodily invasion increases, there was no way without a living will to clearly identify Nancy Cruzan's actual wishes. Expressed intent was key to the Court in this situation.[72]

The right to privacy was not challenged in this case. Rather, the issue was defined in terms of how one can know someone else's private wishes. Nevertheless, Rehnquist's decision for the Court resonates with much of the skepticism about privacy rights reflected in antiabortion and "right to life" rhetoric. In the Cruzan case, Rehnquist argued that life—even vegetative life—should always be privileged. Law professor Ronald Dworkin suggests that Rehnquist assumes that nothing is lost if Nancy Cruzan is kept alive, and something is lost if she dies.[73] Although Rehnquist is writing of a comatose person, it seems likely that his privileging of the sanctity of life as an inherent good, whatever its quality or status, extends to the fetus in the case of abortion.

Justice John Paul Stevens dissented from Rehnquist's position: "Lives do not exist in abstraction from persons. . . . A State that seeks to demonstrate its commitment to life may do so by aiding those who are actively struggling for life and health." He argued that mere life, defined as physical existence, must be distinguished from personhood. Implicated in Stevens's dissent are the ever-changing definitions of and relations between public and private life as they affect the appropriate role of the state. He argues that medical advances have altered the physiological aspects of death through a merger of body and machine.[74] People are less likely to die at home, and more likely to die in public spaces like hospitals or nursing homes. What was once private is now under institutional control. Our judgments about privacy must shift accordingly.

NEW TECHNOLOGIES AND THE
CHANGING CONTOURS OF THE BODY

Scientific discoveries and new technologies have changed not only how we die but also how we are born and how we think about the very process of pregnancy. These shifts clearly affect the way one understands privacy rights, especially in terms of bodily integrity for women in the reproductive realm. Concepts such as "biological mother," once easy to define, have become complicated by technological innovations that can separate the egg donor from the gestational mother as well as from the social mother who rears the child. The parameters of women's bodies become more complex as eggs are fertilized in test tubes and embryos are frozen or transplanted from one woman to another.

At the same time as right-wing and neoconservative forces are using these new developments to combat the rights of women, the shifting nature and meaning of the body and of reproductive concerns provide an open window to the politics involved in defining privacy. The struggle to control our bodies—whether it is to keep them healthy, or to fight against disease, or to end an unwanted pregnancy, or to become fertile if infertile, or even to choose death over endless physical suffering—is at the core of our autonomy. Its very importance explains why the state attempts to control the contours of this struggle.

Technology is always embedded in established societal and political relations and reflects the priorities embodied in those relations. Science and technology are merely part of the web of politics rather than objective and neutral forces. As such, technology also creates new relationships. So it both extends prevailing ideas into new realms and creates new ways of thinking and being which unsettle the old. A new technology—whether it be the computer, the VCR, embryo transplants, or the birth control pill—initiates and defines new social relations, with the attendant complications.

Because technological exploration and innovation always take place within the existing arrangements of power, legal struggles are often initiated in order to legitimize the preferred social relationship. Issues of privacy, property, and copyright are unsettled by technologies such as machine copying and FAX transmissions. Because technological innovations affect the relations of the body and the concept of its ownership, such innovations unsettle existing conceptions of privacy. Bodies and their privacy are in enormous flux as the contours of self and other get redrawn technologically as well as politically. The legal struggles over abortion, over surrogate parenting, and over fetal rights reflect these concerns in the reproductive realm.

Shoshana Zuboff states that "technology represents intelligence systematically applied to the problem of the body." Technology attempts to deal with the body's vulnerability and is often sought as a substitute for bodily presence. Zuboff's discussion focuses on how technology displaces the individual in the workplace—both the factory and the office—and how "computer-based automation continues to displace the human body and its know-how."[75] This displacement of human labor forms a societal backdrop to any discussion of reproductive technologies that seek to control and further enhance the body. The birth control pill, for example, by establishing greater control over unwanted pregnancy, redefined sexual practices and relationships connected with them. Technology is inherently destabilizing. It attempts to control or extend the body (represented as nature); as it does so, technology unsettles existing relations expressing the body. The state's interests, such as its interests in contraception or abortion, establish the political interests that in turn define technological innovation. The self and privacy are redefined in this politico-technical process.

Through the years, science has increased our knowledge and control of sexual reproduction through contraceptive and noncoital reproductive techniques.[76] It is now possible to take preventive measures against pregnancy, and it is also possible to use new forms of insemination. Various contraceptive techniques—birth control pills, condoms, diaphragms, spermicidal jellies—have been developed for greater control over our reproductive bodies. The erratic and changing political context that surrounds these developments has had great impact on contraceptive and reproductive technologies.

Governmental support of the scientific community in the realm of contraceptive and reproductive research remained inadequate throughout the 1980s. Since the early 1960s, new contraceptive research in the United States has been minimal. The Reagan and Bush administrations blocked the distribution and sale of RU 486, an antiprogesterone steroid pill developed in France that can end a pregnancy up to three weeks after a missed menstrual period. The pill has been approved for use in France, Sweden, the Netherlands, and other countries for years.[77] It took the FDA years to approve a condom for use by women; meanwhile, it was easily available in England. The control of contraceptive choice was very much a part of the right-wing political agenda of the 1980s.

So was control of reproductive choice. Technological developments such as artificial insemination, external fertilization, embryo transfer, and surrogate motherhood have altered notions of a woman's body. In vitro fertilization takes place outside a woman's body. The freezing of embryos allows for their sustenance outside a woman's body. Any notion of privacy based on bodily integrity simply does not apply here. The parameters of a woman's body have been extended beyond her corporeal self. Such technological developments necessitate new legal definitions. These definitions can permit government interventions that were previously unknown, interventions that pose new challenges for women's right to bodily privacy.[78]

Science and the differing politics that surround it have brought women both more control and less control as they have created an open window on the embryo.[79] John Robertson argues that in vitro fertilization brings "the formerly invisible process of fertilization and early embryonic development into view." "Extracorporeal" conception and embryo storage redefine the boundaries between self (woman) and other (embryo).[80] Rosalind Petchesky notes that ultrasound images of fetuses have been used to create a vision of a "public fetus" removed from pregnant women's bodies. The fetal images "float like spirits through the courtrooms, where lawyers argue that foetuses can claim tort liability; through the hospitals and clinics, where physicians welcome them as 'patients'; and in front of all the abortion centers, legislative committees, bus terminals, and other places that 'right-to-lifers' haunt."[81]

The legal status of the embryo and the fetus became a central concern of antiabortion activists. In September 1989, a Tennessee state court, against the wishes of the estranged husband (and sperm donor), granted temporary custody of seven frozen embryos to his wife, Mary Sue Davis, who had produced the eggs. The judge ruled that the stored embryos were really "human beings existing as embryos," and that "human life begins at the moment of conception."[82] In this decision, which was later appealed, the judge used the antiabortion framework to legitimize the idea that embryos, like fetuses, are human beings with rights to life.

What complicated this case further is that Mary Sue Davis's lawyer used the fetal rights argument to support her claim to the embryos, whereas her ex-husband invoked "reproductive freedom" (for himself) to defend his right not to become a parent. Tennessee's highest court ruled in June 1992 in favor of the husband, stating that "a man cannot be made to become a parent against his will." Dr. Caplan, Director of the Center for Biomedical Ethics at the University of Minnesota, notes that this decision raises the question whether other courts will extend this reasoning to women. He says it lends credibility to the popular belief that if men could get pregnant, abortion would be an uncontested right.[83] The reproductive rights of women were lost in this case; they were played back in reverse.

However distorted and complicated the case, people desire to control their own procreative options. This desire provides a starting point for reconceptualizing privacy rights in the reproductive realm. John Robertson argues that the "freedom to have sex without reproduction does not guarantee freedom to have reproduction without sex." Full reproductive freedom includes the freedom to reproduce or not reproduce, and to do either by whatever means one chooses. Procreative freedom must allow for the possible separation of the genetic, gestational, and social components of reproduction. Separating and recombining these components in new ways is seen as subversive to present notions of family, upon which the authority of the state rests.[84]

Because it is the infertile who need new procreative technologies, it is important to be clear what is at stake here. Infertility is as much a societal and economic problem as a biological one. The problem of infertility often reflects problems of poverty, work place health, general nutrition, and pollutants in the air and water. Infertility is disproportionately concentrated among older and poorer women, black women, women with high exposure to sexually transmitted diseases, and women with poor nutrition and low access to health care.[85]

Most of the consumers of treatments for infertility are middle- and upper-class white women. Infertility treatments are available only for those who can afford them. There is no vision of public health that requires nontoxic work places and more healthful foods. Instead, the increasing privatization of the Bush administration extended to the realm of health care and environmental regulation.

Women were not recognized as having either the right to procreate or the right to a healthy environment conducive to fertility and healthy babies. Instead, what was recognized was the "right" of the fetus. And new scientific technologies which could be used to rethink and radicalize the rights of women were used to rearticulate male privilege.

Fetal rights takes us full circle to the discourse of reverse discrimination established by Reagan and Bush. Women's rights were set against the rights of the fetus. If fetuses have the status of citizens, they need protection—from women's choice (of abortion) and from fetal neglect and abuse.[86] The fetus became a central player in the rollback of sexual equality and women's right to her bodily privacy.

FETAL RIGHTS

Procreative and reproductive rights are highly contested because they reveal that even the body and the way we think about what is "natural" can change.[87] Who gets to determine whether the fetus is a part of a woman's body or is something separate from it?

Petchesky argues that we must reclaim the fetus from the right wing and recontextualize it back into women's bodies. We must put the "foetus back into the uterus, and the uterus back into the woman's body and her body back into its social space."[88]

Dawn Johnsen states that "the fetus is a physical part of a woman."[89] It has no autonomous existence. In *Roe v. Wade,* the Court held that the fetus is not a person and thus is not entitled to due process or equal protection. The unborn do not have legal standing. Yet fetal rights, fetal abuse, and even a fetal right to health became common terms of state discourse in the 1980s.[90] Within this rhetoric, the fetus is a person with equal legal standing to that of a woman. The woman and the fetus are seen as separate and as in conflict with one another over the issue of abortion. Fetal rights deny the space of a woman's body as her own. Of course, the health of the fetus has always been of concern to the state. It was this concern that led the court in *Muller v. Oregon* (1907) to uphold legislation barring factory work for women for more than ten hours a day.[91] However, the restatement of this concern came to assume the status of personhood for the fetus.

The issue of health—either the woman's or the fetus's—obfuscates the issues at hand. As discussed earlier, throughout the 1980s the state took less and less responsibility for the health of those already born, let alone that of fetuses.[92] Instead, the issue of fetal health was used to set up an adversarial relationship between fetus and mother which required moralistic intervention by the state. The state would protect the fetus from abortion or speak for the helpless fetus of drug-addicted mothers. The fetus emerged as needing protection, while women lost their rights to privacy.

In 1986 Pamela Rae Stewart was arrested and charged with causing her infant son's death by failing to get adequate medical care during her pregnancy. She was charged with failing to protect the life of her fetus.

In 1988, in *United States v. Vaughn,* a District of Columbia woman was given a prison term for cocaine possession rather than the usual sentence of probation when the judge learned she was seven months pregnant. In 1989, Jennifer Johnson, a twenty-three-year-old black woman, was found guilty on two counts of "delivering a controlled substance to a minor" and sentenced to fifteen years' probation for delivering drugs to her fetus through the umbilical cord.[93]

Johnson had sought help for her addiction; she did not intentionally transmit cocaine to her fetus.[94] I have previously discussed how most drug treatment programs do not admit pregnant women, even though the need is great. One in ten babies born in 1988 were drug-dependent.[95] Although many pregnant women seek treatment, it is denied to them.[96]

Almost one-third of all women and one-half of black women who gave birth in 1985 did not receive adequate prenatal care.[97] As a result of lack of care, 13 percent of African American children born in 1988 were low–birth weight babies, according to the Children's Defense Fund. These babies have a much higher risk of developing learning disabilities, which they will carry through most of their lives. In spite of their focus on fetal rights, rightists have not demanded prenatal care or drug treatment programs.

In an increasing number of fetal rights cases, prosecutors have sought arrest and criminal action against maternal drug abuse. Lynn Paltrow argues that women are viewed as "fetal abusers," and criminal prosecutions reflect the punitive stance of the state. One can now be arrested for a new crime, "becoming pregnant while addicted to drugs," even though there is no evidence that criminalization is effective in discouraging or treating drug abuse.[98] Punishment for fetal abuse extends the encroachment of the state into women's lives. As Dawn Johnsen notes, "fetal recognition by the law deprives women of their autonomy on the basis of their pregnancy."[99]

Fetal protection from drug-abusing mothers has initiated other kinds of surveillance. If fetuses need protection from mothers who abuse drugs, they may need protection from other mothers as well. Angela Carder, a woman pregnant and ill with cancer, was forced to have a caesarean section against her wishes and those of her family. She believed that she would be able to birth the child herself. Shortly after the caesarean was performed, the fetus died; Angela Carder also died soon thereafter. Three years later, in 1990, the District of Columbia Court of Appeals, in a 7–1 ruling, decided that a pregnant woman, even if she is terminally ill, cannot be forced to undergo a caesarean delivery in order to save the fetus.[100]

An interventionist stance of protecting fetuses from mothers can be used to justify other infringements of women's rights. Darlene Johnson, convicted of child abuse, was required as part of her sentence to use Norplant, a birth-control implant placed under the skin that releases progestin to inhibit ovulation. The judge, Howard Broadman of Tulare County Superior Court in California, argued that his sentence was constitutionally supportable because the state had a compelling interest in protecting any children Ms. Johnson had not yet conceived.[101]

Former Senator Pete Wilson, now Governor of California, introduced the Child Abuse During Pregnancy Prevention Act of 1989 to encourage criminal sanctions against women whose infants reflect substance abuse during pregnancy.[102] But what effect can criminalization have? It is already illegal to use drugs, yet people continue to use them. Women who birth drug-addicted babies are addicted before they become pregnant. A law specifying drug use during pregnancy as a double violation does not change anything with respect to the initial problem. And the problem is that addiction is an illness. Treating it only as a crime is a defeated solution, especially for the fetus.

Most of the time, drug-addicted babies reflect the horrible poverty and dead-endedness of poor women's choices. Yet the responsibility for the health of the fetus is placed solely on the pregnant woman. No responsibility for healthy newborns is relegated to the state, even though (according to the Children's Defense Fund) the United States has the highest rate of infant mortality among the leading twenty industrial nations.[103] Privatization of the social service state has exacerbated these conditions. It has provided police where doctors and social workers are needed. My point is simple and strategic: criminalization is not the answer because it does not work.

In spite of the discourse of "fetal rights," the reality is that prenatal care is very limited; one out of every five women of childbearing age do not have maternity care coverage. Near the time of Pamela Rae Stewart's arrest, San Diego health care clinics turned away 1,243 pregnant women seeking prenatal care. Thirty percent of women in California are so impoverished they are unable to afford any type of maternity care.[104] If we are really interested in the well-being of the fetus, then to improve fetal health substantially we should make prenatal care available to all pregnant women to help prevent low birth weight—the leading cause of infant death.

When poor white women and women of color have the education, training, and jobs they need, the prenatal care they want, and the access to abortion they might choose, *then,* and only then, could I imagine criminalizing drug use for pregnant women. Such a vision is hard to imagine right now. Even then, my stance would be based, not on the "rights" of fetuses, but on the idea that women, if they freely choose pregnancy while having access to other alternatives, have a responsibility to allow the *potential* life inside them the best chance possible for a healthy survival.

The conflict is not between fetus and mother because they are not separate entities. Rather, the conflict is between women's bodily privacy and a state that has made this privacy increasingly difficult to maintain.[105] Women's sexual and racial equality are at issue here as well. The punitive, moralistic stance has not boded well for women's rights. With the increase in technological and scientific discoveries of new kinds of prenatal harm—such as the effects of smoking and drinking—the pressure to increase the surveillance of pregnant women will likely continue. The moral absolutism of the Reagan-Bush legacy encourages forays into women's lives even as women are defined as mere temporary vessels in which the fetus is housed.

One should not forget the *Maher* or *Harris* decisions when examining fetal rights versus women's rights. If one is poor and lacks monetary support, one cannot get an abortion, and one cannot get prenatal care. If one is also drug-addicted, one cannot afford treatment for the addiction. In spite of almost total lack of choice, one can be prosecuted for fetal neglect. In the ultimate right-wing formulation of reverse discrimination, the rights of the fetus have precedence over the rights of women. We leave the civil rights and women's movements behind: the rights of fetuses and of white men prevail.

BEYOND PRIVACY

The assault on women's reproductive rights has demanded that feminists both defend and push beyond the existing boundaries of a woman's privacy and her right to choose. Our new conceptions must encompass a notion of personal privacy which is also grounded in women's collective and shared need for reproductive control of their bodies. I am indebted to Rosalind Petchesky's formulation of this need. She eloquently advises that we must retrieve reproductive rights from the heavy baggage of liberal exclusivity with which they have been encumbered, and ground ourselves in the actual political struggles of the civil rights and feminist movements. We must develop a definition of rights "that maintains a notion of women's moral and political agency both as individuals and as members of collectivities." [106]

Abortion is individual and collective: specific and universal at the same time. If one starts with reproductive rights, or the right to bodily privacy, at the core of one's theory, one establishes individual rights for women—which speaks of a social collectivity—rather than an individual, private right for a specific woman. The move is transformative of rights theory and of our understanding of privacy. Privacy then encompasses the issues of racial, sexual, and economic quality because it is not simply an individual concern.

Once we move to the collective meaning of our individual status as women, we must push the boundaries of the racialized nature of patriarchal rights discourse. This next level of specificity speaks to the diversity within the collectivity of women. It is to this level that we turn in my final chapter.

SEVEN

Imagining Feminism

Women of Color Specifying Democracy

By specifying the racialized meanings of female bodies, feminists can reimagine a rights discourse which could reinvent democracy. It will be a democracy inclusive of reproductive rights and accountable to women of color. To be accountable to women of color means to encourage diversity and variety. And a reproductive rights agenda will address the needs of all people for work, economic stability, sexual freedom, healthy bodies, prenatal care, and much more. My starting point, then, is women of color and their variety. By specifying diversity, I look to find the commonalities among women. Let me pick this apart more carefully.

Issues of racism and sexism form a major part of the political landscape of the United States. The two issues sometimes require women of color to choose between and against themselves. African American feminist Judy Scales Trent terms this dilemma the "double jeopardy" of black women. They are a discrete group with multiple status as blacks and women.[1] African American feminist Kimberle Williams Crenshaw argues that the "intersectionality" of black women's lives is not recognized. They are said to be discriminated against in the same way as either black men or white women; there is no recognition that they are discriminated against as both.[2] Or as Peggie Smith argues, black women experience "interactive discrimination" or "disproportionate and adverse specificity."[3]

As gender was increasingly racialized throughout the 1980s, two very different possibilities emerged. The racialized aspects of gender could divide women among themselves according to the "power differences" of race, or they could allow for coalition building through the connections of gender. It is the latter development that I want to imagine. It is therefore more important than ever to recognize the complex interconnections of race and gender that allow for a common politics.

In this chapter I will discuss a quite different scenario from the one given us by the antidemocratic, rightist, neoconservative state. I want to renew the imaginings of an antiracist and feminist theory that have been silenced by feminism's defensive posture. I will begin with the insights of Mae Gwendolyn Henderson, who "proposes a model that seeks to account for racial difference within gender identity and gender difference within racial identity." Henderson expands Teresa de Lauretis's notion of a person "en-gendered in the experiencing of race" to include the process of a person " 'racialized' in the experiencing of gender." [4]

Let us imagine a politics that dismantles the racialized patriarchal relations of domination and moves beyond women's fragments and fractures to a more inclusive democratic politics. To become more inclusive, we must begin with a critique of the whiteness of feminism. Throughout the 1980s, women of color resisted racism in their feminist writings. Although they leveled a damning critique of (white) feminism, they also began the difficult process of exploring the relationships between racial and gender oppression. I focus particularly on the voices of black feminists in the United States because they have been in the forefront of these developments.

Although African American voices are not perfectly inclusive of the diversity of the lives of women of color—Latinas, Alaskans, Asian Americans, and Pacific Islanders—they provide a beginning for the process of specifying democracy. The experiences of African American women offer a unique and critically important view of racism in the United States. And although I do not mean to have black women stand in for the many cultural varieties of racialized gender, they are a starting place from which to understand this process. It is a process which, in the end, must recognize the racialized divisions and "power differences" that exist *within* the communities of women of color. And it is a process which must deconstruct the overly simplistic racialized division of black / white, even while recognizing its importance.

RETHINKING THE POLITICAL

Feminism of almost any sort unsettles traditional political theory. Western feminism has rethought and renamed politics by reenvisioning the relationship between public and private life.

Radical feminists in the early 1970s, who were white and Western, argued that politics define private life as much as public life. They argued that the neat divisions between public and private space and between personal and political life were artificial and misrepresented how the relations of power are constructed.[5] They burst the boundaries of traditional politics.

Politics are always shifting to new sites. The activities and sites of power relocate. And in Western societies, power is relocated through the compound lens of private and public spheres. The history of racism in the West has renegotiated these spheres through plantation slave society, the postbellum period, industrialization, and now deindustrialization. Racism—once a much more homogeneous politics—has become more economically diversified as it traverses public and private spaces.

The system of racialized patriarchy has shifted from the construction of the slave woman as an immoral and amoral sexual animal for breeding to the construction of the welfare-dependent and/or crack-addicted woman with AIDS or the emasculating black professional woman. Images of veiled and subservient Arab women further endorse the racial aspect of patriarchy within U.S. borders. These negotiations are threaded through a division between the public and the private that is modeled on an outdated vision of white middle-class family life.

Racism is used in the articulation of gender discrimination, and there are particularly racist ways of depicting women of color *as women*. Racialized gender is structured in and through changes in the family and in the economy. This process of coloring gender also redefines the relationship between women, their families, and the state.

Public and private spaces have different meanings for white women and women of color. Familial patriarchy, which is based on the privileging of the white father as modeled in the traditional white heterosexual family, has different resonance for white women than for women of color. Male privilege is racialized: white men are more privileged than are black men, especially outside the family.

White women's critique of domesticity and housewifery grows out of the particular experience of middle-class white women. There are different traditions among women of color. Married black women have always disproportionately worked in the labor force as compared with white women. Although black women also encounter a sexual division of labor in the home, their response to it grows out of their own history of working as domestics for white women.

The market also shifts the lines between the public and the private. The sexual division of labor within the market exists within a racist division of labor, which disproportionately locates women of color within racial ghettoes within sexual ghettoes. More simply, women's work in the market, be it secretarial or service work, is hierarchically ordered by race. Gender places most women within the sexual ghetto of the labor force, and race further orders that ghetto.

The job market of the 1990s differs from the market of the 1950s and 1960s not only because more married white women are in the market, but also because the economic class differentiations *between* women of color are greater. Though most women of color remain at the bottom rungs of the class structure, some have moved into the middle class. These women share some concerns with white middle-class women, but the problems of racism create ties to their working-class and poor "sisters." Although those groups share *some* concerns, there is definitely no homogeneous group of either women of color or white women. Nor is there a homogeneous group of middle-class women. Race and class intersect with women's identities, needs, and politics. The mix is multiple.

As more married white women have entered the labor force, their experiences have become more similar, though not identical, to those of African American women. Although the market remains racially hierarchical, women of all races share the problems of sexual harassment in the workplace. White women and women of color who work outside the home may also have similar experiences in seeking to control their fertility and sexuality in order to survive outside the traditional boundaries of the patriarchal family. Such experiences may stimulate them to examine the similarities between sex and gender discrimination. So may experiences within the private realm—marital rape, battering, incest, unequal distribution of domestic labor—which cut across racial lines.

As white women become more like women of color, patriarchal controls have shifted to encompass the changes, particularly via the social service sectors of the state.[6] Patriarchal control, although still located with the husband if he is present, can also be exerted through the state welfare system. The social welfare network is redefined as family structures change.

There are at least two processes we need to account for. First, the distinction between private and public spaces and their relations to the system of male privilege are continually renegotiated. Second, this process of negotiation is racially marked: white women and women of color have experienced privacy differently and have often found themselves in conflict with one another even when they have parallel concerns.

To some extent, the problem lies with the feminist short hand for a

complicated issue: the saying that the personal is political. This statement should not be translated to mean that personal and political life
are one and the same. Nor should they be. Rather, feminists must point
out that personal life within a racialized patriarchal society is woven in
and through political structures that seek to maintain systems of
oppression. In order to create a space that is truly private—free from
statist intervention in the reproductive and sexual realms—we must re-
structure the racial divide. Such a restructuring requires a sexual and
racial equality that reenvisions privacy. This restructuring also demands
a politics that moves beyond—although in and through—the personal.

I return here to an earlier point. Because of its racial coding, the right
to privacy has not granted the same protection to women of color that
it has to white women. Feminists need to connect our thinking about
privacy to the discourse of civil rights and the demand for racial (and
sexual) equality.

THE RIGHT TO PRIVACY FOR WOMEN OF COLOR

Feminists of color personalize politics through the lens of racialized
gender: they formulate political thinking from personal experiences, which
speak the specificity of race and gender. Personal experience is used to
theorize a new sense of the political.[7]

Black feminist Patricia Collins argues that the public life of people of
color differs from the public life of white society. Black institutions such
as the church have developed within dominant white culture and operate as simultaneously private and public. The black church functions
not only as a public institution but also "as family" to blacks living in
a white society. In addition, black families house patriarchy in the private domain of black women's lives, at the same time as the racial privileging of patriarchy defines their lives in the public sphere of the market.[8] To the extent that patriarchy infiltrates both the home and the
market, the publicness of white patriarchy also interrupts the division
of public from private life for black women.

One should not assume that patriarchy in the market simply privileges black men as it does white men, or that the privileging of black
men within the African American community is exactly the same as
white male privilege. The racial privileging of whiteness makes it different. Patriarchy does not allow black men the same control over their
lives as it does white men. It instead positions black men against black
women. The privileging of black men is deformed by racism. The mar-

; racially structured via grossly unequal employment opportunities;
.ditionally privileges white men as "providers" for white women
(although white women are increasingly finding themselves heading
families).

Aida Hurtado questions the appropriateness of even thinking in terms
of public and private space for African American women. She argues
that black families have never operated as "havens" from the ruthless
world; they have never had a distance from the state which allows privacy. Women of color have not had the benefit of economic conditions
that allow the separation of these spheres. Instead, black women understand that the "public is personally political." Without privacy, they
"personalize the public"; they attempt to show how public policies need
to connect to their personal choices.[9]

Hurtado's discussion is important to remind white women that privacy has different historical and cultural meanings. However, the fact
that black women have not experienced the same privacy as white women
of the middle class does not mean that privacy is a wrong-headed emphasis or demand for women of color. Black feminist Barbara Smith
has argued throughout her writing that the families of people of color
have been havens, even if the safety or buffer they have provided has
been incomplete. The invasion of the state into black family life does
not negate the protective function of the family and community.[10]

At issue is how one thinks about power. Hurtado assumes that there
is a "center of power."[11] But if power has also been dispersed to multiple locations outside the formal structures of the state, then the division of public from private life is not so stark; it is more fluid and
complex. Privacy becomes a claim of women of color within their own
family structure—as a defense against the patriarchal privileging of the
state.

We must also recognize the power of language as a political discourse. The discourse of public versus private life, which surrounds the
lack of privacy of women of color, can be used to claim the right to
privacy. Feminists need to rewrite the public/private divide, particularly
as it shifts and weaves its way through women's lives. Patriarchal privilege is mystified through the public liberalization of rights for women
even as controls within the private realm are continued—and even rei-
fied.

Mervat Hatem points out that Arab and Egyptian societies now allow women education and the right to work in the market even as they
continue to enforce the patriarchal culture of Muslim family life. State

governments remain male-occupied even though the market has become somewhat gender-integrated; public discourse embraces women's rights even though family life remains restrictive for women.[12] The public sphere is differentiated by messages that are partly in conflict with the private discourse of family life. Martha Njoka, a thirty-three-year-old criminal lawyer in Nairobi, notes: "Men are not ready to be modern inside their homes."[13]

In South Africa, a number of the women activists in the anti-apartheid struggle are also active as feminists. Many of them came to their politics through the experience of being battered wives and victims of incest and through the very particular pain of being mothers of children forced to live in apartheid. RAPE CRISIS is the most powerful feminist organization in South Africa because it addresses the sexual violence that is so much a part of apartheid and the private lives of women of color. Rhoda Bertekmann-Kadalie tells us that this organization fights personal and political issues together. Yet Rozena Maart acknowledges, "When the ANC [African National Congress] is the new government it will definitely still be a male-dominated government."[14]

Privacy has long been criticized by many progressives and some feminists as an inadequate defense of reproductive rights, partly because privacy assumes that the personal is separate from the political, when in fact the political is readily implicated in the private. Feminists who have brought women's reproductive lives out of the private sphere to uncover the politics residing there must turn around and argue that abortion is a private, personal, and individual decision.[15]

The right to privacy is problematic because, as a "liberal" democratic right, it is inflected with the privileging of white heterosexual men's privacy at the expense of everyone else's. It is problematic because the right to privacy never was intended to include black slave women's rights to their bodies, and it is not sufficient to protect women's right to abortion—or the right to medical care of people living with AIDS. Yet privacy is something any woman wants for her body.

RECLAIMING "RIGHTS" FOR WOMEN OF COLOR

Mae Gwendolyn Henderson argues that there are "plural aspects of the self that constitute the matrix of black female subjectivity."[16] It is the matrix of a person's various components that demands privacy. It is the part of the individual which is unique that requires both private space and public nourishment. Public nourishment often allows uniqueness;

being left to oneself is insufficient. Societal conditions must nourish exploration and experimentation in these spaces. Thus "feminism can never be completely comfortable with a rights discourse"[17] that does not move beyond the isolated self.

Black feminist Patricia Williams argues similarly that liberal rights discourse is not trivial for any person who is vulnerable; attaining full rights has been a fiercely motivational source of hope for black people. She believes that the problem is less with "rights assertion" than with a "failure of rights commitment"; less with the restrictiveness of rights discourse than with the restrictions of society on rights.[18] For Williams, the language of rights makes commitments conscious and their possibility real. She therefore wants to broaden and reconfigure the way we think about rights. Kimberle Williams Crenshaw argues similarly that rights discourse is both restrictive and expansive. It restricts to the extent that it covers over inequities of access, but it is also receptive to aspirations that are central to black demands.[19]

Williams argues that even though rights were shaped by whites and parceled out to blacks, until one knows "the crushing weight of total— bodily and spiritual—*intrusion*," one should not think about discarding the concept of rights. Instead, we should "see through or past them so that they reflect a larger definition of privacy and property: so that privacy is turned from exclusion based on self-regard into regard for another's fragile, mysterious autonomy." She wants to unlock rights and give them away—to slaves, to trees, to cows. "Give to all of society's objects and untouchables the rights of privacy, integrity, and self-assertion; give them distance and respect."[20] Once something has rights, it has standing.[21] It is no accident that feminists of color reclaim selves and rights not just for persons but also for the environment. Given the present and probable future condition of the earth, it probably would be better to give trees rights.

Yet this argument creates problems. I do not think Williams really means to grant rights to *everything*. She does not grant the fetus standing. Fetuses are not separate persons from the moment of conception. Rather, she says, the fetus "is interconnected flesh-and-blood-bonded, completely a part of a woman's body."[22] Of course, antiabortionists who have claimed rights for the fetus do not mean rights in the radicalized, egalitarian sense in which Williams uses the term. But they have claimed the same language.

Byllye Avery, a black feminist health activist, is cautious regarding the discourse of rights for black women. She chooses not to use the phrase "reproductive rights" "because there are a lot of us [for] whom it is not a right."[23]

Yet once rights are claimed by women of color, the neutrality of rights discourse is dislodged, uncovering its racialized meanings. Whites do not have to call attention to race because it is not a problem for them. Thus they can easily dismiss affirmative action as an unfair imposition of standards (preference). Williams points out that such neutrality is only a guise for "standardized preference."[24]

THE PROBLEM OF THEORIZING FEMINISM

I need theory because it pushes me to find connections outside myself. In the realm of theory, I generalize from what I know and stretch to think about what I do not directly experience. In the realm of theory, I am allowed to imagine other ways of being.

Theorizing pushes me to find the similarities that exist across and within the specificities that make me different from others. As an individual, I am both uniquely particular and similar to other people. The similarity constitutes what defines me as human; we are enough alike that we are not *completely* different. Without thinking about and theorizing these connections, we only have disparate moments; we are discrete, disconnected individuals, with no possibility of imagining a common politics.

Black feminist bell hooks writes of theory: "I came to theory because I was hurting. The pain within me was so intense that I could not go on living. I came to theory desperate, wanting to comprehend—to grasp what was happening around and within me. . . . I saw in theory then a location for healing."[25]

Feminist theory involves moving beyond the self, when the starting point is the self. It requires a notion of a collective "we," of the collectivities of women. There is a shared sense of other women who are like you, although not identical to you.

Feminists of color have rightly charged white feminists with not imagining far enough beyond themselves. White feminists, of varying political stripes, have tended to equate the experience of white middle-class women with that of all women. Feminists of color, such as bell hooks, Barbara Smith, and Chandra Mohanty, demand that feminism be rethreaded through the imaginings of racial diversity and the problems of racism. Recognizing differences, particularly the racial and economic differences between women, can assist in uncovering the way

power is distributed among and between women. It allows an understanding of power and oppression, discrimination, inequality, and domination among women themselves.

There is a partial conundrum here. Feminist theories must be written
from the self, from the position of one's life—the personal articulates
the political. Yet such theories have to move beyond the self to the
conception of a collective woman, which requires recognizing the diversity of women and the contexts of oppression. Some women are skep-
tical that such theory can be constructed.

Hazel Carby writes that there is no lost sisterhood to be found; that
there are definite "boundaries" to the possibility of sisterhood.[26] White
feminist Adrienne Rich has described the phrase "all women" as a face-
less, raceless, classless category.[27] Black feminist Evelyn Brooks-Higginbotham says it is impossible to generalize womanhood's common
oppression.[28]

Black feminist Barbara Christian believes that theory—particularly
the feminist theory of the academy, which is dominated by post-struc-
turalism—is exclusive and elitist. She is troubled that the overtly political literature of African American women and of the women of South
America and Africa is being preempted by a postmodern view that assumes that "reality does not exist" and that "everything is relative and
partial."[29] Thus, recent insights by women of color are dismissed as
only partial, rather than as a needed corrective to existing views. Black
activist and feminist June Jordan unequivocally argues that post-struc-
turalism and deconstruction reflect the "worshipping of European fathers at their worst." They express the "tyrannies of language that are
anti-democratic and proud of it."[30]

The critiques offered by Christian and Jordan help clarify an important difference between a postmodern focus on diversity and the political focus offered by black feminists since the mid- to late seventies.
Most women of color focus on difference in order to understand problems of oppression: how difference is used to discriminate against people. They struggle to theorize a feminism that is diverse at its core, rather
than to theorize difference as an end in itself. This differs from poststructural theorizing that inadvertently silences politics, because the
connections of similarity are lost. Feminism is then often rejected, along
with any recognition of women's collectivity.[31]

The excesses of postmodernism reject any focus on universalism or
continuity in a trans-historical sense as essentialist. From this vantage
point, specificity is set up in opposition to likeness or similarity. You

must have one or the other. We are left with positions like Judith Butler's statement that gender coherence is a fiction.[32]

I do not mean to position feminism in opposition to postmodernism. Rather, I think that much of black feminist theory pre-dates and informs the developments of postmodern thought. Postmodernism has recently pushed feminism to defend itself as political argument, while feminists of color specify the different meanings of feminism.

Wendy Brown claims that feminists fear the disorientation and depoliticization of postmodern intellectual maneuvers. She sees feminists as too protective of their fixed and circumscribed categories.[33] She obviously is not thinking of black feminists like hooks, Smith, and Williams, who have demanded a rethinking of the concept of sex class. Nor is she thinking, for example, of black feminist Angela Harris, who critiques essentialism and invites readers to subvert her own generalizations.[34]

Black feminist Bernice Reagon recognizes the problems with white feminist categorizations of women. She recognizes the multiple identities of women of color and the problems they pose for women's collectivity. "It does not matter at all that biologically we have being women in common. We have been organized to have our primary cultural signals come from some other factors than that we are women." She says we are not acculturated to be "women people," "capable of crossing our first people boundaries—Black, White, Indian, etc." Yet Reagon argues that political coalitions are necessary and possible. They allow for connection through conflict. Coalition work can create a commonness of experience between women because it recognizes, rather than denies, diversity.[35]

Susan Bordo, a white feminist critical of the abuses of the new poststructural pluralism, argues against the neutralizing of difference. If everyone is simply different, then it is no longer problematic; the problem of discrimination is removed. One needs a way to orient the context in order to distinguish between the differences: to compare and assess them in order to find patterns and similarity.[36] Significantly, Bordo asks: "Could we now speak of the differences that inflect *gender* if gender had not first been shown to make a difference?"[37] When we pluralize our understanding of power, we should not erase the continuities of power, but rather clarify the specific contexts in which continuity exists, in its various forms. The possibility of politics depends on theorizing—on recognizing connections.

Hooks argues that we need to be careful about how we think of theory and about the place of abstraction in theory and politics. She writes of the multiple ways blacks abstract and theorize in their everyday language. She is unwilling to accept the idea that theory is what white Westerners do.[38] It is important not to equate a particular kind of theory—abstracted, overgeneralized, and homogenized—with the very notion of theory. Various kinds of theory already exist within the personal narratives or daily life descriptions of women of color. We must recognize the way women of color express their feminist and antiracist politics in order to find moments of connection.

Audre Lorde argued that a major problem of the white feminist movement was its insufficient response to issues of difference: the refusal to recognize difference in the first place; the misnaming of differences; and the disconnecting of the relations that tie difference together.[39] To say the least, such blindness distorts our differences of race, age, and sexual preference and makes them more problematic. Difference itself is not the problem.

How do we rethread the recognition of "power differences" into a notion of gender and racial equality which could redirect the assault against democracy for women of color and, with them, white women? We must rethink the political once again, as politics shift and are redefined through new locations of gender and racial privilege. The intersections of racialized patriarchy are key for defining feminist activity. By locating the particular relationships of racialized sexual domination, we can better understand the shifting nature of politics and the possibilities of an antiracist feminism.[40]

ON NEEDING FEMINISM

White women and women of color both need feminism, because women need a politics that names the problems of women through the structures of oppression across and through racism. Language is not helpful here. The phrases "women of color" and "white women" wrongly homogenize each and therefore distort the relationship within and between the two. Each group appears monolithic instead of formed of the particulars which define individual women's lives.

White feminist Catherine MacKinnon asks, "What is a white woman anyway?" She argues that the category "white woman" is often used to trivialize white women's subordination. It is used to delegitimize the idea of oppression as a woman—as though white skin insulates white women from the brutality and misogyny of men. Although there is some truth to this point, MacKinnon does not make enough of the complicated dilemma. The category "white woman" is used to divide women from themselves. Yet white women do have privileges as white, compared with women of color. The racialized aspects of patriarchy can be used to subvert the idea of feminism, but it is also the case that white skin privilege necessitates specifying the category "as a woman."[41]

The problem is that women as a homogeneous group do not exist, whereas feminism must posit that women do exist in some sense as a group.[42] Feminists need to distinguish between a false homogeneity constructed by silent exclusions (or silent equations)—such as assuming that white middle-class women represent women per se—and a real, viable collectivity of women rich in diversity.[43] There is nothing inherent in feminism or in the discourse of rights that denies the latter.

The fact that women's experiences are not homogeneous, as they have been falsely depicted as being, does not negate the existence of real similarities. White feminists have solipsistically assumed a stance of homogeneity which denies a truly democratic feminism.[44] Feminists of color have reacted to this stance by radically pluralizing and nurturing new feminist ways of writing and speaking. Susan Willis has called this method a process of "specifying."[45] The pluralization of the term "feminism" to "feminisms" was instigated predominantly by women of color.[46]

Feminist of color bell hooks has been at the forefront of the criticism of white feminism. She has suggested ways to open up and pluralize the relationship between feminism and black women. She distinguishes between advocating feminism and identifying as a feminist, in order to challenge the univocal stance of many white feminists.[47] She thinks of feminism less as a personal identity than as a politics. She fears that politics become reduced to the personal. Therefore, hooks moves from the "I" to the collective "we."[48] The move requires the dislocation of the singular individual to the complex plural. Also, hooks speaks of "women's movement" rather than of "*the* women's movement" in an attempt to use language to refigure our perception of feminism as a process which is open rather than something preformed and exclusive.

For hooks, feminism is not simply a struggle to end male chauvinism, but rather a struggle to eradicate the very ideology of domination.[49] Domination is a large and more plural category that encompasses the specific system of male privilege. Although hooks criticizes white women and "the" white women's movement for its racial and economic class

ias also struggled with black women to "separate feminism as
agenda from white women" in order to "focus on the issue
of sexism as it affects black communities."[50]

Barbara Smith, another significant early voice of black feminism, has
argued that the simultaneity of the oppressions of race, gender, sexual
preference, and economic class make it impossible to choose only one
identity. The systems are integrated and interlocking, not simply added
on to each other. The relations of power implicate each other. The lay-
ers cannot be simply taken apart because they are marbled.[51] Smith
struggles against racism and sexism as a black lesbian feminist; she argues that black women experience racism not as "blacks" but as black
women.[52] From a slightly different angle, June Jordan writes: "Overall,
Black men dominate Black America."[53]

Chandra Mohanty, as an Indian woman of color, also writes with a
critical eye about white women and the white women's movement, but
her skepticism does not require her to reject the import of feminism as
a language or a politics. Mohanty argues that to disembrace the term
"feminism" might be a retreat from the debate where women are central. Although there are keen differences of color, which oppress women
both inside and outside the women's movement, Mohanty wants to
imagine "potential alliances," which are not essentialist, but based in
politics.[54] Cheryl Johnson-Odim similarly argues that we should not
lose sight of the "fair amount of universality in women's oppression."
Problems exist, but they can be addressed by allowing the "potential"
bond of gender to underline feminist politics. This potential bond exists
despite the fact that "women participate in the oppression of other women
all over the world."[55] Conflict exists, but it does not have to be immo-
bilizing. Feminist politics remain possible.

Alice Walker, black feminist and writer, has searched for a language
which would embody the richness of feminism without this racist history. The term she chooses to use is *womanist*. It refers to a black feminist or feminist of color; it refers to outrageous and willful behavior; it
refers to someone committed to the survival and wholeness of an entire
people, male and female. "Womanist is to feminist as purple is to lav-
ender."[56] It is a matter of shading. I wonder what has been gained with
this subtle switch. What is lost is clearer: a language that identifies the
continuity in the politics and history of feminism, however troublesome
it has been.

Gloria Anzaldúa, a Chicana/Mexicana feminist, is wary of the "totalizing identity" called forth by feminist politics. She is eager to create

teorías (theories) that enable us to interpret what happens in the world in specific ways "that will reflect what goes on between inner, outer and peripheral 'I's within a person and between the personal 'I's and the collective 'we' of our ethnic communities." Anzaldúa wants to encompass the overlapping of many worlds, while recognizing that she is always partially inside and partially outside these Western frames.[57]

To create a feminist theory of women of color requires straddling a multiplicity of contexts. Often it requires rejecting the culture that oppresses women to affirm a once-colonized culture.[58] The various contexts do not merely parallel each other; they conflict and demand choices. Because there is no smooth layering that allows for easy separation, one's choice may even feel artificial and unsatisfactory.

Gayatri Spivak explores the further complexities of this point when she argues that one must try simultaneously to affirm feminism and to undo sexism. She writes: "I emphasize discontinuity, heterogeneity, and typology as I speak of such a sex analysis." Spivak does not want to obliterate race or economic class. Instead, she would like to chart "a sense of our common yet history-specific lot." One cannot simply make women's liberation identical with reproductive liberation or allow the problem of oppression to define one's liberation. One has to try to stand outside. In the end, the best one can come up with is provisional generalizations, rather than universals.[59]

Susan Willis's method of "specifying . . . represents a form of narrative integrity" which takes feminists to new sites in order to expand their imagination.[60] Important imaginings are to be found in music, daily conversations, everyday behavior, and actual political organizing.[61] When we explore such places, we hear the voices that explain why 85 percent of black women say they see a need for a strong women's movement (compared with 64 percent of white women).[62] When we visit the homes of strong and hard-working women in the African American community, we see some of the roots of feminism.[63] Feminism is not foreign to black women, even if the white feminist movement has been so.

Feminists of color embrace difference because they must; they focus on complexity and intersection because their lives demand it. So they struggle to find moments of connection and similarity, while recognizing the barriers of racism and economic class privilege. Feminisms of color push to radicalize a more inclusive and cohesive feminism by "specifying." This process moves toward a more inclusive democratic theory that continually reinvents universal claims by particularizing their

meaning. It is a part of the continual process of democratizing feminism. As Trinh T. Minh-ha puts it, "The story never stops beginning or
ending. It appears headless and bottomless for it is built on differences."[64]

RACIAL FRACTURES BETWEEN WOMEN AS A CLASS

Once one agrees on the need for a feminist politics rooted in a race-
conscious, radical pluralism, one must name the complex relations that
define the limits and possibilities of this pluralism. A race-conscious,
radical pluralism embraces the richness of variety and critiques the existing power relations rooted in the hostility to diversity. Radical pluralism is discernibly different from liberal pluralism. Liberal pluralism
speaks of differences as though they are neutral rather than discriminatory. It does not image power. Liberal pluralism does not demand an
antiracist politics, nor does it recognize that differences bespeak power
and privilege. As a result, the standard of white heterosexual maleness
is left in place, and the multiplicity of "others" occupy marginalized
spaces.

Radical pluralism recognizes that processes of discrimination are
complex. It recognizes that racism is debilitating and requires structural
changes. It also acknowledges that some racial differences reflecting history and culture are rich and meaningful, and that the destruction of
racism does not mean the elimination of all racial meanings. Some differences developing from the struggle against discrimination are to be
valued. But differences used to structure and justify inequality must be
dismantled. Radical pluralism anticipates that conflict will occur over
the negotiations of racial privilege. With the restructuring of power,
everyone's lives will change, and many whites and some people of color
will not want change.

Radical pluralism is necessary to white women because racism, as it
is implicated in patriarchy, reinforces gender discrimination, which affects both women of color and white women. Women of color and
white women are defined as women *in relation to* each other, through
a racial privileging of white women.

In racialized patriarchy, racism is differentiated by race *and* gender.
Or, as Evelyn Brooks-Higginbotham states, "Race impregnates the sim-
plest meanings: gender is constructed and fragmented in and through
racialized contexts."[65] The construction of male privilege within the
African American community divides black men from black women. It

also splits black women from themselves, caught between their loyalties of race and gender. Black women get caught between conflicting agendas, as the Anita Hill–Clarence Thomas hearings so painfully revealed.

Against these enormous pressures, many black women refuse to pit racial and sexual oppression against each other. As mentioned in an earlier chapter, a group of 1,603 black women formed a grass-roots network called African American Women in Defense of Ourselves during the Thomas hearings in order to speak for their own complex situation. As black writer Rosemary Bray notes, black women have often chosen race loyalty over the "uncertain allegiance of gender," but this loyalty has also functioned as a way of controlling women within the African American community.[66] Similarly, Joan Morgan wrote in response to the guilty verdict in the Mike Tyson rape trial: "Mike Tyson is a rapist. . . . Saying so doesn't mean that we love black men any less; it simply means that we are not willing to let race loyalty buy us early tombstones."[67]

Patriarchy differentiates gender, gender is differentiated in racism, and racism is differentiated by race and gender.[68] The relations of gender and race are reciprocal. The plural voices of women of color are gendered and racialized.[69]

Chandra Talpade Mohanty writes of "complex relationality" as creating the possibility for feminist action. Although women are not an "automatic unitary group," we can imagine "coalitions and potential alliances."[70] Her imaginings are not utopian. Rather, she attempts to construct political alliances even though she knows they will be fractured ones. Valerie Smith similarly writes of "split affinities" and unstable connections.[71] Mohanty and Smith recognize conflict without letting it have the last word.

Judy Scales Trent describes herself as a black who looks white. As such, she has had to "transgress boundaries" as part of her daily life. She claims that we are often "the same in our differences." She likens the search for similarity to the search for connectedness: it is like finding a home.[72] We most often find what we are looking for. If we are looking for difference, we find it. If we are looking for similarity, we find that, too. Both are there to find—often in a very uneasy mix. As Patricia Williams writes, "What I am saying is that my difference was in some ways the same as hers, that simultaneously her difference was in some ways very different from mine, and that simultaneously we were in all ways the same."[73]

So similarity and difference are not completely separate categories.

Black women are neither simply different from white women, nor the same as black men. Trinh Minh-ha captures this point: "There are differences as well as similarities within the concept of difference."[74] Differences and similarities exist between white women and women of color, and differences and similarities exist within those categories. We are often not as different or as similar as we are said to be. We are similar and different in ways that are not noted. Discontinuities abound.

Pamela Obron, a black woman describing the difficulties she had in starting her own construction company, is quoted as saying, "The white men look at you and see a black. The black men look at you and see a woman."[75] Of course, she is both. White men deny her womanhood while distancing her as black; black men deny her their similarity of race while distancing her as a woman. She is constructed as different, as not equal, through the interplay of racism and patriarchy. Patriarchy even occludes racial similarity for the black man: she is *different* because she is a woman. Both racism and patriarchy deny her womanhood for the white man because she is not a white woman.

There is an important distinction to be made between similarity and sameness. Similarity does not mean identity or unity or universality. Rather, similarity encompasses likeness and variety at the same time. Similar means somewhat alike, but not exactly alike. The space between "somewhat" and "not exactly" is understood by specifying differences *and* similarities. Similarity requires that we move beyond the polarities of sameness and difference: a polarity that problematizes each.

Another way of speaking to this issue is revealed in Pat Parker's poem "For the white person who wants to know how to be my friend." She writes: "The first thing you do is forget that i'm Black. Second, you must never forget that i'm Black.[76] Or, as Audre Lorde has written, black women do not want to shed their differences but rather want to use them for being creative among themselves and with women of other color.[77] Differences are not to be denied or erased. They are to be used. Oppression and discrimination on the basis of difference is what must be destroyed.

Deciphering the relations between racism and racial diversity is not easy. It involves recognizing the history of slavery and of contemporary racism as it has been rethreaded through gender and economic class lines. Many racist practices are gender-specific, and sexual exploitation is structured through racist practices.[78] Race is sexualized, and sexuality racialized. The particular reality of black women's relationship to black men is key for understanding how patriarchy threads racism.[79]

The rape of black women by white men has a specific history deriving from early slave society; the accusation of the rape of white women by black men has been used as a mechanism of control of black men. The rape of black women and children has functioned as part of the system of male privilege in African American communities. Rape and racism intersect to form a complicated and troubled connection for white and black women. Yet all women share the desire to be free from rape.

There are very different, but interdependent, notions of sexuality, motherhood, and womanhood defining white and black women.[80] The nineteenth-century cult of true womanhood excluded black women and white working-class women. White women were mothers; black women were breeders.[81] Black women are now viewed most often as welfare mothers, women with AIDS, pregnant teenagers, or emasculating matriarchs. The view of black women's identity is very often tied up with visions of the underclass: criminality, sexual abuse, promiscuity, drugs.[82] Whether stated or not, the silent subtext of this portrayal is the view of the middle-class white woman as wife and mother.

The variety of black families includes families led by strong and able women teaching survival and resistance effectively to their children.[83] It is amazing how much these women can accomplish, given the way many of them have been forced to live. A recurring barrier for black women is poverty. Statistically, black children in young female-headed households are the poorest in the nation.[84] Twenty-five percent of people with AIDS are black; 52 percent of all women with AIDS-related illnesses are black; black women have a 12–15 percent poorer survival rate from breast cancer as compared with white women.[85] These "power differences" matter.

By calling attention to what Crenshaw has called the "intersectionality" of black women's lives,[86] we focus on the complex interweavings of race and gender. Imbricated in these weavings is the poverty and economic inequality of these women. It is genuinely surprising how infrequently the intersectionality of women's lives is embraced, represented, theorized, or acted on. Disconnected views of racialized patriarchy are reinforced by the everyday cultural politics of newspapers, rap music, television, and movies. Usually we are presented with exclusionary viewings of either race or sex. This nonrelational perspective denies the intersection of race and sex.

When Spencer Holland, head of Project 2000, a school monitoring program in Washington, D.C., spoke in defense of developing schools for black boys in order to counter the problem of racism, he singled out the problem of racism for boys, as though it does not affect girls. He argued that black *boys* need to be taught how to survive.[87]

Partial views that recognize only women's "power differences" set them against each other. These partial views leave those in power scot-free, because power and oppression cannot be combated without acknowledging connection—however fragmented it may be. Yet universal concepts of human rights also leave women out of the picture, by ignoring their specificity and variety. Feminists must start from the specific and move in and through it to the general.

REPRODUCTIVE RIGHTS AND WOMEN OF COLOR

It remains for feminists to address the inadequacy of rights discourse by building a reproductive rights movement which specifies the needs of women of color. We must reconnect the issues of racial and sexual discrimination that underpin the rightist rejection of abortion. Racial and sexual equality are intertwined: the reprivatization and redefinition of access to both—and opportunity for both—are of one (complicated) piece. Reconnecting them moves white women and women of color beyond rights discourse and its assumed unities and presumptions about equality.

So let me return to the female body. Let me make the woman pregnant and a woman of color. Doing so displaces the abstracted male individual to just another specified group. Pregnant women of color destabilize the unity of rights discourse. Pregnancy is a reminder of bodily diversity and of the need for reproductive rights.[88] Women of color remind white women of racial diversity.[89] They press against and challenge the homogeneous viewing of white privilege which is written into the discourse of rights. Woman's biological diversity is sited in pregnancy, and the noting of color unsettles the silent standards of racial homogeneity. Given the political context and history of rights discourse, "pregnant women of color" becomes a more inclusive category of diversification without becoming inclusive in and of itself. Because the category specifies bodies, it comes to include a variety of types. Variety as a standard of inclusion encompasses more than does sameness. The new standard is not the pregnant bodies of women of color, but variety itself.

The category "pregnant women of color" is a specified view that pushes feminist discourse to a more inclusive moment. But this new specificity is not meant to become another overgeneralized statement that occludes the diversity of women of color by positioning or "essentializing" them against white women. On the contrary, the differences are used to spell out a new understanding of commonality. Reproductive rights need to be specified across and through the different needs of different races and economic classes.

The universality of rights discourse is both problematic and necessary for feminists, much in the same way as feminism is. But a feminism specified through women of color allows for a notion of equality that is distinctly compatible with diversity. This radically pluralizes, rather than liberally pluralizes, the meaning of diversity and reinvents the concept of equality, which can no longer mean merely sameness of treatment. A reproductive rights agenda can reconstruct equality through a completely pluralized notion of difference, while recognizing woman's commonality in political coalition. This radical egalitarianism is located between our differences and our similarities.

RADICALIZING PRIVACY THROUGH EQUALITY

White women in the national abortion movement, along with women of color, need to rethink the differences of economic class and race to develop a more inclusive understanding regarding women's different levels of access to health care and abortion. They need to hold onto the universal framing of abortion rights—that any woman has a right to such choice—while recognizing that choices currently differ for women according to their racialized economic situation. The logical starting point for theory and politics is the individual (in her specificity) and her right to reproductive freedom (which is universal). We must connect the discourse of choice to the different meanings that life circumstance affords.

This means reinventing the liberal individualist language of "choice" so that it challenges the inequalities of access women experience in accordance with their race, economic class, geographical location, age, and so on. Feminism needs continually to redefine the meaning of democratic rights to require equality of access via an affirmative and non-interventionist state.

Focusing on reproductive rights as a central facet of a feminist, antiracist, and progressive politics is different than limiting ourselves to abortion politics. Reproductive rights enlarges the issue of abortion to related concerns: affordable and good health care; a decrease in infant mortality and teenage pregnancy; reproductive health; health services for infertility; and access to appropriate contraceptives.[90]

The National Black Women's Health Project and the National Institute for Women of Color criticize the feminist framing of abortion for not addressing the problems of access which many women of color face.[91] These groups emphasize a reproductive rights agenda that includes not only greater access to abortion but also available health care, prenatal care, and economic justice. They locate abortion at the crux of a network of issues related to the economic inequity of racialized patriarchy. For example, the denial of access to abortion directly contributes to increased maternal mortality rates, which are nearly four times higher for black women than for white women in the United States. Moreover, abortion and family planning clinics funded by Title X provide the entry point for reproductive health care and minimal general health care for poor women. These clinics are the only places these women can get pap smears, mammograms, screening for sexually transmitted diseases, and so on.

We must refocus the issue of abortion to the societal framing of how it is available. The lack of prenatal care is as problematic for some women as the lack of an abortion is for others. Teenage pregnancy and the poverty it writes into the lives of newborns is a problem of crisis proportions in the African American community. Contraceptive services, sex education, and AIDS prevention outreach are as important to any woman needing them as abortion is for others. For many black women, who are more at risk for breast and cervical cancer, hypertension, diabetes, lupus, and other problems, abortion appears as only one among many health needs. Recognizing the complexity of the health needs of women of color radicalizes abortion politics for all women. It pushes feminists beyond a notion of bodily privacy limited by middle-class white women's experience, extending it to encompass the experiences of working-class and poor white women, as well as those of Asian and Latina women.

This view of abortion pushes beyond the identity politics of any one group of women by cutting through the racialized and economic class divisions that stunt pro-choice politics. It makes clear that identity is often multiple.[92] But the problem of how to build coalitions in a society so fractured by difference on the one hand and false universality on the other hand remains overwhelming.

Journalist and radical feminist Ellen Willis wonders whether coalition building ever really works. Her experience of feminism is that co-alition work usually waters down the issues, particularly with regard to sexual issues. Much like activists in ACT UP, she worries "that coalition building always seems to mean sexual radicalism gets lost."[93] Women of color wonder the same thing when it comes to the possibility of a radical, antiracist, feminist politics. Many feminist women of color organizations protested in 1991 that the National Organization for Women (NOW) organizers of the reproductive rights march on Washington did not actively seek their participation in the initial stages of organizing the march. The organizations that distributed the letter of protest included Asian Pacific Islanders for Choice, the Asian Pacific Women's Network, the National Black Women's Health Project, the National Coalition of 100 Black Women, the National Latina Health Organization, the Native American Women's Health Education Resource Center, and the International Coalition of Women Physicians.[94]

According to Julia Scott of the Black Women's Health Project and Luz Alvarez Martinez of the National Latina Health Organization, NOW took little, if any, initiative in contacting women of color organizations so that a working coalition could be formed.[95] At the time of this writing, Patricia Ireland, president of NOW, had still not responded directly to any of the organizations regarding their concerns. Yet the NOW National Conference resolutions for 1992 state that NOW members are committed to dismantling racism within themselves, in their organization, and throughout society. The resolutions endorse affirmative action, representative membership, and sensitivity training for NOW members. NOW also formally supported the "Women of All Colors 1993 March" and agreed to send a representative to the planning committee meeting.[96]

Luz Alvarez, whose priority is building coalitions and networks within and between different women's communities, has stated that it is really up to NOW to show that they are serious about coalition work. Obviously, much remains to be done here. Coalitions between and among women of color must be built. And coalitions between sectors of the white women's reproductive rights movement must actively seek connections to the women of color reproductive rights movement.

White feminists must make antiracist coalition work a priority. Reproductive rights is an agenda where there are definite possibilities. Why? Because reproductive rights, as a fundamental democratic right of all women, is located in an *in-between* space: between our rights and our access to them; between our reproductive specificity and our universal human claims; between an affirmative state and our bodily privacy. These issues cut across racialized economic lines.

The narrow focus on abortion (as disconnected from the need for jobs, good health care, and so on) reflects just how narrowed the defensive posture of feminism became during the rightist Reagan and Bush years. Women of color make clear that this narrowing must be reversed. There cannot be bodily privacy for all women without sexual and racial equality. The issues of access and privacy are interwoven. Their connection radicalizes the meaning of privacy for all women.

Democratic rights and equality need redefinition. Reproductive rights require reproductive freedom, and reproductive freedom requires equality of access to health care and abortion, as well as the freedom of individual choice. This is the lesson that liberal democracies and Eastern European societies still need to understand: radical pluralism and radical individuality have to reinvent the meaning of democracy by committing to sexual and racial equality. Starting with pregnant women of color, an antiracist diversity must be at the core of equality and democracy. And a revisioning of democracy must start with reproductive rights.

Postscript

As this book goes to press, the Clinton administration has just completed its first hundred days. I remain hopeful because I feel I must. But I also fear that the "new" Democratic agenda will remain stunted and inadequate.

On the one hand, it seems like much has changed. Bill is no George, and Hillary is no Barbara. They represent a different generation, with different social and personal values. I continue to wonder what, if any, political import this generational difference will have.

This year was supposed to be the "year of the political woman." Yet Zoe Baird lost the nomination for Attorney General because of earlier illegal nanny arrangements. Although it is true that there are many white women and persons of color in the new administration, it is still dominated by white men. And although in some ways Hillary Clinton represents a sea change for American women, long-established constraints continue to limit her.

Bill Clinton, as promised, initiated a lifting of the ban on gays and lesbians in the military as one of his first acts in office. But ever since, he has seemed beaten up by the issue. During the march on Washington for gay and lesbian rights in April 1993, Bill left town.

Meanwhile, the U.S. public awaits the health care proposals from Hillary's committee. We wonder what steps the Clinton administration may take in Bosnia to stop the killing. We await a coordinated plan to deal with AIDS. And we await an effective initiative to deal with the failing economy and the crisis of the cities.

All the mixed signs and signals and false starts define the politics of the 1990s. At least it does not feel as closed down and narrow as the politics of the 1980s. Out of this flux, democracy must be reimaged.

Notes

INTRODUCTION

1. For critiques of traditional political theory, see Christine diStefano, *Configurations of Masculinity* (Ithaca, N.Y.: Cornell University Press, 1991); Zillah Eisenstein, *The Radical Future of Liberal Feminism* (Boston: Northeastern University Press, 1981); Jean Bethke Elshtain, *Public Man, Private Woman* (Princeton, N.J.: Princeton University Press, 1981); Carole Pateman, *The Sexual Contract* (Stanford, Calif.: Stanford University Press, 1988); Mary Lyndon Shanley and Carole Pateman, eds., *Feminist Interpretations and Political Theory* (University Park: Pennsylvania State University Press, 1991). For a more direct feminist critique of democracy, see Susan Moller Okin, *Justice, Gender and the Family* (New York: Basic Books, 1989); and Anne Phillips, *Engendering Democracy* (University Park: Pennsylvania State University Press, 1991).

2. Toni Morrison, *Playing in the Dark: Whiteness and the Literary Imagination* (Cambridge, Mass.: Harvard University Press, 1992), pp. 10–12.

3. Evelyn Brooks-Higginbotham, "African-American Women's History and the Metalanguage of Race," *Signs* 17, no. 2 (Winter 1992): 257–58.

4. Donna J. Haraway, *Simians, Cyborgs, and Women: The Reinvention of Nature* (New York: Routledge, 1991), p. 129.

5. For a full discussion and definition of neoconservatism, see Zillah Eisenstein, *Feminism and Sexual Equality: Crisis in Liberal America* (New York: Monthly Review Press, 1984).

6. I use the terms *sex* and *gender* in their interconnected, but not synonymous, meaning. Whereas *sex* connotes the biological female, *gender* designates the cultural interpretation of being female. "Biology is, in part, gendered—which is, in part, culture; and gender is, in part, biological—which is also, in part, cultural" (p. 2). See Zillah Eisenstein, *The Female Body and the Law* (Berkeley and Los Angeles: University of California Press, 1989), for a full accounting of this relationship.

7. For an interesting discussion of problems with the feminist critique of postmodernism, see Wendy Brown, "Feminist Hesitations, Postmodern Exposures," *differences* 3, no. 1 (Spring 1991): 63–84. Brown argues that feminists fear postmodern intellectual maneuvers because feminists reject fixed metaphysical referents which privilege women's voice. She assumes that feminists fear a "cacophony of unequal voices clamoring for position" (p. 73). But Brown misrepresents feminism in order to position postmodernism favorably. I instead view the relationship between feminism and postmodernism in a more complicated fashion; postmodernism has developed in dialogue with and in critique of feminist insights throughout. There are a series of intersections between feminism and postmodernism that complicate an easy separation of the two.

8. Kwame Anthony Appiah, *In My Father's House: Africa in the Philosophy of Culture* (New York: Oxford University Press, 1992), pp. 140, 142.

9. Sheldon Wolin, "Beyond Marxism and Monetarism," *Nation* 250, no. 11 (19 Mar. 1990): 373.

10. Christopher Lasch, *The Culture of Narcissism* (New York: Norton, 1979).

11. Lane Kenworthy, "What Kind of Economic System? A Leftist's Guide," *Socialist Review* 20, no. 2 (Apr. 1990): 121.

12. Helga Maria Hernes, *Welfare State and Woman Power: Essays in State Feminism* (Oslo: Norwegian University Press, 1987), pp. 46, 123, 131.

13. I do not share Judith Butler's fear that "feminist politics precludes a radical inquiry into the political construction and regulation of identity itself" (p. 11) because such politics accept the regulation inherent in the construction of woman as an identity. See her *Gender Trouble: Feminism and the Subversion of Identity* (New York: Routledge, 1990).

14. Slavenka Drakulic, "In Their Own Words: Women of Eastern Europe," *Ms.* 1, no. 1 (July/Aug. 1990): 36–47; and her "Living in a Le Carré Novel," *Nation* 252, no. 8 (4 March 1991): 261.

15. Inji Aflatun, "We Egyptian Women," in *Opening the Gates: A Century of Arab Feminist Writing,* ed. Margot Badran and Miriam Cooke (Bloomington: Indiana University Press, 1990), p. 350.

16. Nahid Toubia, "Challenges Facing the Arab Woman at the End of the Twentieth Century," in *Opening the Gates,* p. 367.

17. Ghada Samman, "Our Constitution—We the Liberated Women," in *Opening the Gates,* p. 141.

18. Margot Badran and Miriam Cooke, Introduction to *Opening the Gates,* pp. 15, 33.

19. Madhu Kishwar, "Why I Do Not Call Myself a Feminist," *Manushi,* no. 61 (Nov/Dec. 1990), p. 3.

20. As quoted in Karen Grisby Bates, "They've Gotta Have Us," *New York Times Magazine,* 14 July 1991, p. 38.

21. Michael Lowy, "Twelve Theses on the Crisis of 'Really Existing Socialism,'" *Monthly Review* 43, no. 1 (May 1991): 33.

22. Ralph Miliband, "Socialism in Question," *Monthly Review* 42, no. 10 (Mar. 1991): 21, 25.

23. Chantal Mouffe, "Hegemony and New Political Subjects: Toward a New Concept of Democracy," in *Marxism and the Interpretation of Culture,* ed.

Cary Nelson and Lawrence Grossberg (Urbana: University of Illinois Press, 1988), pp. 100, 101.

24. Manning Marable, "Remaking American Marxism," *Monthly Review* 42, no. 8 (Jan. 1991): 42, 46, 53. Also see his *The Crisis of Color and Democracy: Essays on Race, Class and Power* (Monroe, Maine: Common Courage Press, 1992).

CHAPTER 1. EASTERN EUROPEAN MALE DEMOCRACIES

1. As quoted by David Binder in "Two Student Militants," *New York Times*, 10 Jan. 1990, p. A10.

2. John Stuart Mill, "From the *Political Economy*, Book II, Chapter 1," in *Socialism*, ed. W. D. P. Bliss (New York: Humboldt, 1890); Zillah Eisenstein, "J. S. Mill and Harriet Taylor: Liberal Individualism, Socialism, and Feminism," in *The Radical Future of Liberal Feminism* (Boston: Northeastern University Press, 1981).

3. Rosa Luxemburg, as stated in the *Spartacus Letters* and quoted by Irving Howe in "From the Dustbin of History," *Dissent* 37, no. 2 (Spring 1990): 184. Also see her "Reform or Revolution," in *Selected Political Writings*, ed. Dick Howard (New York: Monthly Review Press, 1971).

4. A vast literature deals with the inadequacies of Marxism for feminism. Here are a few titles: Michele Barrett, *Women's Oppression Today: Problems in Marxist Feminist Analysis* (London: New Left Books, 1980); Zillah Eisenstein, *Capitalist Patriarchy and the Case for Socialist Feminism* (New York: Monthly Review Press, 1979); Karen Hansen and Ilene Philipson, eds., *Women, Class and the Feminist Imagination: A Socialist-Feminist Reader* (Philadelphia: Temple University Press, 1990); Sonia Kruks, Rayna Rapp, and Marilyn Young, eds., *Promissory Notes: Women in the Transition to Socialism* (New York: Monthly Review Press, 1989); Catherine MacKinnon, *Toward a Feminist Theory of the State* (Cambridge: Harvard University Press, 1989); and Lydia Sargent, *Women and Revolution: A Discussion of the Unhappy Marriage of Marxism and Feminism* (Boston: South End Press, 1981).

5. V. I. Lenin, *Emancipation of Women from the Writings of V. I. Lenin* (New York: International Publishers, 1934).

6. John Stuart Mill, *On the Subjection of Women* (1869; reprint, Greenwich, Conn.: Fawcett, 1971).

7. Karl Marx and Friedrich Engels, *The German Ideology*, ed. R. Pascal (1939; reprint, New York: International Publishers, 1947).

8. Karl Marx and Friedrich Engels, *The Economic and Philosophic Manuscripts of 1844*, ed. Dirk J. Struik, trans. Martin Milligan (New York: International Publishers, 1964).

9. Hilda Scott, *Does Socialism Liberate Women? Experiences from Eastern Europe* (Boston: Beacon Press, 1974). Also see her "Why the Revolution Doesn't Solve Everything: What We Can Learn from the Economics of 'Real' Socialism," *Women's Studies International Forum* 5, no. 5 (1982): 451–62.

10. Hildegard Maria Nickel, "Women in the German Democratic Republic

and in the New Federal States: Looking Backwards and Forwards," *German Politics and Society*, nos. 24–25 (Winter 1991–92): 38.

11. Ina Merkel, "Another Kind of Woman," *German Politics and Society*, nos. 24–25 (Winter 1991–92): 6.

12. Ruth Rosen, "Male Democracies, Female Dissidents," *Tikkun* 5, no. 6 (Nov.–Dec. 1990): 11. Also see Celestine Bohlen, "East Europe's Women Struggle with New Rules, and Old Ones," *New York Times*, 25 Nov. 1990, p. E1; and interviews with Anna Bojarska of Poland (pp. 4–6), Helke Misselwitz of East Germany (pp. 6–7), and Tatiana Shcherbina of the Soviet Union (p. 8) in *Women's Review of Books* 7, nos. 10–11 (6 July 1990).

13. Scott, *Does Socialism Liberate Women?* p. 86; also see Scott, "Why the Revolution Doesn't Solve Everything," pp. 451–62.

14. Roger Burbach and Steve Painter, "Restoration in Czechoslovakia," *Monthly Review* 42, no. 11 (Apr. 1991): 42.

15. See Myra Marx Ferree, "The Wall Remaining: Reflections on Feminism and Unification in Germany" (Department of Sociology, University of Connecticut, Photocopy).

16. Nannette Funk and Magda Muller, "Dossier on Women in Eastern Europe," *Social Text* 9, no. 2, issue 27 (1990): 88.

17. Marlise Simons, "A Divisive Issue of German Unity: How to Reconcile Abortion Laws," *New York Times*, 19 July 1990, p. A1. Also see Peter Marcuse, "Letter from the German Democratic Republic," *Monthly Review* 42, no. 3 (July–Aug. 1990): 30–62.

18. Dorothy Rosenberg, "The Colonization of East Germany," *Monthly Review Press* 43, no. 4 (Sept. 1991): 20.

19. Brenda Bishop, "From Women's Rights to Feminist Politics: The Developing Struggle for Women's Liberation in Poland," *Monthly Review* 42, no. 6 (Nov. 1990): 15–34.

20. Ruth Rosen, "A Letter to Jirina Siklova: On American Feminism and Gender Democracy," *Dissent* 38, no. 4 (Fall 1991): 533.

21. See Slavenka Drakulic, "Talk to the European Women's Committee on Security and Cooperation" (Paper delivered in Berlin, November 1990), for a careful critique of the new constitutions of Slovenia and Croatia in terms of their stance on abortion rights.

22. Stephen Engelberg, "Abortion Ban, Sought by Church, Is Rejected by Polish Parliament," *New York Times*, 18 May 1991, p. A1. Also see Gabrielle Glaser, "New Poland, Same Old Story," *Village Voice* 36, no. 14 (2 April 1991): 19–21; and her "John Paul Angrily Scolds the Poles over Abortion," *New York Times*, 4 June 1991, p. A11.

23. "Poland Ends Subsidies for Birth Control Pills," *New York Times*, 9 May 1991, p. A11.

24. Ferdinand Protzman, "Germany's Facing Abortion Battle," *New York Times*, 26 Aug. 1990, p. A9.

25. Ferdinand Protzman, "Broader Abortion Law Leaves Germans Somber," *New York Times*, 27 June 1992, p. A3.

26. Robin Morgan, ed., *Sisterhood Is Global* (New York: Doubleday, 1984),

p. 577. Also see Jill Neimark, "Romanian Roulette," *Village Voice* 36, no. 40 (Oct. 1991): 28.

27. Kathleen Hunt, "The Romanian Baby Bazaar," *New York Times Magazine*, 24 Mar. 1991, p. 28. Also see Felicity Barringer, "Birth Rates Plummeting in Some Ex-Communist Regions of Eastern Europe": *New York Times*, 31 Dec. 1991, p. A3; David Binder, "Where Fear and Death Went Forth and Multiplied," *New York Times*, 24 Jan. 1990, p. A12; Celestine Bohlen, "New Rumanian Government Keeps Some Old Ways," *New York Times*, 31 Jan. 1990, p. A1; Meredith Burke, "Ceausescu's Main Victims: Women and Children," *New York Times*, 10 Jan. 1990, p. A27; and Robert Cullen, "Report from Romania," *New Yorker* 66, no. 7 (2 Apr. 1990): 94–112.

28. Elina Haavio-Mannila et al., *Unfinished Democracy: Women in Nordic Politics* (New York: Pergamon Press, 1985), p. 155.

29. Genia Browning, *Women and Politics in the U.S.S.R.* (New York: St. Martin's Press, 1987).

30. Maxine Molyneux, "The 'Woman Question' in the Age of Perestroika," *New Left Review*, no. 183 (Sept.–Oct. 1990): 29.

31. Katrina Vanden Heuvel, "Glasnost for Women," *Nation* 250, no. 22 (4 June 1990): 773.

32. See Natalya Baranskaya, *A Week Like Any Other: Novellas and Stories* (Seattle: Seal Press, 1989), for a compelling description of everyday life for Soviet women.

33. Katrina Vanden Heuvel, "Women of Russia Unite!" *New York Times*, 12 Sept. 1992, p. A21.

34. See A. G. Khomassuridze, "Abortion and Contraception in Georgia," *From Abortion to Contraception* series (World Health Organization Regional Office for Europe, October 1990, Photocopy). Professor Khomassuridze is at the Zhordania Institute of Human Reproduction, Tbilisi, Georgian SSR.

35. Richard Parker, "Inside the Collapsing Soviet Economy," *Atlantic Monthly* 265, no. 6 (June 1990): 70.

36. Molyneux, "The 'Woman Question' in the Age of Perestroika," pp. 28–30.

37. Mikhail Gorbachev, *Perestroika* (New York: Harper and Row, 1987) p. 103.

38. Susan Bridger, *Women in the Soviet Countryside* (New York: Cambridge University Press, 1987), p. 225. Also see Mary Buckley, *Women and Ideology in the Soviet Union* (Ann Arbor: University of Michigan Press, 1989); Ellen Carnaghan and Donna Bahry, *Political Attitudes and the Gender Gap in the U.S.S.R.: Evidence from Former Soviet Citizens*, Working Paper no. 53 (Urbana: University of Illinois at Urbana-Champaign, Soviet Interview Project, October 1988).

39. As cited in Vanden Heuvel, "Women of Russia Unite!" p. A21.

40. Tatyana Momonova, *Russian Women's Studies: Essays on Sexism in Soviet Culture* (New York: Pergamon Press, 1989).

41. Tatyana Tolstaya, "Notes from Underground," *New York Review of Books* 37, no. 9 (31 May 1990): 5.

42. Francine du Plessix Gray, *Soviet Women: Walking the Tightrope* (New York: Doubleday, 1989), p. 37.

43. Betty Friedan, *The Feminine Mystique* (New York: Dell, 1963). See her later *The Second Stage* (New York: Summit Books, 1981) for a rebuttal of her earlier stance equating paid work with equality.

44. Du Plessix Gray, *Soviet Women: Walking the Tightrope*, pp. 97–98.

45. Ibid., p. 97.

46. Ibid., p. 89.

47. Ibid., pp. 35, 47.

48. Yelena Khanga, "No Matryoshkas Need Apply," *New York Times*, 25 Nov. 1991, p. A19.

49. My critique of the limits of Havel's democratic theorizing focuses on his inadequate treatment of gender issues. For other discussions of the limits of Havel's democratic vision, see George Black, "Prague Gets the Chicago Treatment," *Nation* 251, no. 20 (10 Dec. 1990): 717–36; Bill Kovach and Tom Winship, "Havel: Prison for Journalists," *New York Times*, 15 July 1990, p. E19; and A. M. Rosenthal, "Havel and Waldheim," *New York Times*, 29 July 1990, p. E19.

50. Vaclav Havel, *Disturbing the Peace* (New York: Knopf, 1990), p. 9. Also see Vaclav Havel et al., *The Power of the Powerless* (New York: M. E. Sharpe, 1985).

51. Vaclav Havel, "Words on Words," *New York Review of Books* 36, nos. 21–22 (18 Jan. 1990): 6.

52. Havel, *Disturbing the Peace*, pp. 7–9.

53. Vaclav Havel, "The Future of Central Europe," *New York Review of Books* 27, no. 5 (29 Mar. 1990): 19; also see his "History of a Public Enemy," *New York Review of Books* 37, no. 9 (31 May 1990): 36–44; "The New Year in Prague," *New York Review of Books* 38, no. 5 (7 March 1991): 19–20; and "Paradise Lost," *New York Review of Books* 39, no. 7 (9 Apr. 1992): 6–8. Also see Timothy Garton Ash, "The Revolution of the Magic Lantern," *New York Review of Books* 36, nos. 21–22 (18 Jan. 1990): 42–51; Jeri Laber, "Witch Hunt in Prague," *New York Review of Books* 39, no. 8 (23 Apr. 1992): 5–8; Philip Roth, "A Conversation in Prague," *New York Review of Books* 37, no. 6 (12 Apr. 1990): 14–22; and Vit Horejs and Bonnie Stein, "The New King of Absurdistan," *Village Voice* 25, no. 3 (16 Jan. 1990): 31–35.

54. Havel, "Future of Central Europe."

55. Vaclav Havel, *Living in Truth* (Boston: Faber & Faber, 1989), p. 117.

56. Vaclav Havel, "The End of the Modern Era," *New York Times*, 1 Mar. 1992, p. E15.

57. Havel, *Disturbing the Peace*, p. 14.

58. Havel, *Living in Truth*, p. 118.

59. Havel, *Disturbing the Peace*, p. 16. Whether or not Havel's vision of a democratic market will be put in place in Czechoslovakia seems questionable given recent developments instituted by its finance minister, Vaclav Klaus. For a discussion of Klaus's adoption of the economic models of Milton Friedman and Friedrich von Hayek, see Black, "Prague Gets the Chicago Treatment."

60. Havel, *Disturbing the Peace*, p. 13.

61. Havel, *Living in Truth*, p. 23.

62. Alena Heitlinger, a Czech feminist who has been corresponding with me, wonders how I can expect Havel to be a feminist within the present cultural context of Czechoslovakia: personal correspondence, 3 Mar. 1991.

63. As quoted in Jefferson Morley, "Mr. Havel Goes to Washington," *Nation* 251, no. 11 (19 Mar. 1990): 375.

64. Vaclav Havel, *Temptation* (New York: Grove Press, 1986).

65. Havel, *Disturbing the Peace*, p. 156.

66. Vaclav Havel, *Letters to Olga* (New York: Henry Holt, 1988), p. 45. Also see Janet Malcolm, "The Trial of Alyosha," *New York Review of Books* 37, no. 10 (10 June 1990): 35–38.

67. Havel, *Letters to Olga*, pp. 48, 59.

68. Lucinda Franks, "Olga Havel," *People Magazine* 34, no. 10 (10 Sept. 1990): 144.

69. Havel, *Living in Truth*, p. 180.

70. Alena Heitlinger, "The Status of Women in Changing Economies: Czechoslovakia" (Paper presented at the annual meeting of the American Economic Association, New Orleans, 3–6 Jan. 1992).

71. Bohlen, "East Europe's Women Struggle," p. E2.

72. Ibid., p. 159.

73. Rosen, "Male Democracies," p. 101.

74. Drakulic, "In Their Own Words," 36–47. Also see Slavenka Drakulic, *How We Survived Communism and Even Laughed* (New York: Norton, 1991).

75. "East German Feminists: The Lila Manifesto," with introduction by Lisa DiCaprio, *Feminist Studies* 16, no. 3 (Fall 1990): 621.

76. Ibid., p. 627.

77. Ibid., p. 628.

78. Renata Siemienska, "Women and Women's Issues during Systemic Change in Economy and Politics in Poland" (Institute of Sociology, University of Warsaw, Photocopy), p. 34.

79. Eisenstein, *Radical Future of Liberal Feminism*, p. 114.

80. Celestine Bohlen, "Where the Fires of Hatred Are Easily Stoked," *New York Times*, 4 Aug. 1991, p. E3; Judith Ingram, "Hungary's Gypsy Women: Scapegoats in a New Democracy," *Ms.* 2, no. 2 (Sept./Oct. 1991): 17–19; Anthony Lewis, "Hate Against Hate," *New York Times*, 15 Nov. 1991, p. A15; James Ridgeway with Bettina Muller, "Wie Deutsch Ist Es?" *Village Voice* 36, no. 49 (Dec. 1991): 34–41.

CHAPTER 2. UNITED STATES POLITICS AND THE
MYTH OF POST-RACISM

1. For further discussion of the neoconservative attack on sexual equality and abortion, see my *Feminism and Sexual Equality* and *Female Body and the Law;* and Rosalind Pollack Petchesky, *Abortion and Woman's Choice, the State, Sexuality and Reproductive Freedom* (Boston: Northeastern University Press, 1984).

2. See Christopher Lasch, *The True and Only Heaven* (New York: Norton,

1991), for a different and interesting discussion of the place of race and sex in the crisis of liberalism.

3. Anthony Lewis, *Make No Law: The Sullivan Case and the First Amendment* (New York: Random House, 1991), especially pp. 16–19.

4. New York State Judicial Commission on Minorities, *Report*, vol. 1: Executive Summary, April 1991. Available from Clerk, New York State Court of Appeals, 1 Eagle St., Albany, NY.

5. Ibid., especially pp. 12, 37, 41.

6. Jerry Gray, "Panel Says Courts Are 'Infested' with Racism," *New York Times*, 6 June 1991, p. B1.

7. Gary Orfield and Carole Ashkinaze, *The Closing Door: Conservative Policy and Black Opportunity* (Chicago: Chicago University Press, 1991), pp. 11, 15, 68.

8. Andrew Hacker, *Two Nations, Black and White: Separate, Hostile, Unequal* (New York: Scribner, 1992).

9. Orlando Patterson and Chris Winship, "White Poor, Black Poor," *New York Times*, 3 May 1992, p. E17.

10. Michael Omi and Howard Winant, *Racial Formation in the United States* (New York: Routledge, 1986), p. 68.

11. Stephen Labaton, "Few Minority Companies Get Contracts in Savings Bailout," *New York Times*, 4 June 1991, p. A1.

12. Arthur A. Fletcher, as quoted in "Rights Chief Sees Race as Factor in Election," *New York Times*, 1 May 1991, p. A18.

13. *Atlantic Monthly* 267, no. 5 (May 1991): 53–86.

14. Thomas Byrne Edsall and Mary D. Edsall, *Chain Reaction: The Impact of Race, Rights, and Taxes on American Politics* (New York: Norton, 1991), pp. x, 7. Also see Andrew Hacker, "Playing the Racial Card," *New York Review of Books* 38, no. 17 (24 Oct. 1991): 14–18.

15. Edsall and Edsall, *Chain Reaction*, pp. 138, 144–45.

16. Ibid., pp. 3, 12, 13.

17. Adolph Reed, Jr., and Julian Bond, "Equality: Why We Can't Win," *Nation* 253, no. 20 (9 Dec. 1991): 733–37.

18. Gertrude Ezorsky, *Racism and Justice: The Case for Affirmative Action* (Ithaca, NY: Cornell University Press, 1991), pp. 68–70.

19. Stuart Alan Clarke, "Fear of a Black Planet," *Socialist Review* 21, nos. 3–4 (Dec. 1991): 41.

20. *Regents of the University of California v. Bakke*, 438 U.S. 265 (1978).

21. Michel Rosenfeld, *Affirmative Action and Justice* (New Haven: Yale University Press, 1991), pp. 306–308, 325. Also see Andrew Hacker, "Affirmative Action: The New Look," *New York Review of Books* 36, no. 15 (12 Oct. 1989): 63–68; and Tom Wicker, "Justice of Hypocrisy?" *New York Times*, 15 Aug. 1991, p. A23.

22. Mary E. Hawkesworth, "The Affirmative Action Debate and Conflicting Conceptions of Individuality," in *Hypatia Reborn: Essays in Feminist Philosophy*, ed. Azizah Y. al-Hibri and Margaret A. Simons (Bloomington: Indiana University Press, 1990), p. 135.

23. Rosenfeld, *Affirmative Action and Justice*, p. 42.

24. Eleanor Holmes Norton, interviewed in "The Great Divide: Affirmative Action in America" (Transcript from broadcast on National Public Radio, 15–22 Sept. 1991), p. 11. Available from NPR Transcript Office, (202) 822–2323.

25. Rosenfeld, *Affirmative Action and Justice,* p. 336.

26. "Another Yale Panel Urges Hiring Women and Minorities for Faculty," *New York Times,* 24 November 1991, p. A46.

27. Sharon M. Collins, "The Making of the Black Middle Class," *Social Problems* 30, no. 4 (1983): 369–82.

28. Richard L. Zweigenhaft and William Domhoff, *Blacks in the White Establishment? A Study of Race and Class in America* (New Haven, Conn.: Yale University Press, 1991).

29. Don Terry, "Cuts in Public Jobs May Hurt Blacks Most," *New York Times,* 10 Dec. 1991, p. A1.

30. Gerald David Jaynes and Robin M. Williams, Jr., eds., *A Common Destiny: Blacks and American Society* (Washington, D.C.: National Academy Press, 1989).

31. William P. O'Hare, Kelvin M. Pollard, Taynia L. Mann, and Mary M. Kent, "African Americans in the 1990's," *Population Bulletin* 46, no. 1 (July 1991), p. 3.

32. See *Croson v. City of Richmond,* 488 U.S. 469 (1989); *Wards Cove Packing v. Atonio,* 490 U.S. 642 (1989); *Price Waterhouse v. Hopkins,* 490 U.S. 228 (1989).

33. 488 U.S. 469 (1989).

34. Ibid., p. 480.

35. Ibid., p. 470.

36. Ibid., p. 496.

37. Ibid., p. 524.

38. Ibid., p. 527.

39. Ibid., p. 537.

40. Ibid., p. 541.

41. 490 U.S. 642 (1989).

42. 401 U.S. 424 (1971).

43. See Ezorsky, *Racism and Justice,* p. 40, for an insightful discussion of the *Griggs* case.

44. 490 U.S. 642, 653.

45. Ibid., p. 657 (quoting *Watson v. Fort Worth Bank & Trust,* 487 U.S. 977 [1988]).

46. Ibid., p. 673.

47. Ibid., p. 662.

48. 491 U.S. 164 (1989).

49. Ibid., p. 171.

50. Ibid., p. 176.

51. Ibid., p. 177.

52. Ibid., p. 187 (Brennan, J., dissenting).

53. 490 U.S. 755 (1989).

54. 491 U.S. 701 (1989).

55. Linda Greenhouse, "Justices Rule Mandatory Busing May Go, Even If

Races Stay Apart," *New York Times,* 16 Jan. 1991, p. A1. Also see "The Nation's Schools Learn a Fourth R: Resegregation," *New York Times,* 19 Jan. 1992, p. E5.

56. Robert Pear, "Courts Are Undoing Efforts to Aid Minority Contractors," *New York Times,* 16 July 1990, p. A1.

57. See Derrick Bell, *And We Are Not Saved* (New York: Basic Books, 1987), especially pp. 172–75. Also see his *Faces at the Bottom of the Well* (New York: Basic Books, 1992).

58. 110 S. Ct. 2997 (1990).

59. Ibid., p. 3044. Also see Linda Greenhouse, "Justices Bolster Race Preferences at Federal Level," *New York Times,* 28 June 1990, p. B8; and her "Renewing Minority Rights Debate, Court Will Decide on F.C.C. Rules," *New York Times,* 9 Jan. 1990, p. A1; and Neil Lewis, "Court Ruling Encourages Affirmative Action," *New York Times,* 4 July 1990, p. A12.

60. As quoted in Linda Greenhouse, "Supreme Court Decision Limits Scope of '65 Voting Rights Act," *New York Times* 28 Jan. 1992, p. A1. Also see *Presley v. Etowah County Commission,* 112 S. Ct. 820 (1992).

61. As quoted in the "Excerpts from Court Ruling to Lift Curbs on Formerly Segregated Schools," *New York Times,* 1 Apr. 1992, p. B8. See *Freeman v. Pitts,* 112 S. Ct. 1430 (1992).

62. 490 U.S. 228 (1989).

63. Ibid., p. 235.

64. Ibid., p. 251.

65. Ibid., p. 242.

66. Ibid., p. 294.

67. 737 F. Supp. 1202, 1206 (D.D.C. 1990).

68. Ibid., p. 1207. Also see Tamar Lewin, "Partnership in Firm Awarded to Victim of Sex Bias," *New York Times,* 16 May 1990, p. A1.

69. 724 F. Supp. 717, 722 (N.D. Cal. 1989).

70. Nancy Dowd, "Work and Family: The Gender Paradox and the Limitations of Discrimination Analysis in Restructuring the Workplace," *Harvard Civil Rights–Civil Liberties Law Review* 24 (1989), pp. 79–172. Also see Heidi Hartmann and Roberta Spalter-Roth, "Improving Employment Opportunities for Women" (Testimony Concerning H.R. 1, Civil Rights Act of 1991, before the U.S. House of Representatives Committee on Education and Labor, 17 February 1991), available from the Institute for Women's Policy Research, 1400 20th St. NW, Suite 104, Washington, D.C. 20036.

71. 490 U.S. 900 (1989).

72. Ibid., p. 905.

73. Ibid., p. 912.

74. Ibid., p. 914 (Marshall, J., dissenting).

75. Steven Holmes, "Workers Find It Tough Going Filing Lawsuits over Job Bias," *New York Times,* 24 July 1991, p. A1.

76. 111 S. Ct. 1196, 1198, 1210 (1991). Also see Linda Greenhouse, "Court Backs Right of Women to Jobs with Health Risks," *New York Times,* 21 March 1991, p. A1.

77. William Julius Wilson, *The Declining Significance of Race* (Chicago: University of Chicago Press, 1980), pp. 2, 152.

78. William Julius Wilson, *The Truly Disadvantaged* (Chicago: University of Chicago Press, 1987), pp. 10, 11.

79. Ibid., pp. 12, 122–24, 130.

80. William Julius Wilson, "How the Democrats Can Harness Whites and Blacks in '92," *New York Times*, 24 March 1989, p. A31.

81. As quoted in Jason DeParle, "Responding to Urban Alarm Bells at Scholarships' Glacial Pace," *New York Times*, 19 July 1992, p. E7.

82. Stephen L. Carter, *Reflections of an Affirmative Action Baby* (New York: Basic Books, 1991), pp. 74–78. Also see his "I Am An Affirmative Action Baby," *New York Times*, 5 Aug. 1991, p. A13.

83. Carter, *Reflections*, pp. 80, 165, 249.

84. Ibid., pp. 135, 24.

85. Ibid., pp. 6, 34, 199, 47, 27, 69.

86. Shelby Steele, *The Content of Our Character* (New York: St. Martin's Press, 1990), pp. 107, 23, 116, 123, 91.

87. Ibid., pp. 49, 28, 39.

88. Ibid., p. 175.

89. Julianne Malveaux, "Why Are the Black Conservatives All Men?" *Ms.* 1, no. 5 (Mar./Apr. 1991): 60.

CHAPTER 3. THE "NEW RACISM" AND ITS MULTIPLE FACES

1. Jefferson Morley, "Bush and the Blacks: An Unknown Story," *New York Review of Books* 34, nos. 1–2 (16 Jan. 1992): 19–26.

2. Steven Holmes, "When the Subject Is Civil Rights, There Are Two George Bushes," *New York Times*, 9 June 1991, p. E1.

3. *USA Weekend* Survey Poll, June 1991, cited in Jessica Lee, "Why Is Bush Rated the Worst?" *USA Weekend*, Special Report, 28–30 June 1991, p. 7.

4. Anthony DePalma, "Colleges Express Great Confusion on Minority Aid," *New York Times*, 20 Dec. 1990, p. A1.

5. Karen DeWitt, "U.S. Lets Stand Curb on College Aid Keyed to Race," *New York Times*, 19 Dec. 1990, p. A1.

6. Karen DeWitt, "Ban on Race-Exclusive Scholarships Expected Today," *New York Times*, 4 Dec. 1991, p. B16.

7. Anthony DePalma, "Theory and Practice at Odds in Ruling on Minority Scholarships," *New York Times*, 7 Dec. 1991, p. A10.

8. As quoted by Karen DeWitt, "Education Chief Backs Minority Scholarships," *New York Times*, 19 Mar. 1993, p. A15.

9. Anthony Lewis, "Defining the Issue," *New York Times*, 5 Aug. 1991, p. A13.

10. Solicitor General Kenneth W. Starr, as quoted in Linda Greenhouse, "Bush Reverses U.S. Stance Against Black College Aid," *New York Times*, 22 Oct. 1991, p. B6. The case was United States v. Fordice, 112 S. Ct. 2727 (1991).

11. Steven Holmes, "Bush to Order End of Rules Allowing Race-Based Hiring," *New York Times,* 21 Nov. 1991, p. A1.

12. Maureen Dowd, "White House Isolation," *New York Times,* 22 Nov. 1991, p. A1.

13. See Civil Rights Act of 1990, S. 2104, p. 1, and the Civil Rights and Women's Equity in Employment Act of 1991, H.R. 1.

14. Civil Rights and Women's Equity in Employment Act of 1991, H.R. 1, 102d Congress, 1st sess., Rep. No. 102-40, part 1, p. 93. Also see James Ridgeway, "Quota, Unquota," *Village Voice* 36, no. 23 (4 June 1991): 15.

15. Julie Johnson, "What Bush Is Making of Civil Rights," *New York Times,* 3 December 1989, p. E4. Also see Steven Holmes, "Major Civil Rights Bill Heads for Senate," *New York Times,* 10 July 1990, p. A17.

16. Adam Clymer, "Bush Assails 'Quota Bill' at West Point Graduation," *New York Times,* 2 June 1991, p. A32.

17. Sheilah A. Goodman, "Trying to Undo the Damage: The Civil Rights Act of 1990," *Harvard Women's Law Journal* 14 (Spring 1991): 185–221.

18. See the following articles by Adam Clymer: "Debate over Civil Rights Bill Raises Questions about the Law and Job Bias," *New York Times,* 26 May 1991, p. A22; "Bush Denounces Civil Rights Bill Advocated by House Democrats," *New York Times,* 31 May 1991, p. A1; "Rights Bill Passes in House But Vote Is Not Veto-Proof," *New York Times,* 6 June 1991, p. A1; "Impasse Seen in Push for Civil Rights Compromise," *New York Times,* 28 June 1991, p. A12; "Study Says Bush's Stand on Civil Rights Bill Contradicts the Courts," *New York Times,* 28 July 1991, p. A14; "Senate Democrats Back Compromise on Civil Rights Bill," *New York Times,* 26 Oct. 1991, p. A1; "Senate Passes Civil Rights Bill, 95–5, Ending a Bitter Debate over Job Bias," *New York Times,* 31 Oct. 1991, p. A20; and "Bush Heatedly Defends His Record on Civil Rights," *New York Times,* 11 July 1991, p. A17.

19. Tim Rutten, "A New Kind of Riot," *New York Review of Books* 39, no. 11 (11 June 1992): 52. Also see Jack Miles, "Blacks vs. Browns," *Atlantic Monthly* 270, no. 4 (Oct. 1992): 41–68.

20. Cornel West, "Learning to Talk of Race," *New York Times Magazine,* 2 Aug. 1992, p. 24.

21. R. W. Apple, Jr., "Bush Says Largess Won't Help Cities," *New York Times,* 7 May 1992, p. A22; David Rosenbaum, "White House Speaking in Code on Riot's Cause," *New York Times,* 6 May 1992, p. A24; and Michael Wines, "White House Links Riots to Welfare," *New York Times,* 5 May 1992, p. A1.

22. Michael Wines, "President Focuses on 'Family Values,' " *New York Times,* 10 Mar. 1992, p. A15; and his "Bush Tells Graduates That Family, Not Government, Can Cure Nation's Ills," *New York Times,* 18 May 1992, p. A14.

23. For an interesting discussion of how the control of racial and sexual minorities is established through the control of the family, see Carrie G. Costell, "Legitimate Bonds and Unnatural Unions: Race, Sexual Orientation, and Control of the American Family," *Harvard Women's Law Journal* 15 (Spring 1992): 79–171.

24. Michael Wines, "Appeal of 'Murphy Brown' Now Clear at White House," *New York Times,* 21 May 1992, p. B16. Also see Andrew Rosenthal, "Quayle Says Riots Arose from Burst of Social Anarchy," *New York Times,* 20 May 1992, p. A1.

25. Wines, "Appeal of 'Murphy Brown,' " p. A1.

26. Playthell Benjamin, "Uncle Justice Thomas," *Village Voice* 36, no. 29 (16 July 1991): 27–34; John Hope Franklin, "Booker T. Washington, Revisited," *New York Times,* 1 Aug. 1991, p. A21; Linda Greenhouse, "Court Choice Puts Nation's Racial Legacy on Table," *New York Times,* 8 July 1991, p. A9; Neil Lewis, "On Thomas's Climb, Ambivalence about Issue of Affirmative Action," *New York Times,* 14 July 1991, p. A1; Robert Pear, "Court Nominee Defied Labels as Head of Job-Rights Panel," *New York Times,* 16 Aug. 1991, p. A1; and Isabel Wilkerson, "A Remedy for Old Racism Has New Kind of Shackles," *New York Times,* 15 Sept. 1991, p. A1.

27. Clarence Thomas, Letter to the Editor of the *Wall Street Journal,* 20 Feb. 1987, quoted in "Clarence Thomas in His Own Words," *New York Times,* 2 July 1991, p. A14.

28. Clarence Thomas, "Climb the Jagged Mountain" (Excerpt from commencement speech at Savannah State College on 9 June 1985), reprinted in *New York Times,* 17 July 1991, p. A21.

29. Thomas's anti–affirmative action stance led to much debate within the African American community and a lack of support by key civil rights groups. See Maya Angelou, "I Dare to Hope," *New York Times,* 25 Aug. 1991, p. E15; Richard Berke, "Judge Thomas Faces Bruising Battle with Liberals over Stand on Rights," *New York Times,* 4 July 1991, p. A12; Haywood Burns, "Clarence Thomas, A Counterfeit Hero," *New York Times,* 9 July 1991, p. A19; Guido Calabresi, "What Clarence Thomas Knows," *New York Times,* 28 July 1991, p. E15; Steven Holmes, "Black Quandary over Court Nominee," *New York Times,* 4 July 1991, p. A12; Steven Holmes, "N.A.A.C.P. and Top Labor Unite to Oppose Thomas," *New York Times,* 1 Aug. 1991, p. A1; Steven Holmes, "Another Rights Group Is Opposing Judge Thomas," *New York Times,* 14 Aug. 1991, p. A14; Elizabeth McCaughey, "The Real Clarence Thomas," *New York Times,* 9 Sept. 1991, p. A15; and Robert Suro, "Jackson Assails Thomas Selection But Warns Against All-Out Fight," *New York Times,* 11 July 1991, p. A17.

30. Clarence Thomas, as quoted in Neil Lewis, "From Poverty to U.S. Bench," *New York Times,* 2 July 1991, p. A15. Also see Maureen Dowd, "Conservative Black Judge, Clarence Thomas, Is Named to Marshall's Court Seat," *New York Times,* 2 July 1991, p. A1.

31. Marvin Warren, "Letter to the Editor: 'The Judge and His Sister: Growing Up Black,' " *New York Times,* 23 July 1991, p. A20; and Lisa Jones, "The Invisible Ones: The Emma Mae Martin Story, the One Thomas Didn't Tell," *Village Voice* 36, no. 46 (12 Nov. 1991): 27–28. Also see the selections in Toni Morrison, ed., *Race-ing Justice, En-gendering Power: Essays on Anita Hill, Clarence Thomas, and the Construction of Social Reality* (New York: Pantheon, 1992) for further discussion of the role of sexism in the life of Thomas's sister.

32. Carol Delaney, "Letter to the Editor, 'The Lives of Women,' " *New York Times*, 23 July 1991, p. A20.

33. Richard Berke, "Vote on Thomas Is Put Off As Senate Backing Erodes over Harassment Charge," *New York Times*, 9 Oct. 1991, p. A1; Richard Berke, "Thomas Accuser Tells Hearing of Obscene Talk and Advances; Judge Complains of Lynching," *New York Times*, 12 Oct. 1991, p. A1; Neil Lewis, "Judiciary Panel Deadlocks, 7–7, on Thomas Nomination for Court," *New York Times*, 28 Sept. 1991, p. A1; Robert Suro, "Thomas Accuser Defends Her Charge, and Herself," *New York Times*, 8 Oct. 1991, p. A21; and Tom Wicker, "Blaming Anita Hill," *New York Times*, 10 Oct. 1991, p. A27.

34. See Toni Morrison, Introduction to *Race-ing Justice, En-gendering Power*, pp. vii–xxx; and Kimberle Crenshaw, "Whose Story Is It Anyway? Feminist and Antiracist Appropriations of Anita Hill," in Morrison, ed., *Race-ing Justice, En-gendering Power*, pp. 402–440. Also see *Court of Appeal*, ed. The Black Scholar (New York: Ballantine Books, 1992).

35. Clarence Thomas, as quoted in Maureen Dowd, "Taboo Issues of Sex and Race Explode in Glare of Hearing," *New York Times*, 13 Oct. 1991, p. A1.

36. Clarence Thomas, as quoted in Richard Berke, "Thomas Backers Attack Hill: Judge, Vowing He Won't Quit, Says He Is Victim of Race Stigma," *New York Times*, 13 Oct. 1991, p. A1. Also see R. W. Apple, Jr., "Spectacle of Degradation," *New York Times*, 13 Oct. 1991, p. A1.

37. Nell Irvin Painter, "Who Was Lynched?" *Nation* 253, no. 16 (11 Nov. 1991): 577.

38. Barbara Smith, "Ain't Gonna Let Nobody Turn Me Around," *Ms.* 11, no. 4 (Jan./Feb. 1992): 38. Also see other discussions of Anita Hill in this volume by Patricia Williams, Marcia Ann Gillespie, and Eleanor Holmes Norton; and see Patricia Williams, "Clarence Thomas: A Fiction of Individualism," *Radical America* 24, no. 1 (Jan./March 1990; published Jan. 1992): 17–20.

39. Nell Irvin Painter, "Hill, Thomas, and the Use of Racial Stereotype," in Morrison, ed., *Race-ing Justice, En-gendering Power*, p. 209.

40. Anita Hill, as quoted in Felicity Barringer, "Anita Hill Offers Her Version of Senate Hearings," *New York Times*, 17 Oct. 1992, p. A6. Also see proceedings of the conference on "Race, Gender, and Power in America," available from Georgetown University Law Center.

41. Peter Applebome, "Despite Talk of Sexual Harassment, Thomas Hearings Turned on Race Issue," *New York Times*, 19 Oct. 1991, p. A8.

42. Maureen Dowd, "The Senate and Sexism," *New York Times*, 8 Oct. 1991, p. A1; Maureen Dowd, "Facing Issue of Harassment, Capitol Gets Bath in the Mud," *New York Times*, 10 Oct. 1991, p. A1; Alex Jones, "Newspaper Discloses Op-Ed Conflict," *New York Times*, 16 Oct. 1991, p. A21; Anna Quindlen, "Listen to Us," *New York Times*, Oct. 9, 1991, p. A25; Anna Quindlen, "The Perfect Victim," *New York Times*, 16 Oct. 1991, p. A25.

43. For a detailed accounting of the Senate Judiciary Committee's activities, see Timothy M. Phelps and Helen Winternitz, *Capitol Games: Clarence Thomas, Anita Hill, and the Story of a Supreme Court Nomination* (New York: Hyperion Press, 1992).

44. Orlando Patterson, "Race, Gender, and Liberal Fallacies," *New York*

Times, 20 Oct. 1991, p. E15. For a fuller discussion, see Emma Coleman Jordan, "Race, Gender, and Social Class in the Thomas Sexual Harassment Hearings: The Hidden Fault Lines in Political Discourse," *Harvard Women's Law Journal* 15 (Summer 1992): 1–24.

45. Neil Lewis, "Court Nominee Is Linked to Anti-Abortion Stand," *New York Times*, 3 July 1991, p. A1; Richard Goldstein, "Don't Mourn, Organize," *Village Voice* 36, no. 44 (29 Oct. 1991): 26. See also Lewis Lehrman, "The Declaration of Independence and the Right to Life," *American Spectator* 20, no. 4 (April 1987): 22.

46. Of course, all women do not view the problem of sexual harassment in the same light, and all black women did not support Anita Hill's charges. See Felicity Barringer, "The Drama as Viewed by Women," *New York Times*, 18 Oct. 1991, p. A12.

47. Terry Eastland, "Bush and the Politics of Race," *New York Times*, 3 July 1991, p. A19; Robin Toner, "Capturing an Era's Racial Conflicts and Ironies," *New York Times*, 7 July 1991, p. E1; and Robin Toner, "Having Ridden Racial Issues, Parties Try to Harness Them," *New York Times*, 27 Oct. 1991, p. A1.

48. Neil Lewis, "Judge's Backers Seek to Undercut Hill," *New York Times*, 13 Oct. 1991, p. A28.

49. Michael deCourcy Hinds, "Another Surprise May Be Looming," *New York Times*, 26 Apr. 1992, p. A25; Deborah Sontag, "Anita Hill and Revitalizing Feminism," *New York Times*, 26 Apr. 1992, p. A31; and Anna Quindlen, "Gender Contender," *New York Times*, 26 Apr. 1992, p. E19.

50. Patterson, "Race, Gender and Liberal Fallacies," p. E15.

51. Isabel Wilkerson, "Riots Shook Affluent Blacks Trying to Balance Two Worlds," *New York Times*, 10 May 1992, p. A1.

52. Also see Linda Greenhouse, "Justice Thomas Hits the Ground Running," *New York Times*, 1 Mar. 1992, p. E1; Neil A. Lewis, "Lower-Court Ruling by Thomas Backs Affirmative-Action Limits," *New York Times*, 20 Feb. 1992, p. A1; and *Lamprecht v. FCC*, 958 F. 2d 382 (D.C. Cir. 1992).

53. Eric Schmitt, "Ban on Women in Combat Divides Four Service Chiefs," *New York Times*, 19 June 1991, p. A16, and his "Senate Votes to Remove Ban on Women as Combat Pilots," *New York Times*, 1 Aug. 1991, p. A1.

54. Peter Applebome, "Ripples of Pain As U.S. Dips Deeper into Military," *New York Times*, 31 Jan. 1991, p. A12. Also see Adam Clymer, "A Home Front with No Parents at Home," *New York Times*, 16 Feb. 1991, p. A10; Jane Gross, "Needs of Family and Country: Missions on a Collision Course," *New York Times*, 9 Dec. 1990, p. A1; and Jane Gross, "Early Lessons in Wounds of the Spirit," *New York Times*, 19 Feb. 1991, p. A8.

55. Judith Miller, "Saudi Arabia: The Struggle Within," *New York Times Magazine*, 10 Mar. 1990, pp. 27–46.

56. Youssef Ibrahim, "Saudi Women Take Driver's Seat in Protest," *New York Times*, 7 Nov. 1990, p. A1; Youssef Ibrahim, "An Outcry from the Saudis' Liberal Minority," *New York Times*, 9 Nov. 1990, p. A15; and James LeMoyne, "Ban on Driving by Women Reaffirmed by Saudis," *New York Times*, 15 Nov. 1990, p. A19.

57. See Cynthia Enloe, "Womenandchildren: Making Feminist Sense of the

Persian Gulf Crisis," *Village Voice* 35, no. 39 (25 Sept. 1991): 29–32; her *Bananas, Beaches, and Bases: Making Feminist Sense of International Politics* (Berkeley and Los Angeles: University of California Press, 1989), and her *Does Khaki Become You?* (Boston: South End Press, 1983). Also see Ann Scales, "Militarism, Male Dominance and Feminist Jurisprudence as Oxymoron," *Harvard Women's Law Journal* 12 (1989): 25–73.

58. "The General: It's a Great Day to Be a Soldier," *New York Times*, 9 March 1991, 37.

59. As quoted in Michael Ryan, "Here's to the Winners," *Life* 1, no. 4 (18 Mar. 1991): 37.

60. Bay Area Socialist Review Collective, "Warring Stories: Reading and Contesting the New World Order" (Pamphlet), p. 7. Distributed by *Socialist Review*, 3202 Adeline St., Berkeley, CA 94703.

61. Lee Daniels, "With Military Set to Thin Ranks, Blacks Fear They'll Be Hurt Most," *New York Times*, 7 Aug. 1991, p. A1.

62. Brenda Moore, "African-American Women in the U.S. Military," *Armed Forces and Society* 17, no. 3 (Spring 1991): 363.

63. George Bush, as quoted in Daniel Barbezat and Alexander George, "Who Died for Whose Way of Life? Reflections on the Burdens of Race," *Monthly Review* 43, no. 4 (Sept. 1991): 34.

64. Jason DeParle, "Keeping the News in Step: Are the Pentagon's Gulf War Rules Here to Stay?" *New York Times*, 6 May 1991, p. A9. Also see Alex Jones, "Feast of Viewing, But Little Nourishment," *New York Times*, 19 Jan. 1991, p. A10; and Tom Wicker, "An Unknown Casualty," *New York Times*, 20 Mar. 1991, p. A29.

65. See the federal lawsuit filed by the Center for Constitutional Rights on behalf of *The Nation, Harper's, Mother Jones*, and other publications against Richard Cheney, Secretary of Defense: *Nation Magazine v. Department of Defense*, 762 F. Supp. 1558 (S.D.N.Y. 1991). Also see the Press Guidelines available from the Department of Defense.

66. " 'Fighting Words': Novelists, Activists, Scholars, and Poets Take Sides on the War," *Village Voice* 36, no. 8 (19 Feb. 1991): 34–42.

67. See the extraordinarily interesting articles by Doug Lummis and Mojtaba Sadria, "The United States, Japan, and the Gulf War," *Monthly Review* 43, no. 11 (Apr. 1992): 1–16; and Samir Amin, "The Real Stakes in the Gulf War," *Monthly Review* 43, no. 3 (July–Aug. 1991): 14–24.

68. Wicker, "Unknown Casualty," p. 29.

69. Anthony Lewis, "On His Word Alone," *New York Times*, 12 Jan. 1991, p. E19. Also see Theodore Draper, "The True History of the Gulf War," *New York Review of Books* 39, no. 3 (30 Jan. 1992): 38–45; and Jean Edward Smith, *George Bush's War* (New York: Henry Holt, 1992).

70. For important critiques of the Gulf War, see Michael Emery, "How the U.S. Avoided Peace," *Village Voice* 36, no. 10 (5 March 1991): 22–27; Edward Greer, "The Hidden History of the Iraq War," *Monthly Review* 43, no. 1 (May 1991): 1–14; Christopher Hitchens, "Why We Are Stuck in the Sand," *Harper's Magazine* 282, no. 1688 (Jan. 1991): 70–79; Tom Mayer, "Imperialism and the Gulf War," *Monthly Review* 42, no. 11 (April 1991): 1–16; Charles

William Maynes, "Stopping the War," *Nation* 252, no. 8 (4 Mar. 1991): 255–56; Micah Sifry, "America, Oil and Intervention," *Nation* 252, no. 9 (11 Mar. 1991): 296–300.

71. See Mark Crispin Miller, "Operation Desert Storm," *New York Times,* 24 June 1992, p. A21; and his *Spectacle: Operation Desert Storm and the Triumph of Illusion* (New York: Simon and Schuster, 1992). Also see Haim Bresheeth and Nira Yuval-Davis, *The Gulf War and the New World Order* (London: Zed Books, 1992); Stephen Graubard, *Mr. Bush's War: Adventures in the Politics of Illusion* (New York: Hill and Wang, 1992); John R. MacArthur, *Second Front: Censorship and Propaganda in the Gulf War* (New York: Hill and Wang, 1992); Elaine Sciolino with Michael Wines, "Bush's Greatest Glory Fades As Questions on Iraq Persist," *New York Times,* 27 June 1992, p. A1; Hedrick Smith, ed., *The Media and the Gulf War: The Press and Democracy in Wartime* (Arlington, Va.: Seven Locks Press, 1992).

72. "Excerpts from President's Speech to University of Michigan Graduates," *New York Times,* 5 May 1991, p. A32. Also see Maureen Dowd, "Bush Sees Threat to Flow of Ideas on U.S. Campuses," *New York Times,* 5 May 1991, p. A1; and C. Vann Woodward, "Freedom and the Universities," *New York Review of Books* 38, no. 13 (18 July 1991): 32–37.

73. Bruce Robbins, "Tenured Radicals, the New McCarthyism, and 'PC,' " *New Left Review* 188 (July/Aug. 1991): 152.

74. It remains to be seen what impact the Supreme Court decision *R.A.V. v. City of St. Paul,* 112 S. Ct. 2538 (1992), will have on hate speech codes on college campuses. In this decision, the Court found that a St. Paul ordinance used to prosecute a person for burning a cross inside the fenced property of a black family was unconstitutional. The ordinance was found to be too broad and limiting of freedom of speech.

75. Alexander Cockburn, "Bush and P.C.—A Conspiracy So Immense," *Nation* 252, no. 20 (27 May 1991): 685–92. Also see Gary Indiana, "Victory Lite," *Village Voice* 36, no. 24 (11 June 1991): 28–35; and Richard Goldstein, "The Politics of Political Correctness," *Village Voice* 36, no. 25 (18 June 1991): 39–41.

76. Stanley Fish, "There's No Such Thing as Free Speech and It's a Good Thing, Too," in *Debating P.C.,* ed. Paul Berman (New York: Dell, 1992), p. 245.

77. "The Big Chill" (Transcript from a series on political correctness on MacNeil-Lehrer News Hour, broadcast on PBS in the fall of 1991), p. 13. Also see Michael Berube, "Public Image Limited," *Village Voice* 36, no. 25 (18 June 1991): 31–37.

78. Joe Conarroe, "How I'm PC," *New York Times,* 12 July 1991, p. A29.

79. Allan Bloom, *The Closing of the American Mind* (New York: Simon and Schuster, 1987), pp. 391, 34, 88, 30, 320.

80. Dinesh D'Souza, *Illiberal Education: The Politics of Race and Sex on Campus* (New York: The Free Press, 1991), pp. 51, 250, 55, 241, 243.

81. Gene H. Bell-Villada, "Is the American Mind Getting Dumber?" *Monthly Review* 43, no. 1 (May 1991): 41–55.

82. Ibid., p. 251.

83. Karen Houppert, "Wildflowers among the Ivy," *Ms.* 11, no. 2 (Sept./ Oct. 1991): 58.

84. Cockburn, "Bush and P.C.," p. 691.

85. Ibid.

86. Henry Louis Gates, Jr., "Whose Culture Is It, Anyway?" *New York Times,* 4 May 1991, p. A23. Also see his *Loose Canons: Notes on the Culture Wars* (New York: Oxford University Press, 1992).

87. Michel Marriott, "Afrocentrism: Balancing or Skewing History?" *New York Times,* 11 Aug. 1991, p. A1.

88. Martin Bernal, *Black Athena: The Afroasiatic Roots of Classical Civilization* (New Brunswick, N.J.: Rutgers University Press, 1987), vol. 1.

89. Christopher Phelps, "The Second Time As Farce: The Right's 'New McCarthyism,' " *Monthly Review* 43, no. 5 (Oct. 1991): 47. Also see the discussion "Revolution and Reaction," in *The Women's Review of Books* 9, no. 5 (Feb. 1992): 13–18; and Barbara Epstein, " 'Political Correctness' and Collective Powerlessness," *Socialist Review* 21, no. 3–4 (July–Dec. 1991): 13–35.

90. John Leland, "Rap and Race," *Newsweek* 119, no. 26 (29 June 1992): 46–49; Sheila Rule, "Rapper Chided by Clinton, Calls Him a Hypocrite," *New York Times,* 17 June 1992, p. A22.

91. R. W. Apple, Jr., "Jackson Sees a 'Character Flaw' in Clinton's Remarks on Racism," *New York Times,* 19 June 1992, p. A1; Gwen Ifill, "Clinton Won't Back Down in Tiff with Jackson over a Rap Singer," *New York Times,* 20 June 1992, p. A1.

92. For interesting discussion of Perot's candidacy, see James K. Galbraith, "Perot's Plan: Too Much Pain, Too Little Gain," *New York Times,* 31 July 1992, p. A27; Susan Dentzer with Jerry Buckley, "Ross Perot's Bitter Tonic," *U.S. News and World Report* 113, no. 5 (3 Aug. 1992): 28–31; Frank Snepp, "Ross Perot's Private War on Drugs," *Village Voice* 38, no. 23 (9 June 1992): 25–28; Frank Snepp, "Where Perot Dares," *Village Voice* 38, no. 29 (21 July 1992): 33–35; Michael Tomasky, "Regarding Henry: Politics Requires Compromise, Dirty Dealings, and Ruthless Tactics, H. Ross Perot's a Natural," *Village Voice* 38, no. 21 (26 May 1992): 27–35; and Garry Wills, "The Rescuer," *New York Review of Books* 39, no. 12 (25 June 1992): 28–34.

93. Maureen Dowd, "Hillary Clinton as Aspiring First Lady: Role Model or a 'Hall Monitor' Type?" *New York Times,* 18 May 1992, p. A15; Karen Lehrman, "Beware the Cookie Monster," *New York Times,* 18 July 1992, p. A24; Alessandra Stanley, "A Softer Image for Hillary Clinton," *New York Times,* 13 July 1992, p. B1; and Garry Wills, "H. R. Clinton's Case," *New York Review of Books* 39, no. 5 (5 Mar. 1992), pp. 3–6.

94. Alessandra Stanley, " 'Family Values' and Women: Is G.O.P. a House Divided?" *New York Times,* 21 Aug. 1992, p. A1.

95. Garry Wills, "The Born-Again Republicans," *New York Review of Books* 38, no. 15 (24 Sept. 1992): 9–14. See also, in this same issue, Joan Didion, "Eye on the Prize," pp. 57–66.

96. Andrew Rosenthal, "Bush Pulls Close in Poll, But Not with Women," *New York Times,* 11 Aug. 1992, p. A1; Michael Wines, "Bush Seeks to Cast Himself as a Free-Market Feminist," *New York Times,* 19 Sept. 1992, p. A7.

97. Marilyn Quayle argued that her ideas were being falsely represented by the media. See her "Workers, Wives and Mothers," *New York Times,* 11 Sept. 1992, p. A35.

CHAPTER 4. REPRODUCTIVE RIGHTS AND
THE PRIVATIZED STATE

1. "The Battle over Abortion," *Newsweek* 114, no. 3 (17 July 1989): 14–21.

2. Kathryn Kolbert, "Developing a Reproductive Rights Agenda for the 1990's," in *From Abortion to Reproductive Freedom: Transforming a Movement,* ed. Marlene Gerber Fried (Boston: South End, 1990), p. 301.

3. Gina Kolata, "Under Pressures and Stigma, More Doctors Shun Abortion," *New York Times,* 8 Jan. 1991, p. A1; and Jane Gross, "On Abortion, More Doctors Are Balancing Practice and Ideology," *New York Times,* 8 Sept. 1991, p. A18.

4. Stanley Henshaw, Jacqueline Forrest, and Jennifer Van Vort, "Abortion Services in the U.S., 1984 and 1985," *Family Planning Perspectives* 19, no. 2 (Mar./Apr. 1987): 63–65.

5. Tamar Lewin, "Hurdles Increase for Many Women Seeking Abortions," *New York Times,* 15 May 1992, p. A1.

6. 492 U.S. 490, 501 (1989). See also Ronald Dworkin, "The Great Abortion Case," *New York Review of Books* 36, no. 11 (June 1989): 49–53.

7. Ibid., p. 506.

8. 432 U.S. 464, 474 (1977).

9. 492 U.S. 490, 508 (quoting *Maher v. Roe,* 432 U.S. 464, 474).

10. 448 U.S. 297 (1989).

11. 492 U.S. 490, 530 (O'Connor, J., concurring) (quoting *Akron v. Akron Center for Reproductive Health,* 462 U.S. 416, 453 [1983]).

12. Ibid., p. 508 (quoting *Maher v. Roe,* 432 U.S. 464, 474).

13. Ibid., p. 507 (quoting *DeShaney v. Winnebago County Department of Social Services,* 489 U.S. 189, 196 [1989]).

14. Ibid., p. 509–10.

15. Ibid., p. 509.

16. Dworkin, "Great Abortion Case," p. 53.

17. 492 U.S. 490, 515.

18. Ibid., p. 553 (Blackmun, J., dissenting).

19. Ibid., p. 552 (quoting *Thornburgh v. American College of Obstetricians and Gynecologists,* 476 U.S. 747, 778–79 [1986]).

20. Ibid., p. 541.

21. Ibid., p. 518.

22. See Eisenstein, *Female Body and the Law,* for a fuller discussion of *non*-pregnancy as the standard in law.

23. 450 U.S. 464.

24. Dworkin, "Great Abortion Case," p. 52.

25. *Griswold v. Connecticut,* 381 U.S. 479 (1965).

26. 492 U.S. 490, 520.

27. Bertram Gross, *Friendly Fascism* (New York: M. Evans, 1980).

28. 492 U.S. 490, 546.

29. Ibid., p. 528 (O'Connor, J., concurring) (quoting *Ashwander v. TVA*, 297 U.S. 288 [1936]).

30. Ibid., p. 559 (Blackmun, J., dissenting).

31. Ibid., p. 534 (Scalia, J., concurring).

32. 497 U.S. 417 (1990).

33. Ibid., p. 444–45.

34. See Sue Halpern, "The Fight Over Teen-Age Abortion," *New York Review of Books* 27, no. 5 (29 Mar. 1990): 30–32; Linda Greenhouse, "States May Require Girl to Notify Parents Before Having Abortion," *New York Times,* 26 June 1990, p. A1; Tamar Lewin, "Abortion Ruling Likely to Spur Judicial Hearings," *New York Times,* 27 June 1990, p. A14; and Anna Quindlen, "Mom, Dad and Abortion," *New York Times,* 1 July 1990, p. E17.

35. 497 U.S. 417, 464.

36. 497 U.S. 502 (1990).

37. Tamar Lewin, "Parental Consent to Abortion: How Enforcement Can Vary," *New York Times,* 28 May 1992, p. A1.

38. Census Bureau statistics, as cited by Robert Pear, "Bigger Number of New Mothers Are Unmarried," *New York Times,* 4 Dec. 1991, p. A20. Also see U.S. Census Bureau, "Fertility of American Women," [n.d.], available from the U.S. Government Printing Office, Washington, DC 10402.

39. See Ronald Dworkin, "The Center Holds," *New York Review of Books* 39, no. 14 (13 Aug. 1992): 29–34.

40. *Planned Parenthood of Southeastern Pennsylvania v. Casey,* 112 S. Ct. 2791, 2805–6 (1992).

41. Ibid., p. 2818, 2820.

42. Ibid., p. 2821.

43. 462 U.S. 416, 450.

44. 112 S. Ct. 2791, 2825.

45. Ibid.

46. Ibid., 2825–30.

47. 111 S. Ct. 1759 (1991).

48. Linda Greenhouse, "Conservatively Speaking, It's an Activist Supreme Court," *New York Times,* 26 May 1991, p. E1. Also see her "Five Justices Uphold U.S. Rule Curbing Abortion Advice," *New York Times,* 24 May 1991, p. A1. For a discussion of the controversy surrounding the *Rust* decision, see Adam Clymer, "Bill to Let Clinics Discuss Abortion Is Vetoed by Bush," *New York Times,* 20 Nov. 1991, p. A1; Lynnell Hancock, "Piss Poor Decision," *Village Voice* 36, no. 23 (4 June 1991), p. 20; Philip J. Hilts, "House Votes to Overturn Limit on Abortion Advice," *New York Times,* 7 Nov. 1991, p. A24; Philip J. Hilts, "Clinics Seek to Overturn Rule on Abortion Advice," *New York Times,* 25 May 1991, p. A9; Tamar Lewin, "Family-Planning Clinics Face Dilemma over Their Mission," *New York Times,* 26 June 1991, p. A1.

49. 111 S. Ct. 1759, 1777, 1775.

50. *Harris v. McRae,* 448 U.S. 297, 317 (1980).

51. 111 S. Ct. 1759, 1776, 1777.

52. Ibid., p. 1785.

53. "Listen to the Anti-Choice Leaders" (Planned Parenthood Flyer, 1991). Available from 810 Seventh Avenue, New York City, NY 10019.

54. Wayne King, "Florio Signs an Overhaul of Welfare," *New York Times,* 22 Jan. 1992, p. B1.

55. Anna Quindlen, "The $64 Question," *New York Times,* 22 Jan. 1992, p. A21.

56. Tamar Lewin, "Court Says U.S. Violated Law on Abortion Advice," *New York Times,* 29 May 1992, p. A13. Also see Philip J. Hilts, "White House Allows Some Advice at Public Clinics about Abortion," *New York Times,* 21 Mar. 1992, p. A1.

57. *Women's Health Care Services v. Operation Rescue,* 773 F. Supp. 258, 262 (D. Kan. 1991). See also 42 U.S.C. § 1983 (1993). Originally enacted as Section 2 of the Ku Klux Klan Act of 1871, chap. 22, 17 Stat. 18. "The Ku Klux Klan Act," in "Significant Documents in African American History, 1688–1989," *The Negro Almanac: A Reference Work on the African American,* 5th ed., ed. Harry Ploski and James Williams (Detroit: Gale Research, 1989), pp. 249–52.

58. Brief of the United States as Amicus Curiae, *Women's Health Care Services v. Operation Rescue,* 773 F. Supp. 258 (D. Kan., 1991) (No. 91-1303-K).

59. Ibid., pp. 5, 3, 6, 18.

60. Gwen Ifill, "1871 Rights Law at Issue in a Dispute on Abortion," *New York Times,* 11 Aug. 1991, p. A16.

61. Linda Greenhouse, "Court Hears Appeal on Citing Bias to Bar Abortion Opponents," *New York Times,* 17 Oct. 1991, p. A1. Also see William Bradford Reynolds, "Judicial Excess in Wichita," *New York Times,* 1 Sept. 1991, p. E11; Don Terry, "98 Are Arrested As Abortion Foes Defy Judge and Block Clinic," *New York Times,* 10 Aug. 1991, p. A6; and "U.S. Joins Anti-Abortion Group to Shut Clinics," *New York Times,* 7 Aug. 1991, p. A10.

62. Lynn Smith, "An Equality Approach to Reproductive Choice: Rust v. Sullivan," *Yale Journal of Law and Feminism* 4 (Fall 1991): 93–132.

63. Ibid., p. 11.

64. *Jayne Bray v. Alexandria Women's Health Clinic,* 113 S. Ct. 753 (1993). See also Linda Greenhouse, "Supreme Court Says Klan Law Can't Bar Abortion Blockades," *New York Times,* 14 Jan. 1993, p. A1.

65. Meredith Burke, "Ceausescu's Main Victims: Women and Children," *New York Times,* 10 Jan. 1990, p. A27.

66. E.g., Alan Cowell, "Full-Blooded Candor Is Restored, and Evils Not of Dracula Unfold," *New York Times,* 9 Jan. 1990, p. A12. Also see Anthony Lewis, "The Cost of Fanaticism," *New York Times,* 16 Mar. 1990, p. A15.

67. Lynnell Hancock, "Censoring Abortion: The Feds Prepare to Abort the Word," *Village Voice* 35, no. 2 (9 Jan. 1990): 30.

68. Jefferson Morley, "Bush and the Blacks: An Unknown Story," *New York Review of Books* 39, nos. 1–2 (16 Jan. 1992): 24.

69. George Bush, as stated in the Congressional Record, 8 July 1970, pp. 23, 193, and cited in Morley, "Bush and the Blacks," p. 26.

70. Zillah Eisenstein, "Fetal Position," *Nation* 249, no. 17 (20 Nov. 1989): 12–13.

71. Julie Rovner, "Congress Puts Bush on Spot over Funding of Abortion," *Social Policy*, 14 Oct. 1989, p. 2708.

72. Maureen Dowd, "President Hints at a Compromise over Federal Funds for Abortion," *New York Times*, 14 Oct. 1989, p. A1. Also see "President's News Conference on Foreign and Domestic Issues," *New York Times*, 14 Oct. 1989, p. A8.

73. Maureen Dowd, "Veto Nears As Compromise on U.S. Money for Abortion Fails," *New York Times*, 17 Oct. 1989, p. A17.

74. Rovner, "Congress Puts Bush on Spot," p. 2709.

75. Julie Rovner, "Veto over Abortion Funding Pains Some in the GOP," *Social Policy*, 21 October 1989, p. 2789.

76. Hancock, "Piss Poor Decision," p. 29.

77. Tom Wicker, "Bush on the Run," *New York Times*, 27 Oct. 1989, p. A35.

78. Heather L. McCulloch, "Abortion Cutoff," *Nation* 290, no. 14 (9 April 1990): 492.

79. Maureen Dowd, "G.O.P. Congresswomen Hopeful after Bush Meeting on Abortion," *New York Times*, 15 November 1989, p. A1.

80. Andrew Rosenthal, "G.O.P. Leaders Urge Softer Line about Abortion," *New York Times*, 10 Nov. 1989, p. A1.

81. Robin Toner, "Space for All in Abortion Debate, Quayle Says," *New York Times*, 9 Oct. 1991, p. A15; and her "New Worry for Bush," *New York Times*, 22 Jan. 1991, p. A17.

82. Eisenstein, "Fetal Position," pp. 12–13.

83. See Steven Holmes, "Bush Will Veto Bill Requiring Job Leave for Care of Family," *New York Times*, 8 May 1990, p. A1; and his "Bush Vetoes a Bill to Give Workers Family Leave," *New York Times*, 30 June 1990, p. A9.

84. Letter received in the mail from "Republicans for Choice," January 1992. Also see Gwen Ifill, "Two Republican Factions on Abortion Gird for Battle on Party's '92 Platform," *New York Times*, 30 Sept. 1991, p. A15.

85. Richard L. Berke, "Abortion Support Found among Major Parties," *New York Times*, 3 June 1992, p. A17; Beverly G. Hudnut and William H. Hudnut, III, "We're Good Republicans—And Pro-Choice," *New York Times*, 29 May 1992, p. A29; Robert Pear, "G.O.P. Faces Fight on Abortion Issue," *New York Times*, 26 May 1992, p. A1; and David Rosenbaum, "Abortion Issue Rips Away Veil of G.O.P. Unity," *New York Times*, 27 May 1992, p. A1.

86. As quoted in Felicity Barringer, "Clinton and Gore Shifted on Abortion," *New York Times*, 20 July 1992, p. A10.

87. Bill Clinton and Al Gore, *Putting People First: How We Can All Change America* (New York: Times Books, 1992), p. 170.

88. See Adam Clymer, "Law Makers Fear Amendments on 'Abortion Rights,' " *New York Times*, 31 July 1992, p. A11; and Lawrence H. Tribe, "Write Roe into Law," *New York Times*, 27 July 1992, p. A17.

89. E. J. Dionne, Jr., "Poll Finds Ambivalence on Abortion Persists in U.S." *New York Times*, 3 Aug. 1989, p. A18.

90. "Abortion after Webster," *Polling Report* 5, no. 16 (14 Aug. 1989): 2–4.

91. "Abortion: Cutting across Party Lines," *Polling Report* 5, no. 17 (4 Sept. 1989): 6–7.

92. Kirk Johnson, "Connecticut Acts to Make Abortion a Statutory Right," *New York Times*, 28 April 1990, p. A1.

93. "New Maryland Law Protects Right to Abortion," *New York Times*, 19 Feb. 1991, p. A15; and B. Drummond Ayres, Jr., "Filibuster on Abortion Drones On in Maryland," *New York Times*, 22 March 1990, p. A23.

94. "U.S. Judge Strikes Down Louisiana Abortion Law," *New York Times*, 10 July 1990, p. A16; Frances Frank Marcus, "Roemer Keeps Mum on Abortion Bill," *New York Times*, 10 July 1990, p. A17; Ronald Smothers, "Louisiana Abortion Law Is Delayed," *New York Times*, 20 June 1991, p. A14; Roberto Suro, "Nation's Strictest Abortion Law Enacted in Louisiana over Veto," *New York Times*, 19 June 1991, p. A1.

95. Linda Greenhouse, "High Court Takes Pennsylvania Case on Abortion Right," *New York Times*, 22 Jan. 1992, p. A1. Also see Tamar Lewin, "States Testing the Limits on Abortion," *New York Times*, 1 Apr. 1992, p. A4; Tamar Lewin, "Strict Anti-Abortion Law Signed in Utah," *New York Times*, 26 Jan. 1991, p. A10; Tamar Lewin, "Quiet Hearing Could Lead to Resounding Decision on Abortion," *New York Times*, 5 Aug. 1990, p. A24; and Timothy Egan, "Anti-Abortion Bill in Idaho Takes Aim at Landmark Case," *New York Times*, 22 Mar. 1990, p. A1.

96. Roger Rosenblatt, "How to End the Abortion War," *New York Times Magazine*, 19 January 1992, p. 41. Also see Rosalind Petchesky, *Abortion and Woman's Choice: The State, Sexuality, and Reproductive Freedom*, 2d ed. (Boston: Northeastern University Press, 1990) for a full discussion of this issue.

97. See *Polling Report* 5, no. 16 (14 Aug. 1989), p. 3.

98. Ibid.

99. See Petchesky, *Abortion and Woman's Choice*, for a fuller discussion of racial differences in the situation of pregnant teenagers.

100. E. J. Dionne, Jr., "Poll on Abortion Finds the Nation Is Sharply Divided," *New York Times*, 16 Apr. 1989, p. A1.

101. Marla Erlien, "Beyond Roe v. Wade: Redefining the Prochoice Agenda," *Radical America* 11, nos. 2–3 (June 1989): 14–24.

102. E. J. Dionne, Jr., "Advocates of Abortion Rights Seek to Win Blacks' Support," *New York Times*, 16 Apr. 1989, p. A1.

103. Lisa Belkin, "Bars to Equality of Sexes Seen as Eroding, Slowly," *New York Times*, 20 Aug. 1989, p. 26.

104. Lisa Belkin, "Women in Rural Areas Face Many Barriers to Abortions," *New York Times*, 11 July 1989, p. A1.

105. George James, "Newborn Is Thrown in Trash and Dies," *New York Times*, 14 Aug. 1991, p. B3.

106. Elisabeth Rosenthal, "AIDS Infection Often Blocks Abortion Access, Study Says," *New York Times*, 23 Oct. 1990, p. A1.

107. Gina Kolata, "In Late Abortions, Decisions Are Painful and Options Few," *New York Times*, 5 Jan. 1992, p. A1.

CHAPTER 5. THE CONTRADICTORY POLITICS OF AIDS

1. Barry D. Adam, "The State, Public Policy, and AIDS Discourse," *Contemporary Crises* 13, no. 1 (Mar. 1989): 1–15.

2. Dennis Altman, *AIDS in the Mind of America* (New York: Anchor Books, 1987), p. 9. Also see Susan Sontag, *Illness as Metaphor* (New York: Farrar, Straus & Giroux, 1978); Erica Carter and Simon Watney, eds., *Taking Liberties: AIDS and Cultural Politics* (London: Serpent's Tail, 1989); and Simon Watney, *Policing Desire: Pornography, AIDS and the Media* (Minneapolis: University of Minnesota Press, 1987).

3. Janet Dolgin, "AIDS: Social Meanings and Legal Ramifications," *Hofstra Law Review* 14 (Fall 1985): 201. Also see Victoria Slind-Flor, "At the Limits," *National Law Journal* 12 (27 Aug. 1990): 1–31; Eugene Harrington, "A Fatal Bias: AIDS and Minorities," *Human Rights* 14 (Summer 1987): 34–52; and Thomas Mendicino, "Characterization and Disease: Homosexuals and the Threat of AIDS," *North Carolina Law Review* 66 (Nov. 1987): 226–50.

4. Simon Watney, "AIDS: The Cultural Agenda," *Radical America* 21, no. 4 (July-Aug. 1987): 49.

5. AIDS is used to represent a virus *and* a disease, even though it is probably one virus and several diseases. The HIV virus is often loosely and somewhat inaccurately termed AIDS, suggesting a homogeneous illness often excluding individuals with HIV antibodies who are not presently sick. It remains unknown even whether the HIV virus is the cause of AIDS or is itself an opportunistic companion. My discussion focuses on the political discourse of AIDS while recognizing the problematic status of HIV infection. See Kenneth Keniston, "Introduction to the Issue," in "Living with Aids: Part 2," special issue, *Daedalus* 118, no. 3 (Summer 1989): xi.

6. Paula Treichler, "AIDS, Gender, and Biomedical Discourse: Current Contests of Meaning," in *AIDS: The Burdens of History*, ed. Elizabeth Fee and Daniel M. Fox (Berkeley and Los Angeles: University of California Press, 1988), p. 196.

7. Paula Treichler, "AIDS, Homophobia, and Biomedical Discourse: An Epidemic of Signification," in *AIDS: Cultural Analysis and Cultural Activism*, ed. Douglas Crimp (Cambridge, Mass.: MIT Press, 1988), p. 31.

8. David Talbot, "Condom Conundrum," *Mother Jones* 125, no. 1 (Jan. 1990): 46.

9. Susan Sontag, *AIDS and Its Metaphors* (New York: Farrar, Straus & Giroux, 1989), p. 16.

10. See "Facing AIDS: A Special Issue," *Radical America* 10, no. 6 (Nov.–Dec. 1986); and "AIDS: Communities Respond," *Radical America* 21, nos. 2–3 (Mar.–Apr. 1987).

11. Philip Boffey, "Spread of AIDS Abating But Deaths Will Still Soar," *New York Times*, 14 Feb. 1988, p. A1.

12. *Newsweek* 111, no. 11 (14 Mar. 1988); William Masters, Virginia Johnson, and Robert Kolodny, *Crisis: Heterosexual Behavior in the Age of AIDS* (New York: Grove Press, 1988).

13. Gina Kolata, "AIDS Spreading in Teen-Agers, A New Trend Alarming to Experts," *New York Times,* 8 Oct. 1989, p. 30.

14. Jeanne Brooks-Gunn and Frank F. Furstenberg, Jr., "Coming of Age in the Era of AIDS: Puberty, Sexuality and Contraception," *Milbank Quarterly* 68, supp. 1 (1990): 60.

15. Barbara Kantrowitz, "Teenagers and AIDS," *Newsweek* 120, no. 5 (3 Aug. 1992): 45–50.

16. Margaret Cerullo and Evelynn Hammonds, "AIDS and Africa: The Western Imagination and the Dark Continent," *Radical America* 21, nos. 2–3 (Mar.–Apr. 1992): 18. Also see Robert Caputo, "Uganda: Land Beyond Sorrow," *National Geographic* 173, no. 4 (Apr. 1988): 468–91; Richard Chirimuuta and Rosalind Chirimuuta, *Aids, Africa and Racism* (London: Free Association Books, 1989); Bruce Fleming, "Another Way of Dying," *Nation* 250, no. 13 (2 Apr. 1990): 446–50; and Charles Hunt, "Africa and AIDS," *Monthly Review* 39, no. 9 (Feb. 1988): 10–22.

17. Jane Perlez, "Toll of AIDS on Uganda's Women Puts Their Roles and Rights in Question," *New York Times,* 28 Oct. 1990, p. A16. Also see, as part of the same series of articles, Eric Eckholm and John Tierney, "AIDS in Africa: A Killer Rages On," *New York Times,* 16 Sept. 1990, p. A1; Kathleen Hunt, "Scenes from a Nightmare," *New York Times Magazine,* 12 Aug. 1990, pp. 24–51; and John Tierney, "AIDS Tears Lives of the African Family," *New York Times,* 17 Sept. 1990, p. A1.

18. Boffey, "Spread of AIDS Abating," p. 36.

19. Cindy Patton, *Inventing AIDS* (New York: Routledge, 1990), p. 61.

20. Simon Watney, "Missionary Positions: AIDS, 'Africa,' and Race," in *Out There: Marginalization and Contemporary Cultures,* ed. Russell Ferguson, Martha Gever, Trinh T. Minh-ha, and Cornel West (Cambridge, Mass.: MIT Press, 1990), p. 100.

21. Sandor Katz, "HIV Testing—A Phony Cure," *Nation* 250, no. 21 (28 May 1990): 740.

22. Treichler, "AIDS, Homophobia, and Biomedical Discourse," p. 44.

23. Treichler, "AIDS, Gender, and Biomedical Discourse," p. 212.

24. Ibid., p. 39. Also see Peter Davis, "Exploring the Kingdom of AIDS," *New York Times Magazine,* 31 May 1987, pp. 32–40; and Katie Leishman, "Heterosexuals and AIDS," *Atlantic* 259, no. 2 (Feb. 1987): 39–58. For a discussion of the misrepresentation of AIDS through careless misreporting of findings, see Robert Massa, "Unfit to Print," *Village Voice* 35, no. 19 (8 May 1990): 24–26.

25. Bruce Lambert, "AIDS among Prostitutes Not As Prevalent As Believed, Studies Show," *New York Times,* 20 Sept. 1988, p. B1. Also see Katherine Bishop, "Prostitute in Jail after AIDS Report," *New York Times,* 15 July 1990, p. A12.

26. Richard Goldstein, "The Hidden Epidemic," *Village Voice* 32, no. 10 (10 Mar. 1987): 23–30.

27. Joyce Lombardi, "Trail of Tears: AIDS and Native Americans," *Village Voice* 36, no. 53 (31 Dec. 1991): 14.

28. Mendicino, "Characterization and Disease," 226.

29. Mary Catherine Bateson and Richard Goldsby, *Thinking AIDS: The Social Response to the Biological Threat* (Reading, Mass.: Addison-Wesley, 1988), p. 2.

30. Treichler, "AIDS, Gender, and Biomedical Discourse," p. 233.

31. Jeffrey Weeks, *Sexuality* (London: Tavistock Publications, 1986); see especially chap. 2, "The Invention of Sexuality." Also see his *Sexuality and Its Discontents* (London: Routledge & Kegan Paul, 1985).

32. Weeks, *Sexuality*, p. 120.

33. Dan E. Beauchamp, "Morality and the Health of the Body Politic," in "AIDS: Public Health and Civil Liberties" Special Supplement, *Hastings Center Report*, Dec. 1986, p. 31. Also see Dan E. Beauchamp, *The Health of the Republic* (Philadelphia: Temple University Press, 1988).

34. Beauchamp, "Morality and the Body Politic," p. 32. For full and important discussions of homophobia, see Dennis Altman, *The Homosexualization of America* (Boston: Beacon Press, 1982), and Cindy Patton, *Sex and Germs: The Politics of AIDS* (Boston: South End Press, 1985).

35. For a fuller discussion of the effect of AIDS on civil rights for homosexuals, see Mendicino, "Characterization and Disease."

36. Ibid., p. 235; see *Bowers v. Hardwick,* 478 U.S. 186 (1986). Also see Mark Barnes, "AIDS and Mr. Korematsu: Minorities at Times of Crisis," *Saint Louis University Public Law Review* 7 (Spring 1988): 35–43; Susan McGuigan, "The AIDS Dilemma: Public Health v. Criminal Law," *Law and Inequality: A Journal of Theory and Practice* 4 (Oct. 1986): 545–77; Chris Nichols, "AIDS—A New Reason to Regulate Homosexuality?" *Journal of Contemporary Law* 11 (Aug. 1984): 315–43; and Dorenn Weisenhaus, "The Shaping of AIDS Law," *National Law Journal* 10, no. 47 (1 Aug. 1988): 1–33.

37. Douglas Crimp, "How to Have Promiscuity in an Epidemic," in *AIDS: Cultural Analysis and Cultural Activism,* ed. Douglas Crimp (Cambridge, Mass: MIT Press, 1988) p. 253. This is not meant to romanticize safer sex practices. See Robin Hardy, "Risky Business: Confronting Unsafe Sex," *Village Voice* 35, no. 26 (26 June 1990): 35–40, for an important discussion of what he terms "risky sexual relapse": the longing for "one night off" from safe sex practices.

38. Michael Jones, as quoted in *America Living with AIDS* (Report of the National Commission on Acquired Immune Deficiency Syndrome, 1990), p. 34. Copies available from Superintendent of Documents, United States Printing Office, Washington, D.C. 20402.

39. Mireya Navarro, "AIDS in Women Rising, But Many Ignore the Threat," *New York Times,* 28 Dec. 1990, p. B1.

40. Nancy Stoller Shaw, "Preventing AIDS among Women: The Role of Community Organizing," *Socialist Review* 18, no. 4 (Dec. 1988): 77. Also see Helen Singer Kaplan, *The Real Truth about Women and AIDS* (New York: Simon & Schuster, 1987); and *America Living with AIDS,* p. 12.

41. Philip J. Hilts, "AIDS in Women Rising But Many Ignore the Threat," *New York Times,* 11 Dec. 1990, p. A1.

42. Treichler, "AIDS, Gender, and Biomedical Discourse," p. 215.

43. Ibid., p. 212.

44. Robert Massa, "Danger in Numbers," *Village Voice* 36, no. 45 (5 Nov. 1991): 18.

45. Sonia Singleton, as quoted in *America Living with AIDS,* p. 95.

46. Sarah Schulman, "Delusions of Gender," *Village Voice* 35, no. 1 (1 Jan. 1992): 15. Also see Josh Barbanel, "U.S. Sued over Denial of AIDS Case Benefits," *New York Times,* 1 Oct. 1990, p. B3; Peg Byron, "HIV: The National Scandal," *Ms.* 1, no. 4 (Jan./Feb. 1991): 24–29; Marcia Ann Gillespie, "HIV: The Global Crisis," ibid., 17–22; Philip Hilts, "AIDS Definition Excludes Women, Congress Is Told," *New York Times,* 7 June 1991, p. A19; and Mireya Navarro, "Dated AIDS Definition Keeps Benefits from Many Patients," *New York Times,* 8 July 1991, p. A1.

47. America Living with AIDS, p. 28.

48. Suki Ports, "Needed (For Women and Children)," in Crimp, ed., *AIDS: Cultural Analysis and Cultural Activism,* p. 169; and Bruce Lambert, "AIDS in Black Women Seen as Leading Killer," *New York Times,* 11 July 1990, p. B3.

49. Diane Richardson, *Women and AIDS* (New York: Methuen, 1988), p. 29.

50. International Working Group on Women and AIDS, "An Open Letter to the Planning Committees of the Third International Conference on AIDS," in Crimp, ed., *AIDS: Cultural Analysis and Cultural Activism,* pp. 166–68.

51. Presidential Commission on the Human Immunodeficiency Virus Epidemic, *Report* (24 June 1988), p. 15. Available from the Presidential Commission on the Human Immunodeficiency Virus Epidemic, 655 15th St. NW, Suite 901, Washington, D.C. 20005.

52. Gina Kolata, "In Cities, Poor Families Are Dying of Crack," *New York Times,* 11 Aug. 1989, p. A13.

53. Since approximately 1985, increasing attention has been focused on pediatric AIDS. See Marguerite Holloway, "Death by Red Tape," *Village Voice* 35, no. 21 (22 May 1990): 15; David L. Kirp, "The Politics of Pediatric AIDS," *Nation* 250, no. 19 (14 May 1990): 666–68; and Bruce Lambert, "AIDS Legacy: A Growing Generation of Orphans," *New York Times,* 17 July 1989, p. A1.

54. Kimberle Williams Crenshaw, "Race, Reform and Retrenchment: Transformation and Legitimation in Anti-Discrimination Law," *Harvard Law Review* 101 (May 1988): 1331.

55. See Brief Report, "Access to Medical Care for Black and White Americans," *Journal of the American Medical Association* 261, no. 2 (13 Jan. 1989): 278–81; "Health" (special issue), *Sage: A Scholarly Journal on Black Women* 2, no. 2 (Fall 1985); and Gerald David Jaynes and Robin M. Williams, Jr., eds., *A Common Destiny: Blacks and American Society.*

56. Norman Nickens, "AIDS, Race, and the Law: The Social Construction of Disease," *Nova Law Review* 12 (Spring 1988): 1186.

57. Sara Rimer, "Spotlight Fades on AIDS in Town: But the Disease and Stigma Remain," *New York Times,* 14 November 1990, p. A16.

58. Felicia Lee, "Black Doctors Urge Study of Factors in Risk of AIDS," *New York Times,* 21 July 1989, p. B7.

59. Susan Rasky, "How the Politics Shifted on AIDS Funds," *New York Times*, 20 May 1990, p. A22.

60. Sander Gilman, *Disease and Representation: Images of Illness from Madness to AIDS* (Ithaca: Cornell University Press, 1988), p. 263. Also see his *Difference and Pathology* (Ithaca: Cornell University Press, 1985).

61. For an interesting discussion of homophobia and the struggle against racism, see Tseko Simon Nkoli, "An Open Letter to Nelson Mandela," *Village Voice* 35, no. 26 (26 June 1990): 29–30.

62. Evelynn Hammonds, "Race, Sex, AIDS: The Construction of 'Other,' " *Radical America* 20, no. 6 (Nov.–Dec. 1986), p. 31.

63. Lindsey Gruson, "AIDS Is Discovered as Issue by Black Political Leaders," *New York Times*, 9 Mar. 1992, p. A7; Richard Stevenson, "Magic Johnson Ends His Career, Saying He Has the AIDS Virus," *New York Times*, 8 Nov. 1991, p. A1; and E. R. Shipp, "Reluctantly, Black Churches Confront AIDS," *New York Times*, 18 Nov. 1991, p. A1.

64. Sarah Schulman, "Laying the Blame: What Magic Johnson Really Means," *Guardian* (London), 19 Nov. 1991, p. 4.

65. Eugene Harrington, "A Fatal Bias: AIDS and Minorities," *Human Rights* 14 (Summer 1987): 34.

66. Harlon Dalton, "AIDS in Blackface," in "Living with AIDS: Part 2," special issue, *Daedalus* 118, no. 3 (Summer 1989): 208.

67. Nat Hentoff, "Silence = Black and Hispanic Deaths," *Village Voice* 35, no. 9 (27 Feb. 1990): 22. The increase of AIDS among persons of color requires new strategies for AIDS activists. See Frank Browning, "Turf Wars," *Village Voice* 35, no. 28 (10 July 1990): 17–18; Donna Minkowitz, "ACT UP at a Crossroads," *Village Voice* 35, no. 23 (30 May–5 June 1990): 19–22; and Randy Shilts, "The Era of Bad Feelings," *Mother Jones* 14, no. 9 (Nov. 1989): 32–60.

68. "Accelerating, Nation's AIDS Count Hits 200,000," *New York Times*, 17 Jan. 1992, p. A15.

69. Lawrence K. Altman, "Researchers Report Much Grimmer AIDS Outlook," *New York Times*, 4 June 1992, p. A1.

70. Ernest Drucker, "Families Need the Most Help," and Michael Gottlieb, "Leadership is Lacking," both in "AIDS—The Second Decade" (special section), *New York Times*, 5 June 1991, p. A29.

71. Lawrence K. Altman, "Scientists Encouraged by Two AIDS Vaccines," *New York Times*, 22 June 1991, p. A7.

72. Philip Hilts, "Drug Said to Help AIDS Cases with Virus But No Symptoms," *New York Times*, 18 Aug. 1989, p. A1.

73. Robert Massa, "AZT or not AZT," *Village Voice* 36, no. 14 (2 Apr. 1991): 16.

74. Lawrence K. Altman, "Advances in Treatment Change Face of AIDS," *New York Times*, 12 June 1990, p. C5.

75. For an important indictment of the Reagan administration's handling of the AIDS epidemic, see Randy Shilts, *And the Band Played On* (New York: St. Martin's Press, 1987); and Larry Kramer, "A 'Manhattan Project' for AIDS," *New York Times*, 16 July 1990, p. A15. Also see Diane Johnson and John Murray, M.D., "AIDS without End," *New York Review of Books* 35, no. 13

(18 Aug. 1988): 57–63; and Office of Technology Assessment, U.S. Congress, *Review of the Public Health Service's Response to AIDS: A Technical Memorandum* (Washington, D.C.: U.S. Government Printing Office, Feb. 1985).

76. Committee on Government Operations, *The Federal Response to AIDS,* Twenty-Ninth Report by the Committee on Government Operations (Washington, D.C.: U.S. Government Printing Office, Nov. 1983, no. 98–582), p. 4.

77. Shilts, "Era of Bad Feelings," p. 359.

78. Ibid., pp. 93, 94.

79. Crimp, ed., *AIDS: Cultural Analysis and Cultural Activism,* p. 11.

80. Willie L. Brown, Jr., "AIDS: The Public Policy Imperative," *Saint Louis University Public Law Review* 7 (Spring 1988): 12.

81. *Nassau County v. Arline,* 480 U.S. 273 (1987). Also see *Chalk v. U.S. District Court,* 840 F.2d 701 (1988) for a discussion of one of the most sweeping AIDS anti-discrimination cases under section 504. See also Shad-Flor, *National Law Journal,* 27 Aug. 1990; Dennis Hevesi, "AIDS Carriers Win a Court Ruling," *New York Times,* 9 July 1988, p. A6; and Stuart Taylor, "Justices Support Disease Victims: Those with AIDS Could Benefit," *New York Times,* 4 Mar. 1987, p. A1.

82. Philip Boffey, "Expert Panel Sees Poor Leadership in U.S. AIDS Battle," *New York Times,* 2 June 1988, p. A11.

83. Committee for the Oversight of AIDS Activities, Institute of Medicine, National Academy of Sciences, *Confronting AIDS: Update 1988* (Washington, D.C.: National Academy of Sciences Press, 1988).

84. Presidential Commission on the HIV Epidemic, *Report,* pp. xvii, xviii.

85. Ibid., pp. 93, 94.

86. Julie Johnson, "Report by AIDS Panel Gets Muted Reaction by Reagan," *New York Times,* 28 June 1988, p. A16.

87. Warren E. Leary, "AIDS Outlay Matching Cancer and Heart Disease," *New York Times,* 15 June 1989, p. B13.

88. David Rosenbaum, "How Capital Ignored Alarms on Savings," *New York Times,* 6 June 1990, p. A1.

89. Gerald M. Boyd, "Bush Backs Protection of AIDS Victims' Rights," *New York Times,* 29 June 1988, p. A21.

90. Philip Hilts, "2.9 Billion AIDS Relief Measure Easily Wins Approval in Senate," *New York Times,* 17 May 1990, p. B10.

91. Boyd, "Bush Backs . . . Victims' Rights," p. A21.

92. George Bush, as quoted in Andrew Rosenthal, "Bush Plays Down Protest on AIDS," *New York Times,* 3 Sept. 1991, p. A20.

93. Philip Hilts, "AIDS Panel Backs Efforts to Exchange Drug Users' Needles," *New York Times,* 7 Aug. 1991, p. A1.

94. Karen DeWitt, "On Capitol Hill: The Battle for AIDS Funds Heats Up," *New York Times,* 9 Nov. 1991, p. A33.

95. Ibid.

96. Peter Bachrach and Morton Baratz, *Power and Poverty: Theory and Practice* (New York: Oxford University Press, 1970).

97. Philip Hilts, "AIDS Panel Says U.S. Lags on Health Care Policy," *New York Times,* 7 Dec. 1989, p. A26.

98. *America Living with Aids,* p. 4.

99. Ibid., see especially pp. 28–29, 48–49.

100. Magic Johnson, as quoted in Philip Hilts, "Magic Johnson Quits Panel on AIDS," *New York Times,* 26 Sept. 1992, p. A5.

101. George Bush, as quoted in "In Their Own Words," *New York Times,* 31 Oct. 1992, p. A7.

102. Clinton and Gore, *Putting People First,* pp. 36–41.

103. For a rich discussion of the issue of the moral interventionism of the state and neoconservative privatism, see Rosalind Pollack Petchesky, *Abortion and Woman's Choice: The State, Sexuality, and Reproductive Freedom,* rev. ed. (Boston: Northeastern University Press, 1990), pp. 392–96, and the preface to the 1990 edition.

104. Gina Kolata, "AIDS Advocates Find Private Funds Declining," *New York Times,* 7 Aug. 1990, p. A16.

105. For a full discussion, see Bruce Nussbaum, *Good Intentions: How Big Business and the Medical Establishment Are Corrupting the Fight Against AIDS* (New York: Atlantic Monthly Press, 1990).

106. Harold Edgar and David J. Rothman, "New Rules for New Drugs: The Challenge of AIDS to the Regulatory Process," in "A Disease of Society: Cultural Responses to AIDS (Part 1)," special supplement, *Milbank Quarterly* 68 (1990), supp. 1, p. 131.

107. Allan Brandt, *No Magic Bullet* (New York: Oxford University Press, 1987), pp. 202, 182.

108. Committee on AIDS Research and the Behavioral, Social and Statistical Sciences, National Research Council, *AIDS: Sexual Behavior and Intravenous Drug Use* ed. Charles Turner, Heather Miller, and Lincoln Moses (Washington, D.C.: National Academy Press, 1989), p. 383.

109. C. Everett Koop, *Understanding AIDS: A Message from the Surgeon General,* HHS Publication No. (CDC) HHS-88-8404 (Washington, DC: United States Department of Health and Human Services, 1988), p. 4. Available from Department of HHS, P.O. Box 6003, Rockville, MD 10850.

110. William Bennett, "AIDS: Education and Public Policy," *Saint Louis University Public Law Review* 7 (Spring 1988): 2. For an example of the homophobia that underlies the AIDS education campaign, see David Olson, "Read Their Lips: Illinois Moves to Ban AIDS Poster," *Village Voice* 35, no. 30 (24 July 1990): 14.

111. Peter Steinfels, "Catholic Bishops Vote to Retain Controversial Statement on AIDS," *New York Times,* 28 June 1988, p. A1. Also see "Condom Campaign Begins in Massachusetts," *New York Times,* 9 Sept. 1990, p. A28.

112. Joseph Berger, "School Board Backing Off AIDS Abstinence Policy," *New York Times,* 3 June 1992, p. B3; and James Dao, "Critics Decry New AIDS Education Rules as Censorship," *New York Times,* 29 May 1992, p. B3.

113. Talbot, "Condom Conundrum," p. 42.

114. William Honan, "Conferees Reject a Plan to Curb Federal Funds for Obscene Art," *New York Times,* 30 Sept. 1989, p. A1.

115. Maureen Dowd, "Jesse Helms Takes No-Lose Position on Art," *New York Times,* 28 July 1989, p. A1. Also see Elizabeth Hess, "NEA Shoots Itself," *Village Voice* 34, no. 47 (21 Nov. 1989): 63; Michael Oreskes, "Senate Votes

to Bar U.S. Support of Obscene or Indecent Artwork," *New York Times,* 27 July 1989, p. A1; and Elizabeth Whelan, "The Offensive Tactics of AIDS Ideologues," *New York Times,* 8 Aug. 1989, p. A19.

116. Rightists criticized Bush for his position on the NEA. See Richard Viguerie and Steven Allen, "To Bush: The Right Has Other Choices," *New York Times,* 14 June 1990, p. A27.

117. The White House, *National Drug Control Strategy* (Washington, D.C.: U.S. Government Printing Office, Jan. 1990), p. 9. By 1992, Bush was saying much less about the drug war. See Michael Massing, "What Ever Happened to the 'War on Drugs'?" *New York Review of Books* 39, no. 11 (11 June 1992): 42–46.

118. Ellen Willis, "End the War on Drugs: Hell No, I Won't Go," *Village Voice* 33, no. 38 (19 Sept. 1989): 30–31.

119. Daniel Patrick Moynihan, in *Congressional Record,* 101st Congress, vol. 136, no. 76 (14 June 1990): S7945.

120. Playthell Benjamin, "Down with Crack," *Village Voice* 33, no. 38 (19 Sept. 1989): 29.

121. Michael Klare, "The War That Came In from the Cold: Drugs, Militarism and the Monroe Doctrine," *Radical America* 23, nos. 2–3 (Apr.–Sept. 1989): 17.

122. "Text of President's Speech on National Drug Control Strategy," *New York Times,* 6 Sept. 1989, p. B6. Also see Richard Berke, "More of the Same," *New York Times,* 6 Sept. 1989, p. A1.

123. Michel Foucault, *Discipline and Punish: The Birth of the Prison* (New York: Vintage, 1979). Also see his *The History of Sexuality* (New York: Pantheon, 1978), vol. 1, *An Introduction.*

124. James Lyons, "Crime and the Judiciary: Candidates Vie for the Law and Order State," *Village Voice* 37, no. 26 (30 June 1992): 40.

125. White House, *National Drug Control Strategy,* p. 5.

126. Ibid., p. 39.

127. William Bennett, "A Response to Milton Friedman," *Wall Street Journal,* 19 Sept. 1989, p. A30.

128. Milton Friedman, "An Open Letter to Bill Bennett," *Wall Street Journal,* 7 Sept. 1989, p. A14. For other criticism of Bennett from within the neoconservative camp, see Senator Daniel Patrick Moynihan's statements in the *Congressional Record,* vol. 136, no. 76 (14 June 1990): S7945.

129. Ellen Willis, "End the War on Drugs," p. 30; Playthell Benjamin, "Down with Crack," pp. 29–32. Also see Ramsey Clark, "Drugs, Lies and T.V.," *Nation* 249, no. 12 (16 Oct. 1989): 408–9; Michael Massing, "The War on Cocaine," *New York Review of Books* 35, no. 20 (22 Dec. 1988): 61–67; Philip Hilts, "AIDS Panel Says U.S. Lags on Health Care Policy," *New York Times,* 7 Dec. 1989, p. A26; and Jefferson Morley, "Contradictions of Cocaine Capitalism," *Nation* 249, no. 10 (2 Oct. 1989): 341–47.

130. Committee on AIDS Research, *AIDS, Sexual Behavior and Intravenous Drug Use,* pp. 299, 240. Also see the second volume, entitled *AIDS: The Second Decade* (Washington, D.C.: National Academy Press, 1990).

131. Presidential Commission on the HIV Epidemic, *Report,* p. 94.

132. Warren E. Leary, "Sharp Rise in Rare Sex-Related Diseases," *New York Times*, 14 July 1988, p. B6.

133. Peter Kerr, "Crack and Resurgence of Syphilis Spreading AIDS among the Poor," *New York Times*, 20 Aug. 1989, p. A1.

134. Daniel Lazare, "Crack and AIDS: The Next Wave," *Village Voice* 35, no. 19 (8 May 1990): 29.

135. Dean Baquet, "Hearings on Neglect Upheld in Newborn Cocaine Cases," *New York Times*, 30 May 1990, p. B3.

136. Rorie Sherman, "Keeping Babies Free of Drugs," *National Law Journal* 12, no. 6 (16 Oct. 1989): 28. Also see "Punishing Pregnant Addicts: Debate, Dismay, No Solution," in "Ideas and Trends," *New York Times*, 10 Sept. 1989, p. E5; and the work of Lynn Paltrow, Reproductive Freedom Project, American Civil Liberties Union, "State by State Case Summary of Criminal Prosecutions against Pregnant Women Memorandum."

137. Sherman, "Keeping Babies Free of Drugs," p. 29.

138. "Punishing Pregnant Addicts," p. E5.

139. Mark Gevisser, "Women and Children First," *Village Voice* 34, no. 44 (31 Oct. 1989): 18.

140. See Committee on Government Operations, *Federal Response to AIDS*.

141. Ann Giudici Fettner, "Cutting the Cord," *Village Voice* 35, no. 25 (19 June 1990): 16.

142. Ronald Bayer, "AIDS, Privacy, and Responsibility," in *Daedalus*, p. 79.

143. Ronald Bayer, *Private Acts, Social Consequences: AIDS and the Politics of Public Health* (New York: The Free Press, 1989), p. 15.

144. Simon Watney, "The Spectacle of AIDS," in Crimp, ed., *AIDS: Cultural Analysis and Cultural Activism*, p. 86.

145. Sandor Katz, "HIV Testing—A Phony Cure," *Nation* 250, no. 21 (28 May 1990): 738–42; and Bruce Lambert, "In Shift, Gay Men's Health Crisis Endorses Testing for AIDS Virus," *New York Times*, 16 Aug. 1989, p. A1.

146. Charles Rembar, "The A.C.L.U.'s Myopic Stand on AIDS," *New York Times*, 15 May 1987, p. A31. Also see Isabel Wilkerson, "A.M.A. Urges Breach of Privacy to Warn Potential AIDS Victims," *New York Times*, 1 July 1988, p. A1.

147. Jan Hoffman, "AIDS and Rape," *Village Voice* 33, no. 37 (12 Sept. 1989): 36, 38.

148. Dennis Hevesi, "AIDS Test for Suspect Splits Experts," *New York Times*, 16 Oct. 1988, p. A30.

149. Patton, *Inventing AIDS*, p. 38.

150. Lawrence K. Altman, "Guidance for Doctors Carrying AIDS," *New York Times*, 10 Aug. 1991, p. A6; Sarah Lyall, "AIDS Tests Find No Link to L.I. Dentist," *New York Times*, 10 Aug. 1991, p. B21; Elisabeth Rosenthal, "Angry Doctors Condemn Plans to Test Them for AIDS," 20 Aug. 1991, p. C1.

151. William Dannemeyer, as quoted in Philip Hilts, "Mandatory AIDS Tests for Doctors Would Be Useless, Health Experts Say," *New York Times*, 20 Sept. 1991, p. A22.

152. Martin Tolchin, "Senate Adopts Tough Measures on Health Workers with AIDS," *New York Times,* 19 July 1991, p. A1.

153. Philip Hilts, "Mandatory AIDS Tests for Doctors," p. A22. Also see Jane Gross, "Many Doctors Infected with AIDS Don't Follow New U.S. Guidelines," *New York Times,* 18 Aug. 1991, p. A1.

154. Gwen Ifill, "Panel in Congress Drops AIDS Disclosure Plan," *New York Times,* 28 Sept. 1991, p. A7.

155. Kevin Sack, "Albany Plans to Allow Surgery by Doctors with the AIDS Virus," *New York Times,* 9 Oct. 1991, p. A1. Also see Lawrence K. Altman, "New York Won't Tell Doctors with AIDS to Inform Patients," *New York Times,* 19 Jan. 1990, p. A1, and his "U.S. Hears Debate on Mandatory AIDS Test for Health Workers," *New York Times,* 22 Feb. 1991, p. A15; and Stephanie Strom, "AIDS and Privacy: A Bellevue Dilemma," *New York Times,* 28 Jan. 1991, p. B1.

156. Lawrence K. Altman, "U.S. Backs Off on Plan to Restrict Health Worker with AIDS Virus," *New York Times,* 4 Aug. 1991, p. A1.

157. Warren E. Leary, "Mandatory AIDS Test for Doctors Opposed," *New York Times,* 31 July 1992, p. A11.

158. As quoted in Philip Hilts, "Woman with AIDS Seizes Stage, Asking Bush to Help Ease Stigma," *New York Times,* 4 Aug. 1991, p. A1.

159. Philip Hilts, "Sponsors Say AIDS Conference Won't Be Held in U.S. Next Year," *New York Times,* 17 Aug. 1991, p. A6. Also see DeWitt, "In Shift, U.S. Plans to Keep Out People Carrying the AIDS Virus," *New York Times,* 26 May 1991, p. A1.

160. Thomas Morgan, "State Studies Pricing of AIDS Drug," *New York Times,* 8 Oct. 1987, p. B3; Philip Hilts, "U.S. Is Decades Behind Europe in Contraceptives, Experts Report," *New York Times,* 15 Feb. 1990, p. A1; Committee on Contraceptive Development, *Developing New Contraceptives,* ed. Luigi Mastroianni, Jr., Peter J. Donaldson, and Thomas T. Kane (Washington, D.C.: U.S. Government Printing Office, 1990).

161. Presidential Commission on the HIV Epidemic, *Report,* pp. 48, 52.

162. Philip Leder, "Privatizing N.I.H. Is an 'Idiotic Idea,' " *New York Times,* 12 Jan. 1988, p. A27.

163. Philip M. Crane, "Abolish the Arts Agency," *New York Times,* 6 June 1990, p. A27.

164. Bateson and Goldsby, *Thinking AIDS,* p. 118.

165. Morgan, "State Studies Pricing of AIDS Drug," p. B3; Charles W. Hunt, "AIDS and Capitalist Medicine," *Monthly Review* 39, no. 8 (Jan. 1988): 11–25; A. Joseph Layon and Robert D'Amico, "AIDS, Capitalism, and Technology," *Monthly Review* 40, no. 7 (Dec. 1988): 31–36; Mark McGrath and Bob Sutcliffe, "Insuring Profits from AIDS: The Economics of an Epidemic," *Radical America* 20, no. 6 (Nov.–Dec. 1986): 9–26.

166. See Milton Friedman, *Day of Reckoning* (New York: Random House, 1990); and Kevin Phillips, *The Politics of Rich and Poor* (New York: Random House, 1990).

167. Michael Oreskes, "Grudging Public Thinks Tax Rise Now Must Come," *New York Times,* 27 May 1990, p. A1.

168. Patton, *Inventing AIDS*, p. 116. Also see *inside/out: Lesbian Theories, Gay Theories*, ed. Diana Fuss (New York: Routledge, 1991).

169. Robin Hardy, "Die Harder, AIDS Activism Is Abandoning Gay Men," *Village Voice* 36, no. 27 (2 July 1991): 33.

170. Ibid.

171. Donna Minkowitz, "ACT UP at a Crossroads," 20.

172. Frank Browning, "Turf Wars," 18.

173. Donna Haraway, *Simians, Cyborgs, and Women: The Reinvention of Nature*, pp. 109, 113.

CHAPTER 6. REVISIONING PRIVACY FOR DEMOCRACY

1. John Rawls, *A Theory of Justice* (Cambridge, Mass.: Harvard University Press, 1971) for a discussion of contracting for a just state.

2. Adrienne Rich, *Of Woman Born: Motherhood as Experience and Institution* (New York: Norton, 1976), p. 39.

3. Elizabeth Fox Genovese, *Feminism without Illusions: A Critique of Individualism* (Chapel Hill: University of North Carolina Press, 1991), pp. 8, 241, 256, 7.

4. Rosalind Pollack Petchesky, *Abortion and Women's Choice: The State, Sexuality, and Reproductive Freedom*, rev. ed. (Boston: Northeastern University Press, 1990), pp. xxi–xxvi.

5. Helga Maria Hernes, *Welfare State and Woman Power* (New York: Oxford University Press/Norwegian University Press, 1987).

6. See Wendy Brown, "Finding the Man in the State," *Feminist Studies* 18, no. 1 (Spring 1992): 7–34, for an interesting discussion of the patriarchal and limiting aspects of the state.

7. For important critiques of the notion of privacy, see Petchesky, *Abortion and Woman's Choice;* and Aida Hurtado, "Relating to Privilege: Seduction and Rejection in the Subordination of White Women and Women of Color," *Signs* 14, no. 4 (1989): 833–55.

8. See Zillah Eisenstein, *Female Body and the Law,* for a fuller discussion of radical pluralism.

9. Clinton and Gore, *Putting People First*, p. viii.

10. Rosalind Pollack Petchesky, "The Body as Property—A Feminist Re-Vision," in *Reproductive Politics in the 1990's*, ed. Faye Ginsbury and Rayna Rapp (Berkeley and Los Angeles: University of California Press, forthcoming).

11. Paul Veyne, ed., *From Pagan Rome to Byzantium*, vol. 1 of *A History of Private Life*, ed. Philippe Aries and Georges Duby (Cambridge, MA: Harvard University Press, 1987). Also see Jean-Francois Lyotard, *The Postmodern Condition: A Report on Knowledge* (Minneapolis: University of Minnesota Press, 1989).

12. Barrington Moore, Jr., *Privacy: Studies in Social and Cultural History* (New York: M. E. Sharpe, 1984), p. 21.

13. Ibid., p. 9.

14. Nancy Fraser, "Rethinking the Public Sphere," *Social Text* 8, no. 3 / 9,

no. 1 (1990): 77. Also see her *Unruly Practices, Power, Discourse and Gender in Contemporary Social Theory* (Minneapolis: University of Minnesota Press, 1989).

15. Paolo Carpignano, Robin Anderson, Stanley Aronowitz, and William Difozio, "Chatter in the Age of Electronic Production," *Social Text* 8:3, 9:1 (1990): 54.

16. Alida Brill, *Nobody's Business: The Paradoxes of Privacy* (Reading, MA: Addison-Wesley Publishing Co., 1990), p. xii. Also see Joanna K. Weinberg's review of *Nobody's Business* in *Women's Review of Books* 8, no. 7 (Apr. 1991): 1–4.

17. Rosalind Pollack Petchesky, "Foetal Images: The Power of Visual Culture in the Politics of Reproduction," in *Reproductive Technologies,* ed. Michelle Stanworth (Minneapolis: University of Minnesota Press, 1987), pp. 57–80.

18. Donna Haraway, "A Manifesto for Cyborgs: Science, Technology, and Socialist Feminism in the 1980's," in *Coming to Terms,* ed. Elizabeth Weed (New York: Routledge, 1989), p. 193.

19. John Donahue, *The Privatization Decision: Public Ends, Private Means* (New York: Basic Books, 1989), p. 3.

20. Clinton and Gore, *Putting People First,* p. 226. Also see Robert Reich, "Prosperity? Clinton: Spur Growth," *New York Times,* 16 July 1992, p. A25.

21. Arthur MacEwan, "Why the Emperor Can't Afford New Clothes," *Monthly Review* 43, no. 3 (July–Aug. 1991): 79, 86–87.

22. Robert Heilbroner, "Lifting the Silent Depression," *New York Review of Books* 33, no. 17 (24 Oct. 1991): 6.

23. David Alan Aschauer, "Public Investment and Private Sector Growth," in *Economic Policy Institute* (Pamphlet, Economic Policy Institute, Washington, D.C., 1990).

24. Sylvia Nasar, "The 1980's: A Very Good Time for the Very Rich," *New York Times,* 5 Mar. 1992, p. A1.

25. Sylvia Nasar, "Fed Gives New Evidence of 80's Gains by Richest," *New York Times,* 27 Sept. 1991, p. A1.

26. Jason DeParle, "Poverty Rate Rose Sharply Last Year as Incomes Slipped," *New York Times,* 27 Sept. 1991, p. A1.

27. Benjamin Friedman, "The Campaign's Hidden Issue," *New York Review of Books* 35, no. 15 (13 Oct. 1988): 37. Also see his *Day of Reckoning* (New York: Random House, 1988).

28. Friedman, "Campaign's Hidden Issue," p. 26. For a fuller discussion of the problem of disinvestment in the United States economy, as well as the economy's decline, see Barry Bluestone and Bennett Harrison, *The Deindustrialization of America* (New York: Basic Books, 1982); and *The Great U-Turn* (New York: Basic Books, 1988). Also see Paul Kennedy, *The Rise and Fall of the Great Powers* (New York: Vintage Press, 1987); and David Noble, *Forces of Production: A Social History of Industrial Automation* (New York: Oxford University Press, 1984).

29. Robert Reich, "The REAL Economy," *Atlantic Monthly* 267, no. 2 (Feb. 1991): 50–51, 47.

30. Ibid., pp. 51, 46.

31. Anthony Lewis, "The Reagan Effect," *New York Times*, 26 July 1991, p. A27.

32. David Osborne and Ted Gaebler, *Reinventing Government: How the Entrepreneurial Spirit Is Transforming the Public Sector* (Reading, Mass.: Addison-Wesley, 1992), p. 24.

33. Susan Chira, "Lamar Alexander's Self-Help Course," *New York Times Magazine*, 24 Nov. 1991, p. 57.

34. Robert Crain, as quoted in Susan Chira, "The Rules of the Marketplace Are Applied to the Classroom," *New York Times*, 12 June 1991, p. B5.

35. Susan Chira, "Splashy School Venture Creates Lots of Ripples," *New York Times*, 31 May 1992, p. E3. Also see Katherine Bishop, "California Poses Crucial Test to Commercial TV Program in Schools," *New York Times*, 4 June 1992, p. A16.

36. Susan Chira, "Poverty's Toll on Health is Plague of U.S. Schools," *New York Times*, 5 Oct. 1991, p. A1.

37. Robert Pear, "Bush to Propose $500 Million Rise in Budget for Head Start Program," *New York Times*, 19 Jan. 1992, p. A22; and Michael Wines, "Bush Urges Head Start Increase, and Debate on Its Impact Follows," *New York Times*, 22 Jan. 1992, p. A16.

38. Felicia R. Lee, "Immunization of Children Is Said to Lag," *New York Times*, 16 Oct. 1991, p. A5.

39. Robert Pear, "Bush to Make It Easier for Governments to Sell Public Property," *New York Times*, 25 Apr. 1992, p. A5.

40. Sarah Bartlett, "New York Cost-Cutting Idea: City Jobs, Outside Workers," *New York Times*, 7 July 1991, p. A1.

41. James Ridgeway, "Stormy Weather," *Village Voice* 36, no. 24 (11 June 1991): 21–22.

42. Robert Sherrill, "S&L's, Big Banks and Other Triumphs of Capitalism," *Nation* 251, no. 17 (19 Nov. 1990): 589. Also see Robert Pear, "Leap in U.S. Deficit Is Seen Next Year Despite 1990 Law," *New York Times*, 16 Aug. 1991, p. A1.

43. Kevin Phillips, *The Politics of Rich and Poor: Wealth and the American Electorate in the Reagan Aftermath* (New York: Random House, 1990), pp. 170, 218.

44. Robert Pear, "Rich Got Richer in 80's; Others Held Even," *New York Times*, 11 Jan. 1991, p. A1.

45. See Eisenstein, *Feminism and Sexual Equality*, chaps. 4 and 5; and Fraser, *Unruly Practices*, chap. 7, for in-depth discussions of the particular relationship of women and the welfare state.

46. Teresa L. Amott, "Black Women and AFDC: Making Entitlement Out of Necessity," in *Women, the State, and Welfare*, ed. Linda Gordon (Madison: University of Wisconsin Press, 1990), pp. 281, 282–84.

47. Jane Gross, "Collapse of Inner-City Families Creates America's New Orphans," *New York Times*, 28 Mar. 1992, p. A1.

48. 482 U.S. 464 (1977); 448 U.S. 297 (1980).

49. *Roe v. Wade*, 410 U.S. 113, 154–55 (1973).

50. Ibid, p. 154–55.

51. Samuel Warren and Louis Brandeis, "The Right to Privacy," *Harvard Law Review* 4 (15 Dec. 1890): 784.

52. See Melvin L. Wulf's "On the Origins of Privacy," *Nation* 252, no. 20 (27 May 1991): 700–704. Also see Ronald Dworkin, "The Bork Nomination," *New York Review of Books* 34, no. 13 (13 Aug. 1987): 3–10; and his "From Bork to Kennedy," *New York Review of Books* 34, no. 20 (17 Dec. 1987): 36–42.

53. Jed Rubenfeld, "The Right of Privacy," *Harvard Law Review* 102 (Feb. 1989): 804, 784. Also see Anita Allen, "Taking Liberties: Privacy, Private Choice, and Social Contract Theory," *Cincinnati Law Review* 56 (1987): 461–91.

54. *Pierce v. Society of Sisters*, 168 U.S. 510 (1925); *Skinner v. Oklahoma*, 316 U.S. 535 (1942); *Griswold v. Connecticut*, 381 U.S. 479 (1965); *Eisenstadt v. Baird*, 405 U.S. 438 (1972); *Roe v. Wade*, 410 U.S. 113 (1973).

55. *Griswold*, 381 U.S. 479, 483–85; *Boyd v. United States*, 116 U.S. 616.

56. 381 U.S. 479, 495, 499. See also *Poe v. Ullmann*, 367 U.S. 497, 553 (1961).

57. 381 U.S. 479, 508.

58. 405 U.S. 438, 453.

59. Sue Hyde, "Sex and Politics: Challenging the Sodomy Laws," *Radical America* 22, no. 5 (Sept.–Oct. 1988, published in Dec. 1989): 57–63.

60. 478 U.S. 186, 190–91.

61. Ibid., p. 196.

62. Ibid., p. 199, 205–8.

63. Ellen Bigge, "The Fetal Rights Controversy: A Resurfacing of Sex Discrimination in the Guise of Fetal Protection," *University of Missouri—Kansas City Law Review* 57 (Winter 1989): 261.

64. Rubenfeld, "Right of Privacy," p. 744.

65. Dawn Johnsen, "From Driving to Drugs: Governmental Regulation of Pregnant Women's Lives after Webster," *University of Pennsylvania Law Review* 138 (Nov. 1989): 179.

66. Rubenfeld, "Right of Privacy," p. 791.

67. See Petchesky, *Abortion and Woman's Choice*, especially chapters 3 and 4.

68. *Harris v. McRae*, 448 U.S. 297, 315 (1989).

69. Howard Fineman and Evan Thomas, "How Far Right," pp. 19–20; David Kaplan and Bob Cohn, "Good for the Left, Now Good for the Right," pp. 20–23; Barbara Kantrowitz, "Tipping the Odds on Abortion," p. 23; all in *Newsweek* 118, no. 2 (8 July 1991). Also see Linda Greenhouse, "Powers Expanded" and "Justices, 6 to 3, Restrict Rights to Pornography," *New York Times*, 19 Apr. 1990, both on p. A1; and Ira Mickenberg, "Criminal Rulings Granted the State Broad New Power," *National Law Journal* 13, no. 50 (19 Aug. 1991): S10–S14, which is part of the *Journal's* larger "Supreme Court Review Supplement," pp. S1–S28; and *Ohio v. Young*, 525 N.E. 2d 1363 (1988).

70. *Deshaney v. Winnebago*, 489 U.S. 189, 196 (1989).

71. Ibid., p. 197.

72. *Cruzan v. Director, Missouri Department of Health,* 497 U.S. 261, 269, 270 (1990).

73. Ronald Dworkin, "The Right to Die," *New York Review of Books* 38, no. 3 (31 Jan. 1991): 16. Also see Marcia Coyle, "Is the Court Avoiding the Big Question?" *National Law Journal* 12 (9 July 1990): 1–24; Linda Greenhouse, "Justices Find a Right to Die, But the Majority Sees Need for Clear Proof of Intent," *New York Times,* 26 June 1990, p. A1; and Allen, "Court Disables Disputed Legacy of Privacy Right," *National Law Journal* 12 (13 Aug. 1990): S8–S14.

74. 497 U.S. 261, 339, 356–57.

75. Shoshana Zuboff, *In the Age of the Smart Machine: The Future of Work and Power* (New York: Basic Books, 1988), pp. 22, 37.

76. For a sampling of the issues surrounding new reproductive technologies, see Lisa Sowle Cahill, "In Vitro Fertilization: Ethical Issues in Judaeo-Christian Perspective," *Loyola Law Review* 32 (Summer 1986): 337–56; Kelly L. Frey, "New Reproductive Technologies: The Legal Problem and a Solution," *Tennessee Law Review* 49 (Winter 1982): 303–42; William Handel, "Surrogate Parenting, In Vitro Insemination and Embryo Transplantation," *Whittier Law Review* 6 (Summer 1984): 783–88; Matthew R. Eccles,"The Use of In Vitro Fertilization: Is There a Right to Bear or Beget a Child by Any Available Medical Means," *Pepperdine Law Review* 12 (May 1985): 1033–51; Kathryn Venturatos Lorio, "Alternative Means of Reproduction: Virgin Territory for Legislation," *Louisiana Law Review* 44 (July 1984): 1641–76; and Michelle Stanworth, ed., *Reproductive Technologies: Gender, Mother and Medicine* (Minneapolis: University of Minnesota Press, 1987).

77. Laura Fraser, "Pill Politics," *Mother Jones* 13, no. 5 (June 1988): 31–44; Philip Hilts, "U.S. Is Decades Behind Europe in Contraceptives, Expert Report," *New York Times* 15 Feb. 1990, p. A1; Philip Hilts, "Birth Control Backlash," *New York Times Magazine,* 16 Dec. 1990, pp. 41–74; Luigi Mastroianni, Jr., Peter J. Donaldson, and Thomas T. Kane, eds., *Developing New Contraceptives: Obstacles and Opportunities* (Washington, D.C.: National Academy Press, 1990); and Morton Mintz, *At Any Cost: Corporate Greed, Women, and the Dalkon Shield* (New York: Pantheon Books, 1985).

78. Lori Andrews, "Brave New Baby: Biogenetics Is Heralded as a Welcome Scientific Advance, But Will It Turn Big Government into Big Parent?" *Student Lawyer* 8 (Dec. 1983): 25.

79. John Robertson, "Procreative Liberty and the Control of Conception, Pregnancy and Childbirth," *Virginia Law Review* 69 (April 1983): 423.

80. John Robertson, " 'Embryos, Families, and Procreative Liberty': The Legal Structure of the New Reproduction," *Southern California Law Review* 59 (July 1986): 947, 951. See also Lori Andrews, "The Legal Status of the Embryo," *Loyola Law Review* 32 (Summer 1986): 357–409.

81. Petchesky, "Foetal Images," p. 57.

82. See *Davis v. King,* No. E-14496, Tenn. App. Lexis 641 (1989). Also see Ronald Smothers, "Tennessee Judge Awards Custody of 7 Frozen Embryos to Woman," *New York Times,* 22 Sept. 1989, p. A13; "New Divorce Issue: Em-

bryos' Status," *New York Times*, 8 Aug. 1989, p. A11; Rorie Sherman, "Just Whose Embryo Is It, Anyway?" *National Law Journal* 11 (12 June 1989): 1–23; George P. Smith II, "Intimations of Life: Extracorporeality and the Law," *Gonzaga Law Review* 21 (June 1986): 395–424; and Marcia Joy Wurmbrand, "Frozen Embryos: Moral, Social, and Legal Implications," *Southern California Law Review* 59 (6 July 1986): 1079–1100.

83. Ronald Smothers, "Court Gives Ex-Husband Rights on Use of Embryos," *New York Times*, 2 June 1992, p. A1.

84. Robertson, "Procreative Liberty," pp. 406, 408–10.

85. Robertson, "Embryos, Families and Procreative Liberty," p. 943. Also see Lesley Doyal, "Infertility—A Life Sentence? Women and the National Health Service," in Stanworth, *Reproductive Technologies*, 174–90; and Deborah Gerson, "Infertility and the Construction of Desperation," *Socialist Review* 19, no. 3 (July–Sept. 1989): 45–66.

86. See Dawn Johnsen, "The Creation of Fetal Rights: Conflicts with Women's Constitutional Rights to Liberty, Privacy, and Equal Protection," *Yale Law Journal* 95 (Jan. 1986): 599–624.

87. George J. Annas, "Predicting the Future of Privacy in Pregnancy: How Medical Technology Affects the Legal Rights of Pregnant Women," *Nova Law Review* 13 (Spring 1989): 329–53; Gena Corea, *The Mother Machine: Reproductive Technologies from Artificial Insemination to Artificial Wombs* (New York: Harper & Row, 1985); Katha Pollitt, "When Is a Mother Not a Mother?" *Nation* 251, no. 23 (31 Dec. 1990): 825–46; Barbara Katz Rothman, *Recreating Motherhood: Ideology and Technology in Patriarchal Society* (New York: Random House, 1989); Barbara Katz Rothman, *The Tentative Pregnancy: Prenatal Diagnosis and the Future of Motherhood* (New York: Penguin, 1987); and Nadine Taub and Sherrill Cohen, eds., *Reproductive Laws for the 1990s* (Rutgers: State University of New Jersey, 1989).

88. Petchesky, "Foetal Images," p. 78.

89. Johnsen, "From Driving to Drugs," p. 180.

90. Lynn Paltrow, "When Becoming Pregnant Is a Crime," *John Jay Criminal Justice Ethics Magazine* 9 (Winter/Spring, 1990): 41–47. Also see her "Maternal and Fetal Rights" (Paper presented at the National Association of Women and the Law Conference, 16–19 February 1989).

91. 208 U.S. 412, 421.

92. It would make much more sense to provide prenatal care than the intensive medical care needed for premature and unhealthy babies. See Howard French, "Tiny Miracles Become Huge Public Health Problem," *New York Times* 19 Feb. 1989, p. A1; and Barbara Kantrowitz, Pat Wingert, and Mary Hager, "Preemies," *Newsweek* 91, no. 20 (16 May 1988): 62–70.

93. See American Civil Liberties Union Memorandum, compiled by Lynn Paltrow, Hilary Fox, and Ellen Goetz, 7 February 1990, "Case Update: State by State Case Summary of Criminal Prosecutions Against Pregnant Women."

94. Appellant's Initial Brief, p. 24, *Johnson v. Florida*, 578 So. 2d 419 (Fla. Dist. Ct. App. 1991) (No. 89-1765).

95. Johnsen, "From Driving to Drugs," pp. 214, 207. Also see Sherman, "Keeping Baby Safe from Mom," *National Law Journal* 11 (3 Oct. 1988): 1–

25; Molly McNulty, "NOTE: Pregnancy Police: The Health Policy and Legal Implications of Punishing Pregnant Women for Harm to Their Fetuses," *New York University Review of Law and Social Change* 16 (1987–88): 277–319.

96. Paltrow, "When Becoming Pregnant Is a Crime," p. 42.

97. Data from the National Black Women's Health Project, 1237 Gordon St. SW, Atlanta, GA 30310.

98. Paltrow, "When Becoming Pregnant is a Crime," p. 43. Also see Joseph B. Treaster, "Plan Lets Addicted Mothers Take Their Newborns Home," *New York Times,* 19 Sept. 1991, p. A1.

99. Dawn Johnsen, "A New Threat to Pregnant Women's Autonomy," *Hastings Center Report* 17, no. 4 (Aug./Sept. 1987): 38.

100. Linda Greenhouse, "Court in Capitol Bars Forced Surgery to Save Fetus," *New York Times,* 27 Apr. 1990, p. A1.

101. Michael Lev, "Judge Is Firm on Forced Contraception, But Welcomes an Appeal," *New York Times,* 11 Jan. 1991, p. A17. Also see Kate Tentler, "I've Got You Under My Skin," *Village Voice* 35, no. 3 (15 Jan. 1991): 22.

102. Johnsen, "From Driving to Drugs," p. 211.

103. Bigge, "Fetal Rights Controversy," p. 286.

104. W. Lazarus and K. West, *Back to Basics* (Southern California Child Health Network, 1987), pp. 23–24. Also see *The Future of Children: Drug Exposed Infants* 1, no. 1 (Spring 1991). Published by the Center for the Future of Children, The David and Lucile Packard Foundation.

105. Johnsen, "New Threat to Pregnant Women's Autonomy," p. 36.

106. Petchesky, *Abortion and Woman's Choice,* p. 395.

CHAPTER 7. IMAGINING FEMINISM

1. Judy Scales Trent, "Black Women and the Constitution: Finding Our Place, Asserting Our Rights," *Harvard Civil Rights–Civil Liberties Law Review* 24 (1989): 10, 12.

2. Kimberle Williams Crenshaw, "Demarginalizing the Intersection of Race and Sex: A Black Feminist Critique of Antidiscrimination Doctrine, Feminist Theory and Antiracist Politics," *University of Chicago Legal Forum* (1989), pp. 140, 143. She discusses three key cases that deny the intersectionality of black women: DeGraffenreid v. General Motors, 413 F. Supp. 142 (E.D. Mo. 1976); Moore v. Hughes Helicopter, 708 F. 2d 475 (9th Cir. 1983); and Payne v. Travenol, 673 F. 2d 798 (5th Cir. 1982).

3. Peggie R. Smith, "Separate Identities: Black Women, Work, and Title VII," *Harvard Women's Law Journal* 14 (Spring 1991): 22, 31.

4. Mae Gwendolyn Henderson, "Speaking in Tongues: Dialogics, Dialectics, and the Black Woman Writer's Literary Tradition," in *Reading Black, Reading Feminist,* ed. Henry Louis Gates, Jr. (New York: Meridian Book, 1990), pp. 116–17. Also see Teresa de Lauretis, *Technologies of Gender* (Bloomington: Indiana University Press, 1987), p. 2.

5. For classic discussions of radical feminism, see Ti Grace Atkinson, *Amazon Odyssey* (New York: Links, 1974); Shulamith Firestone, *The Dialectic of Sex* (New York: Bantam, 1970); Kate Millett, *Sexual Politics* (New York: Dou-

bleday, 1970); Robin Morgan, ed., *Sisterhood Is Powerful* (New York: Vintage, 1970); and Redstockings, *Feminist Revolution* (New York: Redstockings, 1975).

6. Carol Brown, "Mothers, Fathers, and Children: From Private to Public Patriarchy," in *Women and Revolution,* ed. Lydia Sargent (Boston: South End Press, 1981), pp. 239–68.

7. For interesting discussions of redefining the personal as political, see Carpignano et al., "Chatter in the Age of Electronic Reproduction," pp. 33–55; and Nancy Fraser, "Rethinking the Public Sphere." Also see Ian Angus and Sut Jhally, eds., *Cultural Politics in Contemporary America* (New York: Routledge, 1989).

8. Patricia Hill Collins, "The Emerging Theory and Pedagogy of Black Women's Studies," *Feminist Issues* 6, no. 1 (Spring 1986): 9.

9. Aida Hurtado, "Relating to Privilege: Seduction and Rejection in the Subordination of White Women and Women of Color," *Signs* 14, no. 4 (Summer 1989): 849–50.

10. See, e.g., Barbara Smith, "Home," in *Home Girls: A Black Feminist Anthology,* ed. Barbara Smith (New York: Kitchen Table Women of Color Press, 1983), pp. 64–72.

11. Hurtado, "Relating to Privilege," p. 851.

12. Mervat Hatem, "The Enduring Alliance of Nationalism and Patriarchy in Muslim Personal Status Laws: The Case of Modern Egypt," *Feminist Issues* 6, no. 1 (Spring 1986): 28.

13. As quoted in Jane Perlez, "Elite Kenyan Women Avoid a Rite: Marriage," *New York Times,* 3 Mar. 1991, p. A14.

14. Diana E. H. Russell, *Lives of Courage: Women for a New South Africa* (New York: Basic Books, 1989), pp. 228, 249, 306, 263.

15. Rhonda Copelon, "From Privacy to Autonomy: The Conditions for Sexual and Reproductive Freedom," in *From Abortion to Reproductive Freedom: Transforming a Movement,* ed. Marlene Gerber Fried (Boston: South End press, 1990), p. 33.

16. Henderson, "Speaking in Tongues," p. 18.

17. Elizabeth Weed, ed., *Coming to Terms: Feminism, Theory, Politics* (New York: Routledge, 1989), p. xii.

18. Patricia J. Williams, *The Alchemy of Race and Rights* (Cambridge: Harvard University Press, 1991), pp. 152, 154, 159.

19. Kimberle Williams Crenshaw, "Race, Reform, and Retrenchment: Transformation and Legitimation in Antidiscrimination Law," *Harvard Law Review* 101, no. 7 (May 1988): 2346, 1357.

20. Williams, *Alchemy of Race and Rights,* p. 164–65.

21. Ibid., p. 165; Williams is quoting from Christopher Stone, "Should Trees Have Standing?—Toward Legal Rights for Natural Objects," *Southern California Law Review* 45 (1972): 453, 455.

22. Williams, *Alchemy of Race and Rights,* p. 184.

23. Byllye Avery, "Empowerment through Wellness," *Yale Journal of Law and Feminism* 4 (Fall 1991): 151.

24. Williams, *Alchemy of Race and Rights,* pp. 103, 102.

25. See bell hooks, "Theory as Liberatory Practice," *Yale Journal of Law and Feminism* 4 (Fall 1991): 1.

26. Hazel V. Carby, *Reconstructing Womanhood: The Emergence of the Afro-American Woman Novelist* (New York: Oxford University Press, 1987), pp. 6, 19.

27. Adrienne Rich, "Notes Toward a Politics of Location (1984)," in her *Blood, Bread, and Poetry: Selected Prose 1979–1986* (New York: Norton, 1986), p. 219.

28. Evelyn Brooks-Higginbotham, "The Problem of Race in Women's History," in Weed, *Coming to Terms*, p. 125.

29. Barbara Christian, "The Race for Theory," *Feminist Studies* 14, no. 1 (Spring 1988): 74, 73. For a different understanding of postmodernism and the problem of racism, see Howard Winant, "Postmodern Racial Politics: Difference and Inequality," *Socialist Review* 10, no. 1 (Jan.–Mar. 1990): 121–50.

30. June Jordan, as stated in an interview, "Voices of Change: The State of the Art," *Women's Review of Books* 7, no. 5 (Feb. 1991): 24.

31. See, e.g., several of the articles in Weed, *Coming to Terms*. See also Kathleen Barry, "Deconstructing Deconstructionism (Or, Whatever Happened to Feminist Studies?)," *Ms.* 1, no. 4 (Jan.–Feb. 1991): 83–85, for a highly critical discussion of postmodern feminism.

32. Judith Butler, "Gender Trouble, Feminist Theory, and Psychoanalytic Discourse," in *Feminism/Postmodernism*, ed. Linda Nicholson (New York: Routledge, 1990), pp. 324–40; and Judith Butler, *Gender Trouble: Feminism and the Subversion of Identity* (New York: Routledge, 1990).

33. Wendy Brown, "Feminist Hesitations, Postmodern Exposures," *differences* 3, no. 1 (Spring 1991): 68, 73.

34. Angela Harris, "Race and Essentialism in Feminist Legal Theory," *Stanford Law Review* 42 (Feb. 1990): 585.

35. Bernice Johnson Reagon, "Coalition Politics: Turning the Century," in *Home Girls: A Black Feminist Anthology*, ed. Barbara Smith (New York: Kitchen Table Women of Color Press, 1983), pp. 361, 363.

36. Susan Bordo, " 'Material' Girl: The Effacements of Postmodern Culture," *Michigan Quarterly Review* 29, no. 4 (Fall 1990): 662, 664.

37. Susan Bordo, "Feminism, Postmodernism, and Gender-Scepticism," in Nicholson, *Feminism/Postmodernism*, p. 141.

38. See especially bell hooks, *Talking Back: Thinking Feminist, Thinking Black* (Boston: South End Press, 1989). Also see bell hooks, *Black Looks, Race and Representation* (Boston: South End Press, 1992); and bell hooks and Cornel West, *Breaking Bread, Insurgent Black Intellectual Life* (Boston: South End Press, 1991).

39. Audre Lorde, "Age, Race, Class, and Sex: Women Redefining Difference," in *Out There: Marginalization and Contemporary Cultures*, ed. Russell Ferguson, Martha Gever, Trinh T. Minh-ha, Cornel West (Cambridge, Mass.: MIT Press, 1990), p. 285. For interesting and related discussions of the concept difference, see Carol Lee Bacchi, *Same Difference: Feminism and Sexual Difference* (Boston: Allen & Unwin, 1990); Zillah Eisenstein, *The Female Body and*

the Law; and Iris Marion Young, *Justice and the Politics of Difference* (Princeton, N.J.: Princeton University Press, 1990).

40. Gloria I. Joseph and Jill Lewis, *Common Differences: Conflicts in Black and White Feminist Perspectives* (Boston: South End Press, 1981; New York: Doubleday, 1986).

41. Catherine MacKinnon, "From Practice to Theory, or What is a White Woman Anyway?" *Yale Journal of Law and Feminism* 4 (Fall 1991): 20.

42. Denise Riley, *Am I That Name? Feminism and the Category of 'Women' in History* (Minneapolis: University of Minnesota, 1988), pp. 1, 112. Also see Johnnetta B. Cole, ed., *All American Women: Lines That Divide, Ties That Bind* (New York: The Free Press, 1986).

43. A few representative white feminists who address the issue of racism are Marilyn Frye, *The Politics of Reality* (Trumansburg, NY: Crossing Press, 1983); Ann Ferguson, *Sexual Democracy: Women, Oppression, and Revolution* (Boulder, Colo.: Westview Press, 1991); Minnie Bruce Pratt, "Identity: Skin Blood Heart," in Elly Bulkin, Minnie Bruce Pratt, and Barbara Smith, *Yours in Struggle: Three Feminist Perspectives on Anti-Semitism and Racism* (Brooklyn, NY: Long Haul Press, 1984); Adrienne Rich, "Disloyal to Civilization: Feminism, Racism and Gynephobia," in her *Lies, Secrets, and Silence* (New York: Norton, 1979); and Elizabeth V. Spelman, *Inessential Woman: Problems of Exclusion in Feminist Thought* (Boston: Beacon Press, 1988).

44. For a discussion of white solipsism, see Rich, "Disloyal to Civilization."

45. Susan Willis, *Specifying: Black Women Writing the American Experience* (Madison: University of Wisconsin Press, 1987).

46. Marianne Hirsch and Evelyn Fox Keller, in *Conflicts in Feminism* (New York: Routledge, 1990), p. 2, choose to reject the term *feminisms* as no improvement over the term *feminism.* It merely multiplies the problems contained in its original form.

47. See bell hooks, *Feminist Theory: From Margin to Center* (Boston: South End Press, 1984), p. 30.

48. Hooks, *Talking Back,* pp. 182, 105, 105.

49. See bell hooks, *Ain't I A Woman: Black Women and Feminism* (Boston: South End Press, 1981), p. 194.

50. Hooks, *Talking Back,* p. 180.

51. Barbara Smith, Introduction to *Home Girls,* p. xxiii. Also see Combahee River Collective, "The Combahee River Collective Statement," *Home Girls,* pp. 272–82; and Gloria T. Hull, Patricia Bell Scott, and Barbara Smith, eds., *All the Women Are White, All the Blacks Are Men, But Some of Us Are Brave* (New York: Feminist Press, 1982).

52. Barbara Smith, "Toward a Black Feminist Criticism," in Hull, Scott, and Smith, eds., *All the Women Are White,* p. 162.

53. June Jordan, *On Call: Political Essays* (Boston: South End Press, 1985), p. 38.

54. Chandra Talpade Mohanty, "Introduction: Cartographies of Struggle: Third World Women and the Politics of Feminism," in *Third World Women and the Politics of Feminism,* ed. Chandra Talpade Mohanty, Ann Russo, and

Lourdes Torres (Bloomington: Indiana University Press, 1991), p. 4. Also see Chandra Talpade Mohanty, "Under Western Eyes: Feminist Scholarship and Colonial Discourses," also in Mohanty, Russo, and Torres, eds., *Third World Women*. For an interesting discussion of the complicated meanings of essentialism, see Diana Fuss, *Essentially Speaking: Feminism, Nature and Difference* (New York: Routledge, 1989).

55. Cheryl Johnson-Odim, "Common Themes, Different Contexts: Third World Women and Feminism," in Mohanty, Russo, and Torres, eds., *Third World Women, Feminism*, pp. 316, 325.

56. Alice Walker, *In Search of Our Mothers' Gardens* (New York: Harcourt Brace Jovanovich, 1983), p. xi.

57. Gloria Anzaldúa, "An Introduction: Haciendo caras, una entrada," in *Making Face, Making Soul: Creative and Critical Perspectives by Women of Color*, ed. Gloria Anzaldúa (San Francisco: Aunt Lute, 1990), pp. xxi, xxv, xxvi. Also see Cherrie Moraga and Gloria Anzaldúa, eds., *This Bridge Called My Back* (Watertown, Mass.: Persephone Press, 1981).

58. Uma Narayan, "The Project of Feminist Epistemology: Perspectives from a Non-Western Feminist," in *Gender/Body/Knowledge: Feminist Reconstructions of Being and Knowing*, ed. Alison M. Jaggar and Susan R. Bordo (New Brunswick, N.J.: Rutgers University Press, 1989), p. 259.

59. Gayatri Chakravorty Spivak, *In Other Worlds: Essays in Cultural Politics* (New York: Routledge, 1988), pp. 151, 152, 208.

60. Susan Willis, *Specifying*, p. 16.

61. Patricia Hill Collins, *Black Feminist Thought: Knowledge, Consciousness, and the Politics of Empowerment* (Boston: Unwin Hyman, 1990), p. 202.

62. See Lisa Belklin, "Bars to Equality of Sexes Seen as Eroding Slowly," *New York Times*, 20 Aug. 1989, p. A26.

63. An interesting study of teenage girls by Carol Gilligan raises the question of whether the impact of strong black women on black teenage girls may explain why black teenage girls appear often to have higher self-esteem than white teenage girls. See Suzanne Daley, "Little Girls Lose Their Self-Esteem on Way to Adolescence, Study Finds," *New York Times*, 9 Jan. 1991, p. B6.

64. Trinh T. Minh-ha, *Woman, Native, Other* (Bloomington: Indiana University Press, 1989), p. 2. For a more particular historical discussion of the process of specifying feminism, see Aihwa Ong, *Spirits of Resistance and Capitalist Discipline: Factory Women in Malaysia* (Albany: State University of New York Press, 1987).

65. Evelyn Brooks-Higginbotham, "African-American Women's History and the Metalanguage of Race," *Signs* 17, no. 2 (Winter 1992): 255, 257–58.

66. Rosemary L. Bray, "Taking Sides Against Ourselves," *New York Times Magazine*, 17 Nov. 1991, p. 94.

67. Joan Morgan, "A Blackwoman's Guide to the Tyson Trial," *Village Voice* 37 no. 9 (3 March 1992): 40. Also see Anita Hill et al., "The Nature of the Beast," *Ms.* 11, no. 4 (Jan./Feb. 1992): 32–45.

68. Teresa de Lauretis, "Eccentric Subjects: Feminist Theory and Historical Consciousness," *Feminist Studies* 16, no. 1 (Spring 1990): 134.

69. See the collection *Reading Black, Reading Feminist*, ed. Henry Louis

Gates, Jr. (New York: Meridian, 1990), especially the Introduction, p. 8, for a discussion of the plural and racialized voices of women of color.

70. Mohanty, "Introduction," pp. 13, 7, 4.

71. Valerie Smith, "Loopholes of Retreat: Architecture and Ideology in Harriet Jacob's 'Incidents in the Life of a Slave Girl,' " in Gates, ed., *Reading Black, Reading Feminist,* pp. 212–226.

72. Judy Scales-Trent, "Commonalities: On Being Black and White, Different and the Same," *Yale Journal of Law and Feminism* 3, no. 2 (Spring 1990): 305, 316, 324.

73. Patricia Williams, *Alchemy of Race and Rights,* p. 125.

74. Trinh T. Minh-ha, "Not You/Like You: Post-Colonial Women and the Interlocking Questions of Identity and Difference," in Anzaldúa, ed., *Making Face, Making Soul,* p. 372.

75. Belkin, "Bars to Equality of Sexes," p. A26.

76. Pat Parker, "for the white person who wants to know how to be my friend," in Anzaldúa, ed., *Making Face, Making Soul,* p. 297.

77. Audre Lorde, "The Master's Tools Will Never Dismantle the Master's House," in Moraga and Anzaldúa, eds., *This Bridge Called My Back,* p. 99.

78. Carby, *Reconstructing Womanhood,* p. 53.

79. See Michele Barrett and Mary McIntosh, "Ethnocentrism and Socialist Feminist Theory," *Feminist Review* 20 (Summer 1985): 18–41. See also the responses by Caroline Ramazanoglu, "Ethnocentrism and Socialist-Feminist Theory: A Response to Barrett and McIntosh," pp. 83–86; and Hamida Kazi, "The Beginning of a Debate Long Due: Some Observations on 'Ethnocentrism and Socialist-Feminist Theory,' " pp. 87–91; both in *Feminist Review* 22 (Spring 1986).

80. See Carby, *Reconstructing Womanhood,* p. 20.

81. Angela Davis, "Reflections on the Black Woman's Role in the Community of Slaves," *Black Scholar* 3, no. 4 (Dec. 1971): 3–15; and her *Women, Race and Class* (New York: Random House, 1981).

82. Jacqueline Berrien, "Pregnancy and Drug Use: The Dangerous and Unequal Use of Punitive Measures," *Yale Journal of Law and Feminism* 2 (Spring 1990): 239–250.

83. E. Frances White, "Listening to the Voices of Black Feminism," *Radical America* 18, nos. 2–3 (1984): 7–26.

84. See Marian Wright Edelman, "The Black Family in America," in *The Black Women's Health Book: Speaking for Ourselves,* ed. Evelyn C. White (Seattle, Washington: The Seal Press, 1990), pp. 128–50; Angela Davis, *Women, Culture, Politics* (New York: Vintage Press, 1990); "Scapegoating the Black Family: Black Women Speak," special issue, *Nation* 249, no. 4 (24 July 1989); and Daniel Patrick Moynihan, "Another War—The One on Poverty—Is Over, Too," *New York Times,* 16 July 1990, p. A15. For an interesting discussion of the politics of motherhood of black women, see Eileen Boris, "The Power of Motherhood: Black and White Activist Women Redefine the 'Political,' " *Yale Journal of Law and Feminism* 2 (Fall 1988): 25–50.

85. Alisa Solomon, "The Politics of Breast Cancer," *Village Voice* 36, no. 20 (14 May 1991): 22–27. Also see White, ed., *Black Women's Health Book;*

and Audre Lorde, *The Cancer Journal* (San Francisco: Spinster's/Aunt Lute, 1980).

86. Crenshaw, "Demarginalizing the Intersection of Race and Sex," p. 140.

87. Lynnell Hancock, "Ujamaa Means Controversy," *Village Voice* 35, no. 45 (6 Nov. 1990): 14. Also see Joseph Berger, "New York Panel Backs School for Minority Men," *New York Times,* 10 Jan. 1991, p. A1; Dirk Johnson, "Milwaukee Creating Two Schools Just for Black Boys," *New York Times,* 30 Sept. 1990, p. A1; Felicia Lee, "Black Men: Are They Imperiled?" *New York Times,* 26 June 1990, p. B3; Helen R. Neuborne, "Girls Are Drowning, Too," *New York Times,* 16 Aug. 1991, p. A23; and Isabel Wilkerson, "To Save Its Men, Detroit Plans Boys-Only Schools," *New York Times,* 14 Aug. 1991, p. A1.

88. For a much fuller discussion of bodily diversity and the need for reproductive rights, see Eisenstein, *Female Body and the Law.*

89. See Carby, *Reconstructing Womanhood;* Moraga and Anzaldúa, eds., *This Bridge Called My Back;* Chandra Talpade Mohanty, "Feminist Encounters, Locating the Politics of Experience," *Copyright* 1 (Fall 1987): 30–44; and Willis, *Specifying.*

90. See Charlotte Rutherford, "Reproductive Freedoms and African American Women," *Yale Journal of Law and Feminism* 4 (Spring 1992): 255–90.

91. National Black Women's Health Project, 1237 Gordon Street SW, Atlanta, GA 30310; and National Institute for Women of Color, 1301 20th St. NW, Washington, D.C. 20036.

92. Alisa Solomon, "Identity Crisis: Queer Politics in the Age of Possibilities," *Village Voice* 37, no. 26 (30 June 1992): 27–33.

93. Ellen Willis, "Shaky Ground: The Abortion Fight, Take Two," *Village Voice* 34, no. 29 (18 July 1989), p. 14.

94. See letter from the National Latina Health Organization to NOW, 31 March 1992. Available from: P.O. Box 7567, 1900 Fruitvale Avenue, Oakland, CA 94601.

95. See "Who's Sorry NOW? Women of Color Protest Pro-Choice March," *Ms.* 3, no. 1 (July/Aug. 1992): 88–89; and Catherine Manegold, "The Battle over Choice Obscures Other Vital Concerns of Women," *New York Times,* 2 August 1992, p. E1.

96. See "The National Conference Resolutions," *National NOW Times* 24, no. 6 (Aug. 1992): 12.

Index

Compositor:	Maple-Vail Manufacturing Group
Text:	10/13 Sabon
Display:	Sabon
Printer and Binder:	Maple-Vail Manufacturing Group